SIR HAROLD

PRISONER OF
Japan

A PERSONAL WAR DIARY

SINGAPORE, SIAM AND BURMA, 1941 - 1945

SIR HAROLD ATCHERLEY

PRISONER OF
Japan

A PERSONAL WAR DIARY
SINGAPORE, SIAM AND BURMA, 1941 - 1945

MEMOIRS

Cirencester

Published by Memoirs

MEMOIRS
PUBLISHING

25 Market Place, Cirencester, Gloucestershire, GL7 2NX
info@memoirsbooks.co.uk www.memoirspublishing.com

First published in England, November 2012

Book jacket design Ray Lipscombe

ISBN 978-1-909304-53-6

Printed in England

CONTENTS

DEDICATION

To Anita, Elke, Sally, my Children and Grandchildren.

Publication of this diary took many years, nearly 60 to be exact. That it has seen the light of day is the result of pressure from family and friends. I owe a very special debt of gratitude to my son Martin, who, as a graphic designer with long experience of book design, has generously undertaken all the hard work of transforming an imperfect typescript and incorporating the accompanying illustrations into the finished article. I am also very grateful to Ronald Searle, who generously allowed me to use reproductions of some of the many drawings he made whilst a prisoner. He was, like me, in the 18th Division and we were together throughout most of our captivity. Much hard work, however, had been done many years earlier, before serious thought could be given to possible publication. Anita gallantly typed the first text from the barely legible pages of the diary in its original form, long before PCs had made their appearance on the scene. For this I am deeply grateful. I also received unstinted moral and practical support from Elke, who overcame the pain she so understandably felt at having to read my descriptions of what being a Far East POW meant. I also want to express my thanks to Jamie Bulloch, who generously scanned the first 50 pages of the typewritten text and miraculously transformed them into a document for use on my PC, so that a corrected text could be produced. Thanks to him I equipped myself with a scanner so that I could complete what he had so nobly started.

Harold Atcherley - London.

Drawings by Ronald Searle, originals in the Imperial War Museum

FOREWORD

❧

The diary, which I kept as a prisoner of war of the Japanese, covers the period from the fall of Singapore on 15 February 1942 until 14 September 1945, a few days before I was repatriated to England. There is a gap, however, from April to December 1943, when I was working on the construction of the Burma-Thailand Railway. To have written a diary under the conditions which we had to face during this period would, physically, have been well-nigh impossible.

I have occasionally asked myself – I have certainly been asked by others – why I kept a diary at all. Frankly, I do not really know the answer. Possibly, it was an attempt to maintain some semblance of self-discipline, some structure to my life. It was certainly not written with the thought that anyone else would ever read it, or would even want to, since we were part of the 'forgotten war'. The post-war years have demonstrated that most people are ignorant about the war in the Far East and seem to be generally uninterested; an attitude which is hardly surprising, since it all took place so far away from the war in Europe and so long ago.

Most of my incarceration was spent on Singapore Island, the first fourteen months in Changi Camp on the eastern tip of the island and the last two years in the coolie quarters just outside the walls of Changi Gaol, where there were 7000 prisoners in a gaol designed for 700 civilian prisoners. It was a grim time, during which we never had enough to eat, but as nothing compared with the ten months I was in Thailand – it was always referred to as Siam in those days – and Burma. Although there were one or two who managed to write diaries whilst they were up on the railway, it would for me have been a physical

iii

impossibility. It would also have been far too dangerous. In any event it was never put to the test, since my diary, which I had kept safely in Singapore, was dumped with my pack at the beginning of the long march up to Sonkurai camp near the Burma/Thailand border, and I never expected to see it again. I naturally hoped that it would not be discovered by the Japanese.

I was a member of the so-called F Force, which consisted of 7000 British and American POWs sent to work on the construction of the Burma-Siam railway, in early 1943. When the survivors returned to Kanchanaburi some ten months later, more than half had died. We were told one day by the Japanese, whilst we were in Kanchanaburi, that there were some POW belongings stored in a shed and that, if any of us could claim anything of our own, we were free to take it. A day or two after this, I strolled into the shed, more out of curiosity than from any thought that I might find my own pack. I could hardly believe my eyes, when this was the first thing I saw, and my relief was as great as my surprise, when I saw that my diary was still in it. In my entry for 16 December 1943, I noted that we were shortly to leave Kanchanaburi for Singapore and this must have been a few days after I had recovered my diary. My own record of the time spent on the railway consists of no more than a few pages of rather crude jottings, made so far as I can recall, whilst I was at Kanchanaburi. A brief report on what happened to F Force was submitted by Andy Dillon to the Kempeitai, the Japanese secret military police, at their request in December 1943 and is reproduced under 'F Force Notes' in my diary.

I had been under the impression, until a few years ago, that this was the only effective record of F Force. More recently two books came to my notice. The first 'To the River Kwai: Two Journeys 1943, 1979', was written by John Stewart (known to me at the time as John Ulmann)

iv

and published in 1988. The author had been a corporal on my Intelligence Corps staff in 18 Division HQ and his book is based on notes he kept from April to December 1943, whilst on the railway, initially at Sonkurai in Thailand and later at Tambaya in Burma. Since he and I were both at these two camps during exactly the same periods, his book fills a significant gap in my own diary.

The second book, 'The Tall Man who Never Slept' was published in 1991 and is a biography of Cyril Wild by James Bradley, both of whom I knew well. The former was with us in Changi and at Sonkurai and the latter was one of a group of ten prisoners, who attempted to escape from the camp at Sonkurai in 1943. Their attempt ended in disaster and he was one of only four to survive. Those who did survive were initially condemned to death, reprieved at the last moment, and spent the rest of their time as prisoners condemned to solitary confinement.

Cyril Wild, then a major, was the officer who carried the white flag at the surrender of Singapore in 1942, the photograph of which has been reproduced many times in the press and on television. He had worked before the war in Japan for the Shell Company and was a fluent Japanese speaker. He was with us on F Force as the senior interpreter and 'The Tall Man who Never Slept" provides an authoritative account of the ill-fated F Force and, in particular, of our experiences at Sonkurai Camp, where he was in the same hut as me and the rest of the officers. We arrived in Sonkurai Camp in May 1943. In September, the senior officers, particularly the doctors, in the camp were accused by the Japanese of 'preventing too many prisoners from going out to work' on the railway. As a consequence, they told us that one whole long hut was to be evacuated and 700 prisoners were to be put out into the jungle in order to make way for an equal number of Asiatic coolies. The order to expel 700 seriously ill prisoners, most of whom were near to death, into the jungle was endorsed by the senior Japanese officer, Col. Banno, but, although the coolies did actually arrive at the camp, Cyril Wild succeeded, through sheer force of argument and personality, in having the order rescinded. He was one of the bravest men I have ever met. For less, others might very well have been executed on the spot.

Immediately after the war, he played a major role in the Japanese War Crimes Trials in Tokyo as both chief interpreter and key witness, since he had witnessed more of the atrocities carried out by the Japanese, than any other prisoner. He was tragically killed in an air crash in Hong Kong in September 1946. Cyril Wild said, in his written testimony to the Japanese War Crimes Trials, that Sonkurai was the worst camp of all. I would find it difficult to disagree.

The months I spent in Sonkurai and Tambaya, the so called 'hospital camp' cover experiences so ghastly that I have for many years found it difficult to write or talk about them. Perhaps figures express more eloquently than anything else what we went through. When construction of the bridge at Sonkurai was completed and the camp evacuated, barely 400 out of the original total of 1600 were alive. Of the 400 of us who eventually returned to Singapore, only 182 were alive on our release in 1945. Those who died, did so as the consequence of overwork, starvation, diseases – particularly dysentery, malaria, and cholera – and, in many cases, brutal beatings by the Japanese engineers and camp guards. Of these diseases, cholera took a major toll. I do not recall a single case of cholera which did not prove fatal, and men usually died within 24 to 48 hours in the most appalling agony and physically unrecognisable. We did have our own medical officers in the camp but they had no drugs. Writing this now at the age of 94, it is unlikely that more than a handful of these 182 are still alive.

I was incredibly fortunate to have survived it all – and I like to think –

relatively unscathed. Whilst I have no doubt that luck played an important part, more relevant, perhaps, is the fact that I was one of the relatively few, who were inoculated against cholera by the Japanese, shortly before we left by train from Singapore early in 1943. For many years I wondered why I should have been singled out, until Elke suggested that it was probably because my surname begins with A and any army, when in doubt, would follow alphabetical order. I am sure she is right.

INTRODUCTION

In the latter part of the Second World War, more than a quarter of a million European and American soldiers were taken prisoner by the Japanese in Malaysia, the Dutch East Indies and the Pacific. They went on to suffer years of deprivation and brutality, most of them failing to survive.

I was fortunate enough to be one of the survivors. Throughout my time as a prisoner, from the fall of Singapore on 15 February 1942 until 14 September 1945, I kept a diary, which I was able to bring home with me.

This book is based on that diary, along with other diaries and official documents. I was fortunate enough to count among my friends and comrades the celebrated artist Ronald Searle, whose drawings I have been able to use to illustrate my text; they will give a better impression of what life was like for a POW of the Japanese than mere words can, though neither words nor pictures could ever convey the appalling stench of disease and death on such a scale.

My personal experiences should be put into perspective. Apart from the 40,000 British and Australians captured in Malaysia, 60,000 Dutch were taken prisoner in the Dutch East Indies and a considerably larger number of Americans in the Pacific. I have excluded Indian army troops, since a large number of the 40,000 in Malaysia deserted to join the Indian National Army to fight with the Japanese in Burma. All of us were subjected to inhumane and brutal treatment. The experiences I shall be describing were therefore generally common to all. The death rate for Allied prisoners in Germany (excluding Russian prisoners) was about one per cent. For those held by the Japanese the rate was forty per cent. At Sonkurai camp on the Thailand/Burma border, the worst camp of the lot, the death rate was ninety per cent.

I joined the army on the outbreak of war as a rifleman in a territorial regiment of the King's Royal Rifle Corps. I was then commissioned early in 1940 and, being a German speaker, was appointed Divisional Intelligence Officer at the HQ of the 18th British Infantry Division.

The history of my Division was nothing short of a tragedy. We were never allowed to fight as a division. In the course of six years of war, we were bombed in turn by the Luftwaffe, the Japanese, the American Air Force and finally the RAF, which destroyed a number of the bridges we built on the Burma/Siam railway, killing and badly wounding several hundred POWs. Our Divisional Commander, General Beckwith–Smith died of diphtheria, quite unnecessarily, as a POW in Taiwan. Only some 10,000-11,000 men out of a total strength of 18,000 returned home at the end of the war.

The division spent the first two years in the UK training and, by the end, had become well prepared for war in Europe. In the event we embarked in October 1941 for the Middle East; at least that was our intended destination. Accordingly all our guns, tracked vehicles and transport were painted in desert camouflage.

We sailed from Liverpool and other West Coast ports in convoy, escorted by four WWI American destroyers. We headed west and, to our astonishment found ourselves in Halifax, Nova Scotia. There we were transferred to six American Naval transports. This was two months before America declared war. We embarked on a voyage lasting two months, escorted by eight destroyers, two cruisers, an aircraft carrier and fleet oil-tanker, a total of 18 ships, zigzagging our way for 24,000 miles around the world.

We never got to the Middle East. One brigade was ordered to go from

Mombasa to Singapore and was in action up-country almost immediately. The rest of the division spent a month in India while the War Office made up its mind what to do with us. There were several options – to Iraq for training prior to moving to the Western Desert, the original plan; to Burma or Singapore; or to Russia to reinforce the defence of Stalingrad. This was one of Churchill's madder ideas and the offer was understandably rejected by Stalin.

The fall of Singapore was rightly described by Winston Churchill as "the worst disaster and largest capitulation in British military history". He should have added "and with the highest ever number of desertions". We disembarked in Singapore only two weeks before the surrender, having been sent there largely for political reasons, Malaya being regarded in London as lost before we got there. One of our brigades was on a ship which was sunk by Japanese bombers as it was approaching Singapore harbour. The men had to swim ashore without any of their equipment and a large number of guns and transport was lost.

The loss of Malaysia and Singapore had been rendered inevitable long before the war ever started, thanks to the refusal of the War Office to provide the essential aircraft and tanks, compounded by its incompetence and that of senior commanders in Malaysia before the outbreak of war. Let me give you a few examples, each of which had disastrous consequences:

1. The RAF had located all its airfields in Malaysia without consulting the Army, which was responsible for their defence.

2. We had only a few ancient aircraft, which were quickly shot down by the far superior Japanese planes.

3. We had no tanks because it was believed that they could not operate in Malaysia.

4. Only one regiment, 800 men out of an army of some 120,000, had ever been trained in jungle warfare or, equally important, in rubber plantations.

5. Our radios practically never worked.

This reminds me of the passage in Tolstoy's War and Peace which reflects what we all felt when we surrendered: "The Russians, half of whom died, did all that could be done to attain an end worthy of the nation, and they are not to blame, because other Russians sitting in warm rooms proposed that they should do what was impossible".

The most barbaric incident of all was the murderous attack, by the Japanese, on the Alexandra military hospital in the last days of the battle for Singapore, in which some 200 patients, surgeons and nurses performing operations on the wounded were slaughtered.

Thanks to the Japanese, no information about casualties or the names of those captured could be sent out, with the result that all our next of kin were simply informed by the War Office that we were "Missing, Believed Prisoner of War". It was two years before our families knew whether we were alive or dead, when they received the first of four 24 word postcards. This was all we were permitted to send throughout our captivity. Letters from home took over a year to reach us.

The Japanese were completely unprepared for so many prisoners - we should all have committed hara-kiri, according to them. We received no rations at all initially, but were able to use the considerable food stocks remaining at the submarine base near Changi. After a week or two the Japanese delivered barbed wire with which we wired ourselves in – not that escape was a practical possibility.

Life for the first few weeks was not too bad, although from the beginning our rations were hardly adequate. Our treatment soon became increasingly harsh under the influence of the Japanese military tradition of bushido. This held that any soldier allowing himself to be taken prisoner was guilty of dishonouring both his country and his family. There was only one way out for him and that was to commit suicide. This meant that the Japanese military regarded us as sub-human.

Our Japanese guards were pretty insufferable and the Koreans who replaced them were worse. They were replaced for a time by Indian Army deserters, who were the worst of the lot. I believe they were simply taking revenge for the way they had been treated by their Imperial masters for so many years.

A large number of Indian Army troops deserted. Many Australians also deserted when the Japanese invaded Singapore Island. This was not because they were Australian, but because they were completely untrained, having not even been taught how to fire a rifle.

The Japanese boasted that they had never signed the Geneva Convention on the Treatment of Prisoners of War. Forced labour, or more accurately slave labour, was introduced in the form of working parties to repair bomb damage in Singapore harbour and to load and unload ships.

Some weeks after our imprisonment, four men were caught attempting to escape. They were summarily executed by a firing squad of Indian Army deserters, whose aim was so bad that only two were killed and a Japanese officer used his revolver to kill the other two. This incident led to all prisoners in Changi being ordered to sign an undertaking not to attempt to escape. We refused. Seventeen thousand of us were then marched off to a barrack area designed to hold 800, and we were told we would stay there until we signed.

We received no food; there were only two water points. Machine guns were placed around the perimeter and we were warned that anyone stepping outside would be shot on sight. We had only the clothes we wore and we slept on the ground wherever we could find space. Dysentery and malaria were already prevalent and after two days an epidemic of diphtheria broke out.

The Japanese general in charge of POWs warned us that, unless we signed, the wounded, sick and dying in hospital in Changi would join us. We prevailed upon them to qualify our promise by including the words 'under protest' and we signed.

Early in 1943 we were informed that we were to be sent to "rest camps" in Thailand, where it would be "easier to feed us". We were a party of 7000 and the Japanese ordered us to take 2000 sick men with us. We travelled in trainloads of 600 and it was only after our arrival in Thailand that we learned the truth - we were to work on the construction of the Burma - Siam railway.

This journey took five days on a narrow gauge line, in a train of 20 steel box wagons, which were like ovens by day and freezing at night. The wagons were enclosed, apart from a sliding door with a chain slung across the opening. We were packed so tightly that it was impossible for anyone to lie down.

Twice a day, we were let out briefly to be given a small quantity of rice in onion water. There was no form of sanitation. Practically all of us were suffering from malaria, dysentery or both. The only way to relieve oneself was to hang precariously out of the wagon, the weaker ones being supported by others to prevent them falling out.

On our arrival at the railhead camp near Bangkok, we were told by the Japanese that we would be leaving the next evening on a 200-mile march up to a camp just south of the Burma/Thailand border. The march lasted three weeks, along a rough, winding track, through thick mountainous jungle, up and down steep hills, in constant monsoon rain, often staggering through mud up to our knees. We could only march at night, because the track was used during the day by Japanese Army reinforcements for their southern Burma front. We could only watch with awe as they manhandled their guns and heavy equipment under conditions little better than our own.

Every night of the march a number of prisoners became too weak to keep up. A few officers marched at the rear of the column to carry them on makeshift stretchers, but some had to be left behind because there was no one who had the strength to carry them. We remonstrated with our guards to allow us to rest, but they insisted that we kept going by threatening us with their bayonets. Stragglers were set upon by marauding Thais and many were never heard of again.

The march for our group of 1600 ended at a camp on the Burma/Thailand border called Sonkurai, though it was hardly a camp. There were just a few roofless huts with bamboo platforms down either side of a narrow aisle down the middle. The width allocated to each man was two feet. Asian forced labour had been working there before us and many had died of cholera. Their decomposed bodies still lay in one corner of the camp area, and these had to be cleared up and burned. No one will ever know exactly how many civilian workers died, but it was somewhere around 100,000.

Construction of our section of the railway started immediately, our normal working day being never less than 14 hours and often 18. We worked, ate and slept without any cover, under incessant monsoon rain for the first few weeks on a daily ration, which was supposed to be 250gms of rice and a small quantity of onion stew. We never actually received the full ration since the rice was invariably rancid and full of maggots. To make things worse, the Japanese cut the ration by half for the majority who were too ill to work. In our attempt to stay alive, we resorted to eating whatever foliage we could. We succeeded occasionally in catching snakes to eat, but they were difficult to catch because they hid in bamboo thickets.

Footwear wore out, so that eventually most of us had to go barefoot. Our clothing rotted and with little covering, there was a dramatic increase in cases of jungle ulcers, caused by cuts from razor sharp bamboo splinters and bruises sustained while out working. These ulcers quickly became septic and in the more severe cases extended up to 6 to 12 inches in length, with the bone exposed. The only treatment possible was either to apply maggots or scrape them with spoons to clean out the rotting flesh. Many did not survive.

Our main task at Sonkurai was to build a three-span timber bridge on two levels, rail above and road below. A vast amount of earth and stone had to be moved for cuttings and embankments along the approaches to the bridge. The only tools we were given were chungkols and pickaxes, baskets for carrying earth and stones, and saws and axes for felling trees. There were no mechanical aids to help us with heavier work, such as moving sections of tree trunk down to the saw mill on the river bank.

We did have Burmese elephants to help us and they were clearly our close allies, because whenever the Japanese showed off by trying to take over from the Burmese mahouts, the elephant would not move a foot. These elephants, with their enormous intelligence, were for us the most lovable and helpful co-workers. They had an endearing habit of stopping work at 4 pm, egged on I suspect by the mahouts, who loathed the Japanese engineers as much as we did.

At the end of each day all tools had to be accounted for to the Japanese engineers and something was invariably missing, for which officers, as gang foremen, were the first to be beaten up. I was knocked out myself on two occasions, but I was one of the lucky ones. On returning to camp late at night we had to parade for roll call, when we had to line up the bodies of those who had died while out at work at one end to demonstrate that the numbers returning tallied with those who had gone out in the morning.

The Japanese insisted that the dead should be cremated by POWs who were too ill to work. Since this was quite beyond them, a number of us, mostly officers, took it in turns to help. It was a horrifying experience and one never to be forgotten: one lot of bodies being cremated on the fires and a steady supply of others (up to 14 per day) lined up on the ground nearby awaiting their turn. Death from cholera came so quickly that sometimes men who had been helping in the morning were themselves cremated the same evening.

Many diseases were the cause of death, but common to all were exhaustion through overwork and starvation. Beriberi was one of the more lasting diseases, which caused one's limbs - and in extreme cases one's whole body - to go completely numb. It left one's feet hanging down uselessly from the ankle. We found that by tying one end of a length of liana (that cord-like jungle plant growing up trees) around our big toes and the other around our legs above the knee, our feet could be held up so that we were able, at least, to set out for work.

Operations, mostly amputations, had to be performed without any anaesthetic using sharpened table knives and a saw borrowed from the Japanese engineers for return afterwards, "properly cleaned". Occasionally the Japanese did provide some sake (liquor) in lieu of anaesthetics. Medical supplies were non-existent, banana leaves being used for dressings.

On completion of the railway, a party of some 3000 returned to Singapore. Of our original group of 1600 to arrive at Sonkurai some 10 months before, 1200 were already dead. There were only 182 left at the end of the war.

I and several hundred others were evacuated to a so-called hospital camp at a place called Tambaya in Burma, where deaths continued at about the same level as they had been at Sonkurai. Most of them died.

Shortly after the return of the survivors to Changi, Japanese Army medical staff carried out a health check on us, passing only 125 out of 3000 as fit for light duty only, and this of course by Japanese standards. The engineers took no notice of this and ordered us to start work on construction of an airfield for kamikazi squadrons at Changi. This was like a nine-to-five job compared with what we had endured on the railway. Today the airfield lies under the main runway of the international airport.

By early 1944, we had become quite an international community - British, Australian, American, Dutch and Italian. The Americans were mostly survivors of B29 bombers shot down in raids on Singapore. The Italians had joined us rather earlier after Italy dropped out of the war. The Italians were from four submarines which had docked in Singapore just before Italy capitulated. Their commander was a Captain Grapallo, who gave me Italian lessons and became a good friend. He described to me one evening, how, when his flotilla was patrolling off the coast of Brazil, he sighted our convoy and was disappointed that it was travelling too fast for him to make a torpedo attack.

Sometime towards the end of 1944 our camp administration was shown orders from Japan for the massacre of all prisoners when the allies invaded South East Asia. For those of us on Singapore Island, the plan was for us to be taken by truck to the beaches, where we were to be machine-gunned.

One thing that helped our morale was having radios. These had been constructed to fit into chair or table legs, or for use up on the railway in the bottom half of an army water bottle, a stethoscope being used to listen to the news. Men using these were particularly brave, since they knew they would be executed if they were discovered.

It was difficult on the railway to find a power supply. We were in luck because every night a truck was parked in front of the guard hut. This was usually occupied by one sleepy Korean guard, who kept a fire going all night, which meant that he could not see anything beyond it.

A group of us took it in turn to remove the battery from the truck and carry it up to our hut in a food container, as though we were carrying rice to a late working party. After we had listened to the news, the battery was returned to the truck for recharging. This demanded special care, since one end of the hut was occupied by Japanese guards.

Sometime in the 1980s, a reservoir was built and this covers the site of our camp and the bridge we built at Sonkurai. It is, for me, a fitting epitaph to the thousands who died there.

The war in the Far East was ended abruptly by the dropping of the two atom bombs. This saved the lives not only of all allied prisoners but of hundreds of thousands, possibly millions, of others, both military and civilian of many different nationalities, not least civilians in Japan, who were starving.

I do not believe our treatment stemmed from any innate cruelty in the Japanese population as a whole. It was essentially due to brain-washing by the military commanders to ensure that the army fought with the extreme ruthlessness and brutality demanded. There were, of course, civilised Japanese who did whatever they could to help us.

I have learned that feelings of hatred among those who have to do the fighting are displayed far more by those who have never been directly involved, led by the media. Primo Levi, the well-known writer, a survivor of Auschwitz, wrote in his autobiography Is This a Man? that he regarded "hatred in itself to be bestial and that to hate the whole of any human group would be tantamount to following the precepts of Nazism". He went on to say "I never harboured any hatred for the German people ....I do not understand, I cannot tolerate the fact that a man should be judged not for what he is but because of the group to which he happens to belong". How I agree with every word. I would only like to add that, in the end, hatred only damages those who hate.

As Japanese troops were marched out of Singapore as prisoners shortly after its reoccupation by the Allies, they were watched by our men, by then free. One of them said to his mates "Poor buggers, now it's their turn". This did not reveal any hatred of the Japanese, and I found this to be true of the majority.

It is well-nigh impossible to convey the euphoria of regaining one's freedom. An end to the constant threat of death, to have enough to eat, to have a bath, to have one's own space and be able to go where one wanted. This euphoria was, however, tempered by a feeling of guilt that one had survived when so many thousands had died. This was as common for us as it was for the survivors of concentration camps in Europe.

We must all wonder from time to time whether our world will ever see an end to wars. Although this is highly unlikely, one can at least hope that they will not be on anything like the same scale as WW2 and that governments will learn from the appalling errors of Iraq, Afghanistan and Libya. The world clearly faces huge problems, which are global in nature - population increase, water, food and energy shortages, not to mention climate change, any one of which may well lead to war.

Mohamed ElBaradei, the Nobel Peace Prize laureate, wrote recently "our politics does not sufficiently take into account the increasingly globalized nature of society". Governments have to wake up to the fact that regional organizations and political alliances between nations are dysfunctional. They are based on ad hoc decisions. Global problems have to be dealt with globally.

Worldwide military expenditure in 2010 alone amounted to $1.6 trillion. Official development assistance was only $129 billion. This exposes the folly of believing that international security can be enhanced by spending such an obscene amount on weapons and so little on reconstruction and development.

What then can be done to get governments to change course? I believe the younger generation everywhere has the capacity to start the process. They are far less nationalistic and more globally minded than my generation has been and, provided they use the internet responsibly, are far better equipped than any previous generation has been to influence the political classes.

I would like to end by quoting a few lines from one of John Donne's Essays on Meditation. I am reminded of them whenever I think about war and the world we live in; they are for me especially apt. "No man is an island entire of itself; man is a piece of the continent, a part of the main; any man's death diminishes me because I am involved in all mankind and therefore never send to know for whom the bell tolls; it tolls for thee".

Harold Atcherley

2012

OUTBREAK OF WAR, 1939

I had been greatly looking forward to going to Peking to study Mandarin prior to working in China for the Royal Dutch Shell Group, but it was not to be. By now it seemed certain that we were going to be drawn into war. I knew that I would be amongst the first to be called up for military service. I had in fact already received call up papers, as a twenty year old, in the summer of 1938 ordering me to report to a heavy anti-aircraft training regiment in Hampshire. This was under the so-called Militiaman Scheme, in typical civil service verbiage. I felt that this particular form of military employment would be exceedingly dull. Fortunately the scheme was almost immediately abandoned, when the government introduced general mobilisation, so that I never became a 'heavy anti-aircraft gunner', for which my weight was not, in any case, ideally suited. Today I would regard such a posting as being a relatively safe option and therefore quite attractive.

For the next few weeks I was in a form of limbo, in which Shell no longer had a job for me and I had been sent down to Teddington to work temporarily as an auxiliary fireman at the company's Lensbury Club. At least the company continued to pay me. I was a member of a team of some six trainees, under a senior member of staff who was the Chief Fireman and knew about as little as we did about the art of fire fighting. Our duties were not onerous; all we had to do was to push the fire pump and hoses, which sat on a two-wheel trailer, out of its garage near the club house and take it down to the river bank, where one of us put one end of the hose into the water, whilst others uncoiled the main length of hose in the general direction of the club buildings. When all was ready the order was given to start the pump. This created a jet of water of considerable pressure, strong enough to need two of us to hold the nozzle and point it in whatever direction the situation might demand. Our first effort at doing this created great excitement, combined with shock and amazement on the part of several members of staff working in one of the offices, as our jet of water scored a direct hit on one of the windows facing us. We were fortunately just far enough away not to break the window. Three members of our team, who had been in the Cambridge University Air Squadron, left soon afterwards for their training as fighter pilots in the RAFVR. Two of them were killed in the first six months of the war.

There was a short gap between the ending of the militia scheme and conscription which meant that I was free either to join a Territorial Army Regiment or await conscription. I decided to take the initiative and I became a rifleman in one of the London territorial regiments, the Queen's Westminster Rifles, which was affiliated to the King's Royal Rifle Corps (KRRC), also known as the 60th Rifles. The regiment had originally been formed in North America in 1755 as the 60th Royal American Regiment of American Colonists. Among the more distinguished foreign officers given commissions in the regiment was a Swiss citizen named Henri Bouquet, who introduced new tactics, training and man management; battle dress, which only became universal 150 years later and unofficially, the use of the rifle to replace the smoothbore musket.

I thus embarked on my wartime military career in the late summer of 1939. The Queen's Westminster Rifles offered two distinct benefits over the majority of other regiments in the British Army: the uniform had black buttons and belts and thus there was no brass to be cleaned and one did not have to slope arms and carry one's rifle on one's shoulder – a particularly uncomfortable, not to say impractical, method of carrying a gun – but carry it in one's right hand, as one would a shopping bag. Everything has its disadvantages, however, and the regimental marching pace was considerably faster than that for most other infantry regiments. This stemmed from the fact that the KRRC and its sister regiment the Rifle Brigade (both now combined to form the Green Jackets) had been created at the time of the American War of Independence as a fast moving scouting regiment, trained to carry out all sorts of complicated manoeuvres at great speed, often at night. This meant that we had to march extremely fast taking very short steps, which always conjured up for me the image of a bunch of young secretaries, late for work, walking as fast as their high heels would carry them over London Bridge. Compared to this, the guards' regiments have a much more relaxed and unhurried style of getting from A to B.

I reported for duty in due course with about twenty other equally apprehensive young men of similar age, at an underground gym, which had an almost invisible entrance facing the ramp, down which taxis brought passengers to catch their trains at Liverpool Street station. Here we were issued with 1917 rifles, battle dress uniform, boots, thick wool underwear, even thicker grey socks, web belts, pack, haversack, water bottle, tin hats and, to crown it all, instead of army greatcoats, which were in short supply, dark blue London Passenger Transport Board bus drivers' overcoats. The latter had leather patches over the elbows. We did not consider that such equipment was in keeping with our status as brave young soldiers going off to war. Our initial enthusiasm was dampened further by our being issued with civilian gas masks instead of the much more professional looking khaki military version. Civilian gas masks were much smaller and were packed in little brown cardboard boxes, which might have been designed for carrying sandwiches for a lunch break. These were attached to a piece of string so that they could be carried from the shoulder.

Having changed into this new gear and packed our kit bags, we were ordered to 'fall in' on the ramp outside the gym by a corporal, by which time we felt like a group of bag ladies. To the fascination of a crowd of city types, which had assembled to watch these strange goings on, our corporal ordered us to 'fall in'. This operation took some time to complete, as we struggled with our unaccustomed possessions but eventually we were brought to attention, ordered to do a 'left turn' followed by 'quick march', and headed up the ramp into Liverpool Street, behind our corporal shouting 'left, right, left, right'. Apart from myself and one or two others, none of our little group had ever marched in formation in their lives. After a 'left wheel' into Bishopsgate, we came to a halt after about 100 yards in front of an ABC teashop, where we were each given a cup of tea and a bun. Thus refreshed, we were marched back into Liverpool Street station and 'entrained' on the District Line for Pinner, an inner London suburb consisting of rows and rows of little 'two-up, two-down' houses, all identical.

One of the first things we had to do was to fill our palliasses, which was an entirely unexpected experience for all of us. We were each issued with a flat coffin-shaped canvas bag, about six feet long and three across at the widest point, which we had to fill with straw to form a mattress. On 'going to bed' on our first night, we quickly discovered that we had all filled our bags with too much straw so

4

that they resembled large canvas sausages, on which it was impossible to lie without rolling on to the floor. We spent our first two or three weeks in Pinner being drilled by a sergeant in the street under the eyes of the local housewives. I cannot believe that they could have been over-impressed by the sight offered. The tedium of morning drill was broken by a twenty-minute break, in which we each bought a pint of milk and a 2d apple pie, supplied by the United Dairy man, who could not believe his luck at suddenly having such valuable captive customers. He soon learned to time his arrival to coincide with our regular morning break.

In due course we 'entrained' again on the District Line to join the battalion, which was then billeted in St Alfred's School at the top of Hampstead Heath. The battalion then consisted of some 500 men, considerably below strength for an infantry battalion, the full complement of which should have been some 750. We spent two or three weeks at the school, going on route marches, carrying out sentry duty and the usual round of fatigues, such as peeling potatoes, washing up and cleaning out latrines. The most unpleasant part of our training by far was bayonet practice, when we were ordered to 'fix bayonets' and stick them into straw-filled sacks, to the accompaniment of the most bloodthirsty noises we could muster. This however did have its funny side, since we tended to sound more like people vomiting. This caused great mirth, to the annoyance of our sergeant instructor, who did his best, without much success, to get us to take all this seriously. The only lesson I learned from it was that I would be utterly incapable of ever sticking a bayonet into anyone, however much I might be under attack.

Once our initial training had been completed, we were sent off in small groups to do what was euphemistically called 'guarding vulnerable points' or, as we soon called it, 'doing VPs'. Such duties lasted forty-eight hours with two hours on guard and four off, when we had to remain fully equipped without being allowed to take our boots off. We were never able to see the point of this. We had to guard such disparate places as the railway bridges taking trains into Victoria, where we stood with trains thundering by every few minutes within a few feet of our noses; Willesden Junction signal box, where we were billeted in a District Line coach; an underground power sub-station under Leicester Square, where we were billeted with prostitutes in a house on the south side of the Square, which in those days still consisted of houses. A number of Fleet Street journalists, several well-known young actors and people working in the city had joined the battalion before war had been declared. Amongst the actors were Nigel Patrick and Frank Lawton, who was married to the musical comedy actress, Evelyn Laye. She was extremely attractive and became very popular with us when we were doing VPs in and around London, particularly at Willesden Junction, where she would frequently come up after the theatre to see her Frank, laden with whatever bottles of wine, gin or whisky she had been able to lay her hands on.

Later, we were sent to guard Woolwich Arsenal, where we had Nigel Patrick as our platoon commander. He became a leading actor after the war but he was an absolute pain as a young army officer. He had started as a rifleman in the Queen's Westminster's and returned to the battalion with a commission after I had joined. From the start he made himself extremely unpopular, behaving like a martinet. He tried to get us to march at the full regimental pace of 140 paces per minute. He even expected us to do this when we were returning from forty-eight hours guard duty, tired, unwashed and generally browned off with army life.

He did not succeed. As we marched out through the gates of the

Arsenal on our way up the hill to the Royal Military College, where we were billeted, he would try to up the pace, whilst the three leading riflemen, who always seemed to include Rifleman Atcherley, slowed the pace to a guardsman's stroll with the satisfying result that our platoon commander found himself marching on his own far ahead of the column. This invariably caused him to go berserk and scream at us, to our immense satisfaction. He appeared not to be aware that we were not supposed to march at the full regimental pace unless it was on a formal occasion.

We had, some weeks before, at last been issued with proper army great coats and gas masks and this made us feel rather more soldierly, but life in the ranks did not appeal to me greatly and it was not long before I saw an opportunity to do something more interesting. A notice appeared one day on the battalion office notice board calling for volunteers, who could ski, to apply for training with the Chasseurs Alpins in the French Alps, with a view to going to Norway or Finland with the ski troops. This was, for me, a heaven-sent opportunity to get away from 'doing VPs' and to improve my skiing. I immediately sent in my application, but to my great annoyance the battalion commander turned down my request. This prompted me, a few weeks later, to apply for a transfer to the army air reconnaissance branch, for which volunteers were being sought to train as Lysander pilots. I must have been mad since Lysanders, which were designed as observer planes, were extremely slow, flew at very low altitudes and were sitting targets for anything shooting at them from the air or from the ground. This second application was also refused, which was probably just as well.

After these disappointments, and in my quest to find more interesting things to do, I applied to join the Bren gun carrier platoon as a driver, was accepted and sent up to the tank driving school at Dunstable for two or three weeks, at the end of which we received our complement of carriers which we drove back to the East End of London where we were then stationed, guarding London Docks. Carriers were fun to drive as they could do over 50mph and were very manoeuvrable but they were absolute death traps. Unlike tanks, which were then, incidentally, steered by two levers controlling each track, carriers had steering wheels and were far more dangerous than a tank, since they were open and consequently provided no cover at all. It was rather like sitting in a square steel bath; when it rained hard one was even supplied with bath water.

My enjoyment of driving a carrier proved to be short lived, since the battalion received some 200 new recruits to build us up to strength. They had to undergo concentrated training, and were spared time-wasting chores such as peeling spuds and cleaning out latrines. This is where members of the carrier platoon came in; our carriers were parked under tarpaulin covers whilst we spent the next few weeks wielding potato peelers, buckets and mops.

INTELLIGENCE CORPS, 1940

All this encouraged me to apply for a commission in the Queen's Westminster Rifles and after an interview with a brigadier, who appeared to think that I was suitable material to be a 'leader of men', I was ordered a few weeks later to report to 164 Officer Cadet Training Unit, known as an 'OCTU', at Goojerat Barracks in Colchester. All I can recall now about this interview is being asked why I wanted to become an officer and I cannot remember how I replied. Whatever I may have said it was unlikely to have revealed the truth, which was that it was for me the only available route to a more civilised life in the army. We were a group of some 200. We lived in barrack rooms, each of which accommodated about 20 cadets so that our living arrangements continued to resemble life at boarding school. We wore our army battle dress, the only distinguishing feature being a white band worn round our forage caps to show that we were officer cadets. We were shouted at daily by our hut corporal; we were shouted at by sergeants, by warrant officers and by officers at every level. We drilled, were issued with bicycles, went out – in all weathers of course – on weapon training, on field exercises by day and night, map reading, and what were known as Tactical Exercises Without Troops or TEWTS.

Not surprisingly, life at OCTU was hard, but frequently hilarious, not least when we paraded for TEWTS complete with bicycles. We lined up two abreast and waited for the first cavalry command, 'Prepare to mount!', at which point we had to place our left foot on the left pedal. This was followed by the second command 'Mount!', when we all swung our right legs over our saddles and teetered off across the parade ground. There was no need for a further command because after 'mounting' we had to move in order to avoid falling off. I seem to recall that we never succeeded in getting away without at least two cadets colliding with each other. We naturally found the performance highly amusing and felt that we must resemble a bunch of women heading for the village shop. Our unmilitary behaviour annoyed our sergeant major, who told us more than once that if we wanted to become commissioned officers we had better mend our ways. In the evenings, we frequently went out to one of the surrounding pubs in Colchester, or to the canteen with our NCOs, who by then had stopped shouting at us and with whom we actually had very friendly relations.

My time at Colchester coincided with the invasion scare and half way through our training, which was supposed to last three months, about 120 of us were ordered out to the Essex coast, south of Clacton at St Osyth, to guard no less than seven miles of coastline. We were equipped with only one Bren gun between the lot of us. During the day we looked out to sea from a slit trench, which we had dug along the top of the beach, complete with a revetment of wooden planks to stop the sides from collapsing. At night we were supposed to withdraw into a small reinforced-concrete 'pill box' some 100 yards behind the beach. The air inside the pill box was so fetid that we always slept outside under the sky, unless it was raining. When later I was posted to the 18th Division in Norfolk, I learned that there had been no troops in reserve behind us and that there were no guns or tanks anywhere in East Anglia, this being a direct result of most of our equipment having been lost in France after the retreat from Dunkirk. I also discovered later, when

I joined the 18th Division in Norwich, that there had in fact been a Newfoundland artillery battery of First World War howitzers, which was reported to have had a total of only 50 shells. Since no more shells existed, they would not have been very effective.

To my amazement I passed out second at my OCTU, being beaten into first place by a very conscientious cadet from the Royal Scots. I can only assume that I took things rather more seriously than I was conscious of at the time. Whilst I was at Colchester, I was interviewed by a colonel from the War Office, who asked me if I would consider a commission in the Intelligence Corps. I must have put down on a form somewhere that I could speak German and French. As I had very little idea what this might involve, I asked him to explain what I might have to do as an Intelligence Officer. What he had to tell me sounded more interesting than being an infantry officer and I agreed to my name going forward with the result that I was commissioned into the Intelligence Corps as a Lieutenant, rather than a Second Lieutenant, which was standard practice in line regiments.

My first posting was to the War Operations Room in the Home Office. The room was in the basement of the building, the entrance to which, as with all other Whitehall buildings, had been heavily sandbagged. There were three of us in the team and we were responsible for transmitting direct to GHQ Home Forces every hour, or more frequently if circumstances dictated, reports about all air raid damage which might affect military movement, i.e. roads, railways, bridges etc. We wrote our reports in longhand on signals forms, which we then handed to one of a number of motorcycle despatch riders, who were constantly in attendance, to take to Intelligence at GHQ, Home Forces, which at the time was stationed in St Paul's School, then in Hammersmith.

There were normally some twenty or thirty people on duty at any one time in the Operations Room and one wall was covered by a large map of the British Isles and the northern coast of Europe from Scandinavia to central France. The Blitz had just started and as soon as information on the build-up of attacks, their strength and direction, started to come in, this was plotted on the map by a group of WAAFs (Women's Auxiliary Air Force). The first clue as to what we might expect began to emerge on the map as the Luftwaffe bombers and fighters took off from their many airfields dotted along the continental coastal belt. As they formed up and headed towards the British coast we began to get an idea as to their likely destination. The information was not always very reliable since in those days, before electronic gadgets had been invented, we had to rely on relatively primitive equipment. Speculation naturally tended to be concentrated on London, Liverpool and Manchester but it was often impossible to know until bombs started to drop which city or target had been singled out for that particular raid.

We sat at a table at the back of the room, with our backs to the wall, which no doubt the civil servants considered appropriate for members of 'the military', who tended to be regarded as interlopers on their territory. The three of us were billeted in the Charing Cross Hotel and were thus able to walk to and from the Home Office along Whitehall. We walked regardless of air-raid warnings in order to report on time. One morning, shortly after the all-clear had been sounded on my way to work after a particularly noisy night, I was astounded to see a bus up ended by the blast, presumably from a land-mine, with all four wheels against the wall of the building not far from the entrance to the Cabinet Office, on the edge of a large crater in the road. Another morning I and a number of other service officers were having breakfast in the hotel dining- room, which ran along the side of the station. A stick of bombs hit the station, killing a large number of people, who had just arrived by train on their way to work, and blowing in all the windows running along the side of the dining-room. A group of us were having breakfast together at the same table when we were blown on to the floor, and after recovering from the shock found ourselves covered in bacon and eggs, toast, tea and soot, the latter blown out of the chimneys at each end of the room.

Wherever one was in Central London during an air-raid, one was subjected to the constant noise of bombs exploding and anti-aircraft guns firing, interspersed by the ear-splitting whine and crash of bombs falling close by, followed a few seconds later by the sound of falling masonry and breaking glass. Each of us did two hours on and four hours off duty for a period of some two months. Sleep in wartime is always at a premium, and when this particular assignment ended after two months, I was greatly relieved.

This was my first direct experience of being bombed and I found it terrifying. In the years to come, I was to experience many more air attacks by the Luftwaffe, the Japanese and US air forces and even one by the RAF in Thailand, which killed a number of POWs. Looking back I realise that I was unbelievably lucky that none of them hit me, but at the time I could not help wondering why they should all be picking on me; I thought it was all very unfair. The most terrifying raids of the lot were, for me, the American B27 attacks on Singapore, which we experienced when we were sent to work in the docks, if only because of the sheer number and weight of bombs dropped in a comparatively small area. It was, I suppose, some consolation that I was never bombed by the Russians.

Following my assignment in the bowels of the Home Office, I was appointed Intelligence Officer at HQ 18th Infantry Division, then stationed in Norwich, with its units spread all over Norfolk, Suffolk and Cambridgeshire. The 18th was a Territorial division and soon after my joining its strength had been built up to its full complement of some 18,000. We were being trained as a Motorised Infantry Division, its primary role in the UK being to provide rapid reinforcement at short notice, wherever needed in the event of invasion. This meant that we would be carrying out exercises all over the country. We were, I think, the only division of our type in the British Army and after about a year of frequent exercises we became quite proficient. We would find ourselves in Southern England one week, the North of England a couple of weeks later, followed by Wales or Scotland. We learned how to move at considerable speed, and bearing in mind that we were a division of three infantry brigades and all the attendant artillery, engineer, supply and medical units, with our guns, tracked vehicles, not to mention hundreds of trucks, large and small, ambulances, staff cars and motorcycles, we became quite proud of ourselves. More than once our guns and heavy transport got stuck, on one occasion on the narrow bridge over the river at Ludlow, and on another in deep snow in the Scottish Borders. Our divisional commander was a Welsh Guards officer, Beckwith-Smith, who as a brigadier had brought the Guards Division back to England at the time of Dunkirk, after their divisional commander, Major-General Paget, I think it was, had been promoted to take command of an army corps in England. Becky, as we all called him, was promoted to Major General. He was an outstanding professional soldier and a wonderful human being, who was admired, respected and indeed loved by all who knew him. Little did any of us realize that he was later to die, quite unnecessarily, as a prisoner of war of the Japanese.

The majority of the senior staff officers at Divisional HQ were regulars and with few exceptions were highly capable. The two senior staff officers under Becky were Lt Col Hutchison, 'Hutch', who covered the operations side and Lt Col Dillon, 'Andy', who covered the administration, supply and legal side. Hutch had been a gunner and Andy, who had served in the Indian Army Service Corps, had seen action on the North West Frontier. Both were highly professional although Hutch had a singularly un-military bearing, always wearing his cap on the back of his head, being round shouldered with a paunch, and frequently being seen with a cigarette dangling from the centre of his mouth.

I joined the division as a Lieutenant and soon after taking up my appointment was promoted to Captain as a G3 (Grade 3) staff officer. As the Divisional Intelligence Officer my job initially meant that I spent a lot of time out and about at brigade and battalion level, lecturing on the German army, its organisation, weaponry and equipment, and getting to know the intelligence officers. I was, to start with, very ignorant about anything to do with the German Army, but fortunately for me, and much more important for the division, I was sent almost immediately on a War Intelligence Course at Matlock in Derbyshire. This lasted some six weeks and those attending were billeted very comfortably in Smedley's Hydro, then a well-known and long-established health spa.

In the course of visiting all our units, I got to know Norfolk, Suffolk, North Essex and Cambridgeshire very well. This could be quite fun, since all village and town signs had been removed in order to fox the Germans, or so it was believed. I found this an enormous help in improving my map reading, which I had always enjoyed and continue to do to this day. The British authorities were reportedly unaware that the German air force was already carrying out a comprehensive programme of aerial photography covering the whole of the country, which produced highly accurate large-scale maps.

My colleagues at Divisional HQ, who were all captains, included Tufton Beamish, a regular from the Northumberland Fusiliers, who was the GSO3 operations. He and I became good friends. Not only did we have a close working relationship, but also spent a lot of time together. Another was Peter Jamieson, one of our Motor Contact Officers, who became a particular friend. Tufton and I were part of the group of some 500 ordered away from Singapore on Friday 13 February 1942, about forty-eight hours before we surrendered. He fortunately made it whereas I did not. He escaped first to Sumatra, crossing to the west coast of the island where he and a group managed to get hold of a dhow and sail to Colombo. Tufton had earlier served in France, where he had been wounded and lost a finger, so this was the second time he had avoided becoming a prisoner. After spending some time in India he was posted to the 14th Army in Burma.

There was also a very conscientious and busy subaltern by the name of Tomkinson, who wore large tortoiseshell spectacles and was a wartime officer like me. He did his best to turn himself out like a regular by buying himself a pair of field boots and riding breeches, in which he strutted around on every possible occasion. Breeches did not form part of an officer's essential uniform in wartime and were normally only worn by regular army officers, who had them anyway. He took himself more seriously than we did and he soon became known as 'Puss in Boots', much to his fury. He was, like Peter, one of the three Motor Contact Officers, whose responsibility was to act as despatch riders, providing a vital link between divisional and the three brigade headquarters. They had to spend an unconscionable amount of their time dashing around the country at great speed on their Norton motorcycles. They really came into their own when radio communication failed, which it did frequently, particularly in Malaysia where radios seldom worked at all. Then there was Kerr Paxton, a Scot, who was the Divisional Education Officer, who had been with the British Council in Rome before the war. He was a great asset, being extremely well educated and highly civilised. He returned to the British Council in Rome after his release as a POW, from which experience he never fully recovered, becoming an alcoholic and committing suicide a few years later. Sadly, he was not the only one; I knew two others who never got over their experiences and did the same.

The division remained in East Anglia until late autumn 1940, when we were moved to Scotland. We had an eventful journey as it had snowed hard and much of our transport and guns got stuck for several hours in Northumberland, just south of the border - a good example of the difficulties facing any army which is foolish enough to fight a war in northern Europe in winter. We set up our Divisional Headquarters in Melrose and our units were stationed right across the Borders from Dumfries to Duns. Whilst there, we carried out several divisional exercises in the Lowlands and Highlands of Scotland and in the north of England.

North of the Firth of Forth, a large number of allied army units were stationed. They had successfully escaped from the continent and included a whole army corps of some 30,000 Poles and smaller numbers of Norwegians, Belgians and Czechs. The latter regarded exercises as being not far short of the real thing, well-illustrated on one occasion when one of our brigadiers, who had been 'captured' by a Czech unit, refused to give himself up and before he could drive off had the windscreen of his staff car smashed by rifle butts.

On one occasion when Becky's ADC went on leave I was asked to stand in for him. This coincided with the Duke of Buccleuch giving a reception for the senior officers of all the allied forces stationed in Scotland, and other VIPs. Becky and his wife were naturally there and I had to attend them. It was a memorable occasion since all the Polish, Norwegian and Czech generals and other senior officers wore their full dress uniforms, their chests covered by medals from the 1914-18 war. It took one back to Europe in the nineteenth century.

Whenever we were engaged on exercises, Becky operated from his advance HQ, staffed by his operations officers, who included Hutch, GSO1; 'Whiskers' Sutherland, GSO2; Tufton Beamish GSO3, myself as the GSO3(I) and the three MCOs (Motor Contact Officers). Field officers, who were all those of the rank of major and above, travelled in staff cars with their own driver. The Motor Contact Officers and I were equipped with Norton motorcycles. At the rear of the convoy came a mess truck with cook and batmen, a signaller's truck and a number of transport vehicles carrying HQ defence troops and military police. By day when the weather was fine, I thoroughly enjoyed it, but when we had to move at night, in rain or snow, with head lights blacked out on icy, winding roads, it was sheer hell. Occasionally vehicles went into ditches at the side of the road and it was amazing that none of us was killed.

We enjoyed an active social life in Melrose, thanks to the incredible hospitality of the local residents. Having had experience of being stationed in different parts of the British Isles in the course of the first two years of war, I came to the conclusion that the further north one was, the more hospitable people became. We put the south of England at 0-2 on a scale of 10 and Scotland at 8-10. Melrose is situated in Walter Scott country and we met lots of people of the same name although he had not fathered all of them. The house in which Walter Scott lived at Abbotsford was only a few miles away. One of the many Scotts, who lived in a large attractive house just outside Melrose, generously put the whole of the ground floor at our disposal for use as an officers' club. They then organised a large party for us shortly afterwards and we thus met most of the locals, who all seemed to be delighted by our invasion.

One of the girls I met at this party was Bridget Elliot, the daughter of the 5th Earl of Minto. She and I used to go out together whenever we had the opportunity. I remember returning one particular night to my room in the Abbey Hotel, which had been taken over for the junior mess, to find the walls covered with messages saying 'Harold loves Bridget'. The following morning I asked my batman, Hipperson (a milk roundsman in Norwich in civilian life) if he would kindly remove them. This he did with amused embarrassment, saying to me that he assumed I had had a pleasant evening. Bridget married a colonel in 1944.

Hipperson was considerably older than me and had spent all his life in Norwich, never leaving it until he was called up on the outbreak of war and posted to the 18th Division. Batmen had a rather more important role than acting as officers' servants as they formed part of the divisional defence company; nevertheless, hindsight tells me that it was utterly ridiculous for junior officers to be provided with a personal servant. It was hardly surprising that when I became involved with armed forces pay in the early 1970s I discovered that, by then, batmen were only allotted to lieutenant colonels and above.

In May 1940, whilst I was stationed in Scotland, there was a combined Naval and Army action in the Lofoten Islands, off the north coast of Norway. This was part of the so-called Norwegian campaign, which proved a fiasco and had to be aborted a month or so later. Most of the fighting against German forces, which were then in Norway, took place around Narvik, where a Polish brigade, then based in the Highlands, played a major part. Some 1200 prisoners were brought back from the Lofoten Islands and were initially interned in a temporary holding camp at Corstorphine, on the outskirts of Edinburgh. The intelligence officers of the three divisions stationed in Scotland were ordered up to Edinburgh to interrogate them. This was known in Intelligence jargon as the 'initial squeeze'. The three of us from the 51st Highland, 52nd Lowland and 18th Division were billeted in the North British Hotel on Princes Street for about a month.

Each morning I was collected by an ATC driver, who took me out to the camp in Corstorphine, a suburb of Edinburgh. At lunchtime she would drive me into Edinburgh for lunch, after which she took me back for the afternoon session of interrogation. She was an extremely attractive girl about my age. As the ATC was, at that early stage of the war, a purely voluntary organisation with the girls providing their own uniforms, they were very smartly dressed in tailor-made uniforms and silk stockings. This was in sharp contrast to the ATS, whose members were all conscripts and had to wear army issue clothing, with skirts which looked as though they had been run up by a sail-maker, and thick woollen stockings.

It was not long before my driver, whose name, sadly I cannot remember, and I decided to have lunch together and we ate most days at the Aperitif, one of the better restaurants in the centre of Edinburgh, which I seem to remember was situated in one of the side streets linking Prince's Street with George Street. This restaurant was frequented by many senior service officers and the situation was somewhat tricky since officers and other ranks were not supposed to mix socially, at least in public. However no-one ever said anything and I have little doubt that this was due to the attractiveness of my driver, both in looks and dress, and the fact that we both spoke educated English. Whatever the reason, we were never challenged. One of the unfortunate features of the war was that we were constantly being moved from place to place and this meant that whenever one was lucky enough to meet anyone who could have become a good friend, one was soon forced to part, with little prospect of meeting again.

Whilst the 18th Division was stationed in Scotland, we were warned that we were soon to embark on overseas service. The War Office clearly regarded the word 'soon' as being thoroughly elastic, since we were not actually ordered overseas until October 1941. Instead, in the spring of that year we moved to an area bounded roughly by Liverpool, Manchester and Birmingham and we established our Divisional Headquarters on the banks of the River Severn at Ribbesford House, near Bewdley, where we had to work in largely unheated Nissen huts. The location was beautiful, as the lawns ran down to the river. We established our mess in a large house in the vicinity. Our unattractive working conditions encouraged me to visit units as much as possible, and this proved especially valuable as I got to know all the other intelligence officers at brigade and battalion level far better than I would have done otherwise. I had been issued with a baby Austin van because for some unknown reason my motor cycle had been withdrawn for use elsewhere. I was naturally delighted since it was far warmer and safer to drive on four wheels.

Towards the end of 1940, prior to our move to Scotland, I had been sent on a German interrogation course in Cambridge and, throughout the four weeks we were there, we were expected to speak German. The course was primarily devoted to role playing, either as an interrogating officer or as a German prisoner. The two participants were, of course, briefed separately in considerable detail about the circumstances leading up to their 'capture'. The idea that I might one day become a prisoner of war myself never for one moment entered my head. Being captured or killed was something that only happened to others.

After we had been in Bewdley for some weeks, rumours suddenly resurfaced about our embarking for service overseas. It was about this time that I received a signal from the War Office ordering me to report to a colonel in the Intelligence branch. I drove up to London in my van and parked in Whitehall. After the usual pleasantries, the colonel pointed to several well used tea-chests, stacked in the corner of his office, and told me that they contained various items designed to assist anyone who had been taken prisoner to make a successful escape. He told me that I should distribute these to as many units as possible within the Division, adding that he could only let me have a limited quantity. He then gave me a secret code, which I had to commit to memory, so that in the event of my being captured, I would be able to transmit whatever important information I might be able to pick up about the enemy to the War Office. I spent most of my drive back to Bewdley repeating the code, so that it stuck in my memory.

The unexpected sequel to this visit to the War Office occurred some two years later when I had already been incarcerated in Changi for more than a year. When the first batch of letters from home had, at last, been allowed through by the Japanese, I received several from the family and one from an 'Aunt Annie'. At first I thought that there had been some mistake, since I certainly did not have an aunt of that name. After a day or two the penny dropped and I remembered that this was the person to whom I should address my letters giving information about Japanese military activities. It took a day or two for me to recall the code, which I had been given nearly two years before. After an hour or two of deciphering, I was able to read that they wanted me to pass on any information I could about Japanese troop movements between Singapore Island and the Malaysian mainland and Japanese naval movements in and out of the naval base situated on the North side of Singapore Island. I was incapable of doing anything to help since I was never allowed to send more than four 24 word postcards throughout the whole of my captivity.

Following the War Office meeting, I returned almost immediately to Ribbesford and together with my staff sergeant and several other intelligence staff got down to unpacking the contents of the cases. To our astonishment they contained nothing more sophisticated than a large quantity of celluloid front and back collar studs, which after much scratching revealed compass needles. There were also several hundred silk maps, about the size of a large handkerchief, of Europe. I had been told by the colonel that the studs should be worn at all times and that the maps were to be sewn into the lining of our battle dress. We were not exactly overwhelmed by what we had been given. So far as the maps of Europe were concerned, their value depended on our destination, which was unknown.

During the Division's stay in the Midlands, the Luftwaffe started bombing the Liverpool docks in earnest. Most of the dock labour was Irish – the so-called 'Liverpool Irish', who had always been regarded with some suspicion. This was confirmed when they downed tools and hurriedly cleared off when bombs started falling on the docks. Unloading came to a standstill. We were ordered by Eastern Command to send in several hundred troops immediately to take over the unloading of the ships, which had to be turned around as quickly as possible so that they could return to the US without delay to maintain the flow of essential war material and food, without which the country would have been incapable of continuing the war. It took some weeks before the problem of dock labour was sorted out, enabling our troops to return to normal military duty, but not before we suffered quite a few casualties, including a number killed, in the constant air raids.

The Division finally received embarkation orders in October, but we were not given any information as to our destination. Our transports were waiting in the ports of Bristol, Liverpool and Glasgow. Divisional Headquarters was to sail on the Reina del Pacifico, even then a relatively old ship, which in peacetime plied between Liverpool and the West Coast of South America through the Panama Canal. There is an account of what proved to be a journey of nearly three months at the beginning of my diary.

A few weeks before we left, Becky and his wife had invited all his team at Divisional HQ to a cocktail party in the senior officers' mess to meet local people. Amongst those invited were two extremely attractive girls, one dark and one blonde. The first was Jean Palethorpe and the other Diana Bean, whose father had been the founder and managing director of a well-known engineering firm which, amongst other things, manufactured the car of that name. Jean was to become Tufton Beamish's girlfriend, and Diana mine. The four of us went out together whenever we could get away from soldiering and in Diana's case farm work.

One of our favourite destinations was Shuthonger Manor, some miles south of Bewdley, a combined restaurant and night club. Here we frequently dined, drank and danced away the night, doing our best to forget the war, until daybreak compelled us to return to hard reality. On other occasions I used to have dinner with Diana and her parents at their lovely country house a few miles away. We all worked quite hard as soldiers but I think Diana had a much tougher time as a 'land girl', working from dawn to dusk on a local farm. She and I fell in love at first sight and I recall our last evening together at Shuthonger Manor the night before I sailed. It was a very happy but tearful occasion; we could only hope that the war would at least allow us to keep in touch. This was not to be. I received a pile of letters from her on my arrival in Singapore, but I was only able to write to her twice in reply before Singapore fell. It is unlikely that she ever received them because Singapore was soon cut off by a Japanese naval task force. I did receive two letters from her some two years later in captivity.

EMBARKATION, 1941

Recently, Anita gave me a bundle of letters of mine, which she had just discovered in turning out a lot of old papers. These included a number of letters I had written home in the course of my voyage to the Far East and the extracts which follow describe our time in Cape Town and India and my views, admittedly rather naïve, on the war at the time.

27th November 1941. On board MV Wakefield somewhere in the South Atlantic: The only news we get is from a daily news sheet issued on board but it is practically impossible to glean from this what exactly is happening in this war. Things seem to be moving fast in North Africa at last but with what success it is difficult to make out. The longer the war goes on the more I feel how unnecessary it all is. I have just finished reading Shirer's Berlin Diary, which brings home to me yet again what complete fools and sheer incompetents we were in the few years preceding the outbreak of war in 1939. If only there had been just one group of men capable of uniting the French and English at the time Hitler reoccupied the Rhine land, we could have stepped in and headed off war. The German army, such as it was in 1936, was far from ready to fight a war.

I am now a strong advocate of the US declaring war in the near future, not least for the moral effect it would have on Germany. I think that after what appears to be the German failure in Russia, the Nazis must be beginning to realize that they have got little hope of winning this war. That will not however make them fight any the less as they are probably afraid of the consequences of a peace which would put Versailles in the shade.

1st November 1941. I am rather anxious to give Diana some small present for Christmas as I know she would appreciate it. I wonder whether you could find something suitable? You and I have much the same tastes in clothes and books. I am afraid I am not in a position to do much.

16 December 1941. Still on board the American troopship Wakefield: Since my last letter, I have spent four and a half days in a South African Port (Cape Town – censorship forbade me to mention the name)… After spending nearly seven weeks on board ship without ever setting foot on land, it was absolute heaven. We first sighted land in the early morning. High green mountains with villages and red-roofed houses dotted about near the water's edge with, here and there, wedge-shaped deposits of sand, leading down to the beaches, very pale in colour and reminiscent of glaciers. The peaks of the hills just visible through an early morning mist, the whole scene moving nearer. I felt rather like the Flying Dutchman. Everything descended into crude reality when large advertising hoardings became visible – GEC Ltd, Shell Company of South Africa. Before going alongside, the whole convoy anchored for a short time in the harbour. It must have been an impressive sight from the shore. We learned later that everybody in the city was puzzled by seeing all the ships flying the Stars and Stripes.

We were finally able to go ashore early in the afternoon. Tufton and I accompanied by two other officers walked as far as the dock gates where we got a taxi, asking the driver to take us to 'the best hotel' in Cape Town for our first drink in seven weeks. The US navy is unfortunately 'dry'.

Before going ashore, all the officers had been given an invitation to a dance that evening at Kelvin Grove, a club on the outskirts of the city. Tufton and I went off to reserve a table for dinner at the Café Royal where we had an excellent dinner with crayfish and the most delicious peaches I have ever eaten.

Soon after we arrived at the club, which we did fairly early, my eye picked out a very attractive girl, tall with long dark hair, dressed in black and I decided that this was where I stepped in before anyone else could beat me to it. Her name was Yone May, who became my constant companion throughout our five day stay. Her mother and father were extremely hospitable....

About 10.00pm Field Marshall Smuts, Premier of South Africa, gave a speech of welcome, the first time he had done this on the occasion of convoys passing through Cape Town, so we felt very honoured. He is a fine looking man with a neat pointed beard. He had led the United Party in South Africa and had been appointed to the British War Cabinet in 1941.

On the day after the party, Yone drove us, in her very smart open sports car, up to Stellenbosch, the seat of the Afrikaans University, a very attractive town in Dutch style and apparently a hive of nationalism. It was a lovely drive through open rolling country with many fields of sweet corn, or mealies as it is called here, and many vineyards. Every few minutes we passed Dutch farmsteads, with their water mills, so reminiscent of the Argentine. The countryside in Cape Province is extremely beautiful, lush green and undulating, with eucalyptus trees, mimosa and many others with dark blue and mauve blossom, the names of which I have forgotten.

After returning to Cape Town, Tufton and I had dinner with Yone and her parents at their house and afterwards we went out to Kelvin

Grove and later to a night club called the 'Bohemian' – very good and far cheaper than any London night club – sadly we had to return to the ship by 2.30am. I shall never forget the beauty of Cape Town at night; such a contrast with blacked-out Europe, with its street lighting, neon signs, car headlights, floodlights in the dock area and the sparkling water in the moonlit night.

It all seemed unreal and I did not feel that I belonged there. Yone's father was head of BAT in South Africa and when war broke out in 1939, was six months overdue for home leave and did not expect to return to England until after the war. Yone's sister is working at GHQ in Cairo and her brother is a gunner officer in Singapore.

One evening Tufton and I invited Becky, to come out with us to have dinner and dance. He gets very fed up with all the official parties he has to attend and rather likes being with the 'nursery' as he calls us in C Mess, which contains all those of captain and subaltern rank, who by definition are mostly in their twenties. We took him to dinner at the 'Café Royal' and then went on to the 'Bohemian', where we danced until 2.0am. We were quite a large party as Tufton and I had invited Archie Bevan, Becky's ADC and Kerr Paxton, the Divisional Education Officer and Yone had invited two or three of her girl friends. The whole evening was a great success and I think Becky enjoyed it immensely and was very touched.

The following morning we met two South African millionaires, who entertained Tufton and me royally. On the last evening, Friday, we dined again with Yone at home and danced away the night at the 'Bohemian'. We knew that we were sailing early on the Saturday morning. I awoke at 7.30am to feel the vibration of the ships' engines and going on deck saw that we were already slipping out into the bay. There we remained until the afternoon when we finally up-anchored, each ship and our naval escorts taking up their position in convoy, leaving civilisation behind us. What a stay it was. The hospitality for both officers and men had been quite unbelievable. The government of South Africa and the city of Cape Town had each voted £5000 to enable both transport and entertainment to be provided free for the troops.

Now we have got these God-damned little Japs to fight. What a world this is. At the moment they appear to be doing well and Hong Kong and Singapore seem to be seriously menaced. By the time you receive this letter, however, things will no doubt have altered considerably. Meanwhile the news from Russia is excellent and if only they keep up their guerrilla tactics throughout the winter, the Germans might possibly be broken by the spring. In any case the German army will not be able to hold a line. This is no longer possible in modern warfare. The only thing one can do is to hold a series of all round defensive localities each of which is independent. This of course leads to the possibility of being outflanked and this the Russians may well try to do by a concentrated attack in one area on a narrow front.

As for the Japs, they will presumably go all out for the oil supplies in Indonesia, which would seem vital to their taking over South East Asia.

We are all getting fed up with sailing for ever without knowing where the hell we are going. I long to get ashore and stretch my legs wherever it is, even in the middle of a lot of Japs! It is getting hotter and hotter every day.

As for my relations I regret to say that they have been slightly neglected.

Give them my love and say that I will endeavour to write in due course.

4 January 1942. Bombay: India is smelly, dirty, dusty and the plumbing is that of the Middle Ages. We arrived in the harbour of Bombay in the early afternoon and immediately knew that we were in the Far East. There was bright sun over the harbour but a thick haze over the city and along the shore. We naturally wondered what had brought us here and speculated on where we might head next; it could only be one of two directions, the Middle East or Singapore. On disembarking the following morning, I was detailed to supervise the unloading of baggage and equipment and its loading into railway wagons. We left that night and rolled slowly through the outskirts of the city. I have never in my life seen anything to compare with the general squalor, filth and cramped conditions in which people lived. We arrived in Ahmednagar the following morning and settled into our accommodation in the fort. We shared this with a group of British Indian Army officers of a particularly repugnant type, who went around looking as though they had an unpleasant smell under their noses and clearly regarded us as something the cat had brought in. They certainly think that the war is unlikely to affect them.

There was a dance in the club on New Year's Eve, but the whole atmosphere was so ghastly that we left early and repaired to our senior officers' mess where we drowned our sorrows in the usual manner. The bugs in India are too numerous to count; there are cockroaches, ants of every conceivable size, flying insects and jackals can be heard in the night as they scrounge in the refuse around the fort.

16 January 1942. Bombay: We have spent a little over a fortnight in India and I am not sorry to see the end of it. It is often said that the best view of it is 'from the stern of a ship leaving Bombay'. I feel as though it will take several days to get rid of the dust from

my lungs and throat. At the moment I am sitting on the Wakefield in the harbour, a most unsavoury place. The water is a deep brown and reminds me of the River Plate. We are still travelling, but in which direction we still have no idea, except Becky and his senior officers I assume. I leave India with the possibly erroneous impression that here is a vast country with great potential wealth, which has not yet been fully awakened to the fact that there is a war on. Indian troops, however, could hardly have done more as they are now fighting on almost every front.

SINGAPORE FEBRUARY 1942

Special Orders

～

Special Order of the Day by General Wavell.

It is certain that our troops on Singapore Island heavily outnumber any Japanese, who have crossed the straits. We must destroy them. Our whole fighting reputation is at stake and the honour of the British Empire. The Americans have held out in the Bataan Peninsular against far heavier odds. The Russians are turning back the picked strength of the Germans. The Chinese with an almost complete lack of modern equipment have held the Japanese for four and a half years. It will be disgraceful if we yield our boasted fortress of Singapore to inferior enemy forces.

There must be no thought of sparing the troops or civil population and no mercy must be shown to weakness in any shape or form. Commanders and senior officers must lead their troops and if necessary die with them. There must be no question or thought of surrender. Every unit must fight it out to the end and in close contact with the enemy.

Please see that the above is brought to the notice of all senior officers and by them to the troops. I look to you and your men to fight to the end to prove that the fighting spirit that won our Empire still exists to enable us to defend it.

Singapore
10 Feb. 42. (Signed) AP Wavell. General.

From Lieutenant General Percival:

I attach a copy of an order I received from the C in C South Western Pacific Command, General Sir Archibald Wavell, GCB, CMG, MC.

The gist of this order will be conveyed to all ranks through the medium of all commanding officers. In some units the troops have not shown the fighting spirit which is to be expected from troops of the British Empire. It will be a lasting disgrace if we are defeated by an army of clever gangsters, many times inferior in numbers to our own. The spirit of aggression and determination to stick it out must be inculcated in all ranks. There must be no further withdrawals without orders.

There are too many fighting men moving about the back areas. Every available man, who is not doing other essential work, must be used to stop the invader.

HQMC, 11 Feb. 42. (Signed) A Percival, Lieut. General, GOC Malaya.

WAR DIARY

May 1942 to July 1942

❧

I started to write this diary in May 1942. The original, written in pencil, partly on paper scrounged from wherever I could find it and which I bound together in brown paper covers by needle and thread and partly in Malayan school exercise books, is in the archives of the Imperial War Museum. It had become very difficult to read and needed proper preservation. The text that follows is identical to the original, except for corrections to spelling and grammar, where I felt this was called for in the interests of greater clarity.

It is now 26 May 1942. I left England seven months ago and arrived in Singapore after a voyage of three months, which took me nearly 24,000 miles around the world. During this trip I set foot in North America, South Africa, India and spent three days in sight of South America in Trinidad harbour. At the end of January 1942 I disembarked in Singapore and fifteen days later woke up to the unpleasant fact that I was a prisoner of war.

It has long been my intention to start a diary to put on record my experiences during this time but it has taken three months of captivity for me to make a start. I must turn my thoughts back to those few hectic days, which we all spent between the time orders were received for us to go abroad and the day we actually left Bewdley to go by rail to Liverpool for embarkation. It was not until

Friday 22 October 1941 that we were told definitely that our day of departure from Bewdley was fixed for the following Tuesday the 26th. Friday evening found the mess in good form although, looking back, I think most of us were leaving with mixed feelings. I know Tufton and I were. By the Saturday morning work had ceased and I spent most of the day arranging a farewell party at Shuthonger Manor. The party consisted of Archie, the Perrins, Tufton, Jean Palethorpe, Diana and myself. It was a wonderful evening and I don't think I was in bed until after 4.00 am. Diana called for me at Ribbesford at midday on the Sunday morning and we had lunch together in Droitwich. After a really delightful day we drove over to A mess for drinks with the Perrins and Becky (Maj. Gen. Beckwith-Smith, our Divisional Commander). Becky was in great form and it was not until about 9 o'clock that Tufton, Jean, Diana and I were able to get any dinner. We decided to pay a farewell visit to the 'Whittington'. That night I said goodbye to Diana and by mutual consent we decided not to ring each other before I left, our parting was difficult enough as it was. Monday we all spent packing up as everything was to be ready for en-training early on the Tuesday morning. The evening was spent working off what still remained of the drink stock and this was done quite satisfactorily.

Tuesday came; a sunny, cold day with a biting wind which I often wish would blow here in Changi. There is nothing I should like to experience more than a damp London fog, after all these months of sun and heat. We pulled out of Bewdley station at about half-past ten and after a journey in which we proceeded in fits and starts and which seemed never ending, we arrived in Liverpool at about 4 o'clock in the afternoon. We detrained but could see no signs of any troop-ships. We had not quite completed our journey by land as we caught sight of a long line of old and dilapidated buses, into which we had to pile. Our trip through the docks came to an abrupt halt after a mile or two and on getting out we suddenly saw the Reina del Pacifico and the Andes looming above our heads. We were to embark on the former, a much older ship and we looked somewhat wistfully at the Andes, which had only been launched shortly before the outbreak of war and was a fine sight as she lay over on the opposite side of the dock.

Embarkation for officers of Divisional HQ was simpler than I had imagined and we walked straight up the gang-plank onto the ship. There was a long line of troops on the quayside reaching along the whole length of the ship and seeing how many men already appeared to be on board I rather wondered how they would all fit in. However, I had not yet had the doubtful pleasure of travelling on a troop ship. I had a lot to learn about the use of space. Officers were allotted accommodation in first class cabins and I could see at a glance we should not be too badly off. The appearance and general lay-out of the Reina reminded me very much of the Asturias, on which I had travelled to Buenos Aires as a boy, but it had undergone a major transformation since her peace-time role. Everything was painted grey, three Bofors guns were mounted forward and two in the stern. Her decks were already littered with men's kits and the dull khaki mass of the troops to whom they belonged.

Tufton and I took a look into the public rooms and found them filled with timber frames, providing tiers of bunks three high. Even the forward end of the promenade deck, where it was covered, had been turned into accommodation for troops. Latrines were on the open deck aft and consisted of wooden constructions. After the first few days at sea, we were glad that they were aft and we had a head wind.

We were to be roughly 150 officers and between 2,500 and 3,000 troops. Tufton and I were lucky in that we found we had been allotted a cabin together with Stephen Lee, our Gas Warfare officer. Our cabin was small but quite pleasant. At 7 o'clock we had our first surprise, when we descended to the dining-saloon for dinner. This was the one part of the ship still left intact and we sat down to a six course dinner. The food was every bit as good as that one used to have in peace time. It was most unreal to sit down and see all this food when everybody on shore would be sitting down to a meal of rations. That night the ships were towed into the river, where we were to remain until the morning of the 28th. Up river we could see some of the other ships which were to make up our convoy. The Andes – Royal Mail Line, Orcades – Orient Line, and the Warwick Castle –Union Castle Line. We slipped down stream and after we had passed New Brighton on the port side we were able to see our destroyer escort. The remainder of the convoy was sailing from Glasgow and we were to go up to the rendezvous off the north coast of Ireland to form up. It was a bitterly cold day with a driving wind and showers. Everything was grey. The destroyers, the ships in the convoy, the sky, the sea and the day could not be described as cheerful. In the bar, however, the officers had a small lounge. There was plenty of alcohol at the usual ridiculously low prices. Cigarettes could be bought by the hundred. When I disembarked from the Reina in Halifax, I took a thousand cigarettes in my suitcase, as I thought it advisable to build up a stock. However, I am getting ahead and at the time our first port of call was being kept highly secret; why I don't know. It was not as though anybody could pass the news on to a fifth column. Just another indication of the illogicality of security in the army.

It was not until several days later that the rumour of our going to

Halifax became known. None of us could make out why we should be going in that direction and of course rumours started thick and fast. And what of our daily life on board? Well, food played the most part. Meals were quite staggering. One started off breakfast with fruit then went on to porridge or cereals, fish, bacon and eggs and toast and marmalade. I can hardly realise that I have ever eaten anything but rice, rice and yet more rice; however, this is another story and the meals of the Reina belong to another world. Most of the morning was taken up with boat drill, which was a rather more serious business than it could ever have been in peace time. We then did an hour or so of P.T. on the boat deck, after which we were more than ready for lunch. The afternoons we had to ourselves and I spent most of them reading or writing letters. The deck was too cold a place except for walking around briskly at that time of year in the north of the North Atlantic. Dinner at 7.00 pm was something to look forward to and we never went down to it without the odd drink or two in the bar upstairs. We usually opened a bottle of South African wine, sweet but quite acceptable under the circumstances, since the ship, oddly enough, had no dry, white wine. We were told that all the better wines had been drunk by Canadians, who had been on the Reina del Pacifico on her previous trip from Halifax to Liverpool. The Reina had, before that, been used as a transport ship in the Norwegian expedition. So it is not surprising that little drink in the way of good wine was left. The bar was otherwise well stocked. Many of the more senior officers tended to get drunk most nights, but that is something one gets used to.

The third day out dawned bright and cheerful though extremely cold. The morning was not far gone before we caught sight of a vast concentration of shipping to the north and, as it loomed nearer, we could distinguish an aircraft-carrier and at least one battleship with their accompanying cruisers and destroyers. Away on our starboard bow was a large convoy of merchantmen, which these vessels appeared to have been escorting. We were puzzled as to what was going on but were not left long in doubt since suddenly our four escorting destroyers wheeled round together with the anti-aircraft cruiser and made off in the direction of the convoy of merchantmen. Simultaneously destroyers came in from the port bow and took up station, where the others had been, with four more spread out round the convoy.

The flags of our new naval escort were the Stars and Stripes and we suddenly woke up to the fact that we were witnessing a completely unexpected event. This was the first time during the war, so far as we knew, that US naval vessels had escorted British ships. While this change-over was going on, planes from the aircraft-carrier zoomed overhead, more and more of them taking off from the deck of the carrier, until we counted 34 planes in the air at the same time. It was all very noisy and impressive and in fact reminded us very strongly of a Hollywood film. Our convoy then consisted of the 9 troopships, for we had picked up, off Glasgow, the Dunbar Castle, the Oronsay, the Duchess of Atholl, a Polish ship called the Sobieski and another Duchess, the name of which I forget. These with the Reina, Andes, Orcades and Warwick Castle made the total of 9, which hitherto had been escorted by the four first world-war, American 'lend-lease' destroyers and one old RN anti-aircraft cruiser. We now had fourteen destroyers. Some more naval ships joined us the following day; two cruisers, a battle-ship, the aircraft-carrier Ranger, and a fleet oiler. We felt no safer, however, than with our four destroyers which had a distinct air of quiet efficiency. This was all rather flash and we wondered what would happen in an emergency.

The convoy was now as follows:

Three destroyers
Duchess of Atholl / MV Sobieski / MV Dunbar Castle / Battleship / Destroyer
Destroyer / Aircraft Carrier / SS Andes / Duchess of Bedford / Cruiser / Destroyer
Reina del Pacifico / SS Oronsay / Orcades / Cruiser
Three destroyers

The rest of the destroyers formed an outer circle. We proceeded without incident until we were almost off Newfoundland, when a U boat was reported. We then ran into one of those fogs, which are so common off Newfoundland and the following day, during boat-drill, I happened to be looking over the side when the cry went up "Man overboard". I looked down and saw an American sailor in the water, floating by some fifty yards from the side of the ship. The wretched man looked up and somebody threw him a life-belt. This landed some way from him however. He did not appear to be struggling at all and the sea was very calm albeit cold, but nothing could have saved him. I realised he would not be picked up, since the convoy was unable to stop.

The first part of our journey was coming to an end as we were due in Halifax on the Saturday morning November 8th. Tufton and I got up early and at about 8 o'clock land came in sight. Our escort gradually dispersed and when the last of the destroyers left us, the nine troopships of the convoy went into line-ahead formation for the entry into Halifax harbour. It was a lovely morning with bright sunshine and a fresh breeze. Soon we could pick out ships in the harbour and details of the coast-line gradually came into view. The coast here is barren and wild looking, most of the low hills being barely covered by a sort of low scrub, but it all looked very cheerful. Rumours started flying around the ship almost immediately- "We were just putting in to re-fuel", "We were going to be transhipped" and finally, the best of all, "We were to be disembarked and travel by train across Canada". Nobody knew where we were going.

Actually, Tufton and I had already heard that transhipment was the next thing on the programme. As we got into the inner harbour, we were able to pick out several large ships. There was the America, completed at the beginning of the war and the largest ship ever to be built in American shipyards, now renamed the Westpoint and used as a troop transport. Then there were the Manhattan and the Washington, now renamed Mount Vernon and Wakefield respectively. The other three alongside were the Orizaba, a small two funnel ship, which used to do the run from New York to Central America; the J.T. Dickman and the Leonard Wood, both of the latter originally belonging to the President line. When we had picked out all these ships, their names of course we did not learn until later, it suddenly dawned on us that we were about to be transhipped on to US naval transports and clearly we were making history as the US was not yet in the war. We were the first convoy to be escorted by ships of the US Navy and now we were about to be the first British troops to be transported in US ships. It was all being kept very quiet, which is not surprising as we were certain that American public opinion, being divided as it was in those days, would receive a rude shock if it had known of the uses to which American shipping was being put, namely to transport and escort a complete British Infantry Division of some 18,000 men several weeks before America came into the war.

But to resume: by about 11.00 am we had anchored in the harbour and we were to be one of the second group of ships to go alongside for unloading. By now the breeze had died right down and the sun was pleasantly warm. The rest of the morning we spent sitting on deck and at 12 o'clock we descended to the bar for a drink. As usual, of course, we found it full of senior officers of Divisional Headquarters. The usual few of whom were already hardly sober. This particular habit of our senior officers getting tight was to annoy us for many weeks to come, particularly as it meant that, each morning, we had to put up with their foul tempers, which were invariably vented on us. The trip, so far, had been quite pleasant in spite of crowded conditions and the food was excellent, so good in fact that I did not, for one moment, expect such a high standard to be maintained on the American ships.

We were all wondering, naturally, what our ultimate destination would be now that we were going to travel in US naval ships for they had all been taken over by the navy and were crewed entirely by naval personnel. The afternoon we spent quietly scanning the shore. Everything looked incredibly peaceful and war might never have existed. All those grey painted ships looked as if they did not belong there. Dozens of big American cars could be seen on the roads and when darkness fell their headlights combined with all the street lighting and electric signs made a beautiful sight.

Even the deck lights were put on on the ships in the harbour and the whole scene seemed quite unreal. I stood against the rail taking it all in with something of a lump in my throat. I thought of Europe three thousand miles away in complete darkness, although I suppose that Portugal was still able to keep the lights burning in that small corner of Europe. Somehow she seemed to me then to be the last bulwark of civilisation, the last hope where, beyond, was nothing but blackness. Tufton's mind, I realised, was running on very much the same lines and we both discussed the futility of it all, particularly as one realised that the US would be unable to keep out much longer. We were due to go alongside the quay in the evening and by about midnight everything was ready for unloading. Troops were to embark on the Wakefield on the Sunday so most of them were able to get a good night's rest. 2.00 am found me on the quayside supervising the unloading of baggage and equipment belonging to Divisional H.Q. There was a lot of stuff to come off and a considerable shambles on the quayside. I was to get to know that quay quite well as I was there practically continuously until 4 o'clock on Sunday afternoon, when the last baggage had come off. I then went for a stroll with Peter into the town but this we did not find impressive at all, particularly as it was Sunday afternoon, never an ideal time to see any town for the first time.

After an hour or so we returned to the dock and in a few minutes got a lift on a truck piled high with packing cases to the dock where the Wakefield lay. She was a lot bigger than the Reina and we were to be 5000 on board. We had a bit of trouble at the gangway as there was no berthing card made out in my name. I said "Fine I'll go back to the Reina again" but I was merely given someone else's card and told that that would be all right. Pity – I might never have had to come any further on this fool's errand. The first thing we did when we got on board was to go in search of something to eat. This was not so easy. The ship seemed crowded with men everywhere and the passages were blocked with baggage. Eventually we found what we were looking for, the dining saloon. This consisted of a number of long tables and a lot of black boys making the most awful noise with knives, forks and plates. The heat was unbearable and as soon as we had finished we went up to A deck where I was told I should find my cabin. This I eventually did and entered quite a large cabin which four of us were to share. In fact this proved quite comfortable as we were not too crowded and we had our own shower. The other three were Archie Bevan, ADC to

Becky, Bobby Trench, DAPM and Kerr Paxton, Divisional Education Officer. I had the camp bed which was in the middle of the cabin, presumably as I had arrived last. This was to prove a great advantage, however, when we got down into the tropics as Tufton, who was in a cabin a little further along, and I started sleeping up on the boat deck. We woke on Monday morning to find we were already out in the harbour and all set to go. We sailed after breakfast and the second stage of our journey had begun. Little did any of us think then, on 10 November, that we would still be on the Wakefield on 29 January 1942.

The convoy was now as follows:

Three destroyers

Fleet Oil Tanker / Cruiser

Destroyer / Orizaba / J T Dickman / Leonard Wood / Destroyer

Aircraft Carrier / Cruiser

West Point / Wakefield / Mount Vernon

Three destroyers

The three larger vessels sailed in one line on the starboard side and the three smaller ones on the port side. Soon after leaving Halifax we picked up the escort. An aircraft-carrier, two cruisers and eight or ten destroyers. The Americans certainly made use of their aeroplanes as they circled round and zoomed over our heads practically every day. Rumours abounded, naturally, as to what was going to be our next port of call. We had already learned that this was to be Port of Spain, Trinidad, where the destroyers and the three smaller ships of the convoy were to be re-fuelled. It took several days to create any order out of the chaos which prevailed on board at first. The Americans must have received rather a shock when they suddenly realised the task they faced of feeding some 5000 troops in one dining saloon. During the first few days men literally spent the whole day in the queue, since by the time they had received food for one meal they had to get into the end of the queue for the next. However, everything settled down eventually but one of our earliest shocks was to realise that the US Navy was dry. In practice this was something that worried the senior officers more than the junior. There were no lounges and we were forced to make much more use of our cabins than had been the case on the Reina del Pacifico. It was not long before this did not trouble us since it was steadily getting warmer as we proceeded southwards and so we were able to spend all day on deck. The American officers were a pleasant lot and we got on well with them. This was apparently not true on some of the other ships, particularly on the West Point, as we learned later, where there was considerable friction. I felt I knew where the fault lay with the inability of the Englishmen to understand the Americans, but maybe both sides were equally responsible.

Most of the time we spent reading and in the afternoons we played medicine ball up on deck. We had no official duties to carry out on board, other than those of inspecting men's meals and quarters. This only came round every sixth or seventh day. They were not very onerous. As we neared Puerto Rico we were accompanied by an escort of Catalina flying boats, which remained with us the whole of the day. We entered the Mona Passage in the early hours of the morning and some three or four hours later we sighted Mona Island. This is a small island mid-way between Puerto Rico and Dominica, very flat without much sign of habitation, except a lighthouse and something which looked very like a watch-tower. We were also able to pick out several small islands on the port side –

we passed Mona on the starboard side – but they all appeared to be uninhabited. The weather during this part of the trip was glorious and the sea was as calm as I have ever seen it. From Mona to Port of Spain was 600 to 700 miles and the trip was uneventful until we sighted the mainland of South America, the Paria Peninsula, on the morning of 17 December.

The entrance to the Gulf of Paria is very narrow and we soon went into line ahead formation, the cruisers leading. As we entered, we passed the mainland of Trinidad on the port side and a small island on the starboard, both heavily wooded; details of the trees stood out so clearly that one felt as though one could stretch out both arms and touch each side. Further in we could see dozens of small bungalows dotted about on the hillsides but nowhere very far above the water's edge. It was a pleasant sight with the green of the mountains and the bright reds and pinks of the house tops. We were wondering if we would be allowed ashore, when we suddenly turned to starboard and dropped anchor about seven miles out in the bay and it became clear that we would be highly unlikely to have any opportunity of thumbing a lift ashore in any of the jolly-boats. We sat in Port of Spain from 17 to 19 November and it was very hot indeed in the shelter of the high hills. One or two of the luckier ones did manage to get ashore but I gather they found the town very hot and dirty and there is only one good hotel, the Queen's Park. The only ship to go alongside was the Orizaba, the rest of the ships being re-fuelled and watered by lighter. We finally sailed at 2.00 pm on the afternoon of the 19th and after steaming north for a short time we turned east and then south-east, after passing Tobago on our port side, although visibility was so bad we were unable to see it.

Reports were received from time to time during the first few days after leaving Port of Spain of U-boat activity off Pernambuco, whether there was any truth in these rumours I never discovered. Life went on, in fact quite peacefully, reading, writing letters and sunbathing. I had managed to get letters posted at Halifax and Port of Spain. Archie Bevan was able to send off a cable for several of us when he went ashore with Becky. We passed quite close to the island of Fernando de Noronha and I suddenly wished we were en route for Buenos Aires. A day or two later re-fuelling began and the convoy slowed down to nine knots. This was the first time, and indeed the only time, I had ever seen re-fuelling done at sea. The Orizaba and all the destroyers were eventually re-fuelled and some of the destroyers returned to America with the aircraft-carrier. We were now left with the two cruisers and three or four destroyers. It was about this time that our precious 'G' staff started us all off, Divisional HQ and 54th Infantry Brigade HQ staff, on three hours 'work' each morning. This was pleasant enough in so far that it helped us pass the time but I learned very little and found it all exceedingly dull.

However, it kept our senior officers quiet since they love to have something to do so long as it is military. Regular officers have few interests outside the army and find it very difficult to amuse themselves on board. It was about this time that Tufton and I decided that it would be preferable to sleep up on the boat deck as we could no longer stand the heat in the cabin. The conditions for the men were ghastly. They were of course extremely crowded and the smell of all those thousands of bodies was indescribable. We found this particularly annoying as we had to walk through it all going to and from meals. However, we had to remember that it might have been us, who had had to travel in those conditions. Indeed, looking back on all this, I find it quite incredible that the difference in treatment between the officers and the other ranks was so great and could not have been justified on any grounds at all.

When we were some 1500 miles from Cape Town, which we heard in due course was to be our next port of call, we received further reports of submarine activity and we had to make a long detour around to the south until we were some 500 miles south of Cape Town and then approach it from the south east. We arrived in Cape Town eventually on 9 December and by now we were all more than ready to set foot on shore. We had, to all intents and purposes, been at sea from 28 October until 9 December and the men, in particular, had been travelling under the most appalling conditions. Indeed, how they remained as cheerful as they did is past my comprehension. None of us even then had the slightest idea of our ultimate destination. Not even, so far as I can recall, did Becky. But this was, in a sense, of secondary importance then, since all we wanted to do was to get ashore as soon as possible. The view across Table Bay to Table Mountain is too well known to need any description from me but it was certainly a wonderful sight, perhaps doubly so for us who had been travelling so long.

The convoy slowed down and went into line ahead. We heard that the Wakefield was going to be first in, so Tufton and I dashed down to get a quick lunch so that we did not miss anything of interest on the way in. By the time we returned to the deck we had just got under way again and were sliding slowly passed the ships ahead of us. It was a glorious afternoon and the setting was perfect. By about half-past two we were tied up but we had to wait a couple of hours before there was any chance of getting ashore. We had no passes and no money. We had now heard that we should get at least three days ashore, possibly more. The 9th was a Tuesday, we hoped we might have until the end of the week. Tufton and I had decided to spend our days ashore together.

We had heard, while we were still on board, that there was to be a dance for all officers at some club just outside Cape Town that evening and we thought that this would be a good kicking off point. The first two things to be done, however, were to get something to drink and then something to eat. After that we decided it was essential to find somebody with a car. At about half-past five in the evening we stepped off the ship and walked to the dock gates and collared a taxi, telling the driver to do a quick tour of the centre of the city and then drop us at the best hotel for a drink. This he did, chattering away all the time. The first thing that struck me about Cape Town was the bright colouring of its buildings and the cleanliness of the streets. The whole scene was very cheerful. In time we arrived at the Mount Nelson Hotel which is quiet, not that it was quiet for long, and situated in the most pleasant gardens. We told George, our taxi driver, to come back for us in an hour's time to take us to the Cafe Royal restaurant where he claimed we would get the best food in Cape Town. After a month on a dry ship and an hour at the Mount Nelson, life had taken on a definitely pleasant aspect and we felt ready for a good dinner. George was already waiting when we got outside and by half-past seven he dropped us outside the Cafe Royal. We told him to collect us later to take us out to the Kelvin Grove Club where a dance was to take place. We certainly did have an excellent dinner and washed it down with a couple of bottles of La Gratitude, a South African white wine which is supposed to be one of the better white wines produced locally.

The dance at the Kelvin Grove was scheduled for 8.45 pm and we left the Cafe Royal feeling no pain at all, just before 9.00 pm finding George waiting patiently outside. George was a great character; he never ceased to extol the beauties of Cape Town and kept up a

50

continual flow of conversation. He had to speak at the top of his voice, however, as he had his car radio on at full volume the whole time he was talking. He drove at a furious pace and never seemed to keep his eye on the road. How we got to our destination I don't really know. It was a great sight to see all the lights of Cape Town and we felt as if we had come into another world with all the cars' headlights full on, neon signs winking, and shop lighting shining out onto the streets. The Kelvin Grove is a country club some 5 or 6 miles from the centre of Cape Town and had recently been the scene of two similar dances given for officers of visiting convoys or warships. In fact the Prince of Wales, later to be sunk with the Repulse with very few survivors, had put in for a few days on its way to Malaya about two weeks before.

We arrived at the club shortly after 9.00 pm and found a large crowd already there. Quite soon I met a girl by the name of Ione May and discovered she had a car. Tufton and I had thought that if we could find someone with a car, this would be an ideal way of seeing Cape Town and certainly the most pleasant. About half way through the evening, General Smuts addressed us. He spoke for some 10 minutes, welcoming us to Cape Town and wishing us good luck, wherever we might go in the future. It was interesting to realize, from what he said, that he clearly assumed that we would be heading for the Far East and that we would probably be fighting Japs and not Germans. For our part, we did not think for one moment that we would end up in the Far East. We returned to the ship about 1.00 am after a very enjoyable evening. I arranged to meet Ione at 11.00 am the following morning for a drink and a trip in her car outside Cape Town. In fact she collected Tufton and me at the quayside in her very smart open roadster. We drove out to Stellenbosch, the seat of the Dutch university, the English university being in Cape Town. Stellenbosch we found to be a very attractive small town about 30 miles inland. In the evening, we all returned to Cape Town and had dinner with Ione's parents, who were extremely hospitable. Her father was the BAT representative in South Africa. He had been due for home leave in 1939 and, as a result of the war, would have to wait until the end, before he and his wife could return to the U.K. He told us that his son was a gunner and, so far as he knew was in Singapore. In fact he is supposed to be in the same camp as I am, but I have not so far been successful in contacting him. There is an elder sister working in Cairo at GHQ so the family is well spread out. After dinner we made up a party and went to a very good nightclub where one had to take one's own drink, since it did not have a licence.

Before going any further, I must say a word about hospitality in Cape Town, which we found quite astounding. Troops had free access to places of entertainment and could use the city's transport facilities for nothing. Literally hundreds of troops of 18 Division must have been taken out by people ashore and were entertained for the whole of the four days we were there. These days will not be forgotten in a hurry by any of us and the Americans from the ships had an equally good time and were very well received. On the Thursday, Tufton and I did some shopping in the morning and met Ione for lunch at the Del Monico restaurant. In the afternoon we went out in her car to a beach at Duisenburg to swim. It is a well-known beach with heavenly sand and excellent surf bathing. We made full use of surf-boards. The war seemed very far away that afternoon, the glorious blue of the sky and the sea, the gold of the beach and the green hills forming the edge of the bay. We just relaxed and drank it all in, but had to return to Cape Town early as Tufton and I had invited Becky out to dinner that evening at the Cafe Royal and Ione joined us. I think she was the only woman present and this certainly made the occasion more enjoyable, not least for Becky. In fact, the evening was a great success and I think Becky enjoyed himself thoroughly. Certainly he was able to relax. We invited him out, not only because we liked and admired him immensely, but partly because we knew how tired he was of all the official dinners and parties, to which he had to go and we knew how much he enjoyed a party with the 'nursery' as he called us. We all returned to the Wakefield in great form.

Friday morning we heard that we were sailing on Saturday and this would be our last day ashore. We made the most of it and finished up once more at the Bohemia having to leave early as we had to be on board by mid-night. The scene at the dock gates was indescribable – a mass of cars and hundreds of troops in varying stages of drunkenness but most of them on top of their form and well able to get on board under their own steam. Drinking for Tufton and myself continued on board with Hutch and Andy, who appeared to have a good supply of liquor in their cabin and we were not in bed until about 4.00 am We had little to do the following day but sleep it off. From all of this, it would appear that drink played the most important part of our stay in Cape Town, but in fact only a very minor part of our time was spent drinking and I was only really tight once.

We now said good-bye to our American naval escort and our convoy was taken in charge by a RN cruiser, which is to accompany us as far as Bombay. We started now what I regard as the third part of our journey. We left Cape Town early on Saturday afternoon and were sorry indeed to have to leave South Africa so soon. In fact I left with the firm intention of returning there one day to see more of the country which I thought very beautiful. It was an afternoon of bright sunshine when we left and we had an excellent view of the Cape of Good Hope, which incidentally is not the most southerly point of South Africa as I had always assumed. Cape Agulhas extends some fifty miles further south and is over a hundred miles south-east of the Cape of Good Hope. It is interesting to note that the distance from Southampton to Cape Town is just under 6000 miles but by the way we had travelled we had done well over 13,000 miles.

The news that we were in fact destined for Bombay, and not our original destination Suez, was soon public knowledge and we toiled on up the east coast of Africa. There is really not much to tell of this part of our trip. Life went on much the same as usual. We had sailed from Cape Town on 13 December and it soon became apparent that at our then rate of progress we should be spending Christmas Day on board. In fact by then we were prepared to travel the rest of our days on board and, indeed, the Division had become a sort of 'Flying Dutchman' Division. We thought that the War Office had probably forgotten our existence. We steamed up the coast until we reached Mombasa, and here the Orizaba left the convoy to re-fuel. It had been the original intention for the convoy to slow down while the Orizaba caught us up again. However, the next day, the Mount Vernon, the flagship of the convoy, was ordered into Mombasa as well. The reason for this was not known at the time; in fact not until after we had arrived in Singapore. All we heard then was that she was headed for some different destination but nobody knew where. Christmas Day came and we were still a day or two from Bombay. On Christmas Eve we presented all the senior officers with Christmas stockings, which were filled with anything from a packet of Chesterfield cigarettes to a potato. However, the gesture was well received, particularly by Becky.

Two days later we arrived in Bombay. It was a hot, muggy day and the first thing we saw was a whole crowd of sampans. Here we first realised that we were in the East and by the time we had entered Bombay harbour, we were already able to feel its influence. It was not only hot and sticky, but a smoky haze hung over the harbour and city. One could already pick up some of those ghastly smells and there were plenty of them, as we were to discover almost too soon. Our convoy anchored in the harbour, where there was a considerable amount of shipping. It was dark by the time we started to glide up to the dockside. There was apparently some trouble in getting us alongside as the tide was turning and the Wakefield was no small ship. Eventually they managed to get a line ashore from the bow but it was a full half hour before the stern was brought round. We wondered whether we would have to disembark that night. Luckily it was decided to spend the night unloading stores and the troops were to disembark the following morning. Most of us, therefore, managed to get some sleep but early on the Sunday morning I had to go along to the platform at Bombay station to supervise the stacking of baggage, prior to loading it into the train. It was exceedingly hot and smelly, although the scene was quite colourful with all the hundreds of coolies about the place. Later in the morning, I was joined by Peter and we got most of the work done by lunch-time. We returned on board in search of some food and enjoyed one of the best meals we had had, which is not saying very much as food on the Wakefield was not good.

Bombay looked very unattractive in the heat and haze of the afternoon. Peter and I thought we would have a look round for an hour or two. Our train was due to leave at 5.00 pm and we returned to the station at about 4.30 with our first impressions confirmed; Bombay was not an attractive city. We wondered whether our next abode –Ahmednagar– would be any more attractive. We were due to arrive there at 7.00 am the following morning. Kerr Paxton and I were due to share a compartment, which consisted of one bunk above the other, small but comfortable. Tufton arrived about 15 minutes before we were due to leave and found he had no compartment and he joined us, which was particularly fortunate as he was laden with 12 bottles of beer and a large supply of excellent sandwiches from the Taj Mahal Hotel. He had been attending a conference in Bombay somewhere.

The train eventually started off and we moved out through what appeared to be the slum quarters of the city. Never have I seen human beings living in such crowded and filthy conditions as those we saw that evening. The smells were the most unpleasant part of it all. We were not long in polishing off the beer and sandwiches, after which we prepared for sleep. This I found impossible. It was a beautiful starry night with a gentle cool breeze. I just sat, hour after hour, looking out of the window up at the starry sky, wondering what fate held in store for us. I did not think for one moment that we should remain in India for long, but were we to go East or West from there? There still seemed to be an air of doubt about it. Not even Becky had had any definite orders until then. The train jolted to a standstill every time we came to a wayside station, to let another train pass and eventually at about 2.00 am we arrived at Poona. I never thought I should live to see Poona of all places on God's earth, but there it was and I rubbed my eyes. We halted there some time but I was unable to make out much of the town. This I was able to see later as we went through it by daylight on our return trip.

After another five hours crawling along with innumerable halts we arrived at Ahmednagar more or less on time. I could see the station, but no other form of human habitation. Eventually I heard someone explaining that the town itself was two miles from the station and I was somewhat reassured. After the usual hanging about, we all clambered on to a truck and were driven off to our new home. The native city lies some distance from the military camp area, which centres on the fort. We caught a glimpse of the city as we skirted one side of it on our drive to the camp and thought it extremely ugly, dirty and squalid. After another mile or so we arrived at the fort where we were told divisional headquarters was to be situated. It took us a long time to find anybody, who could tell us where our mess was to be, but eventually we found it at about 9.30 am. Our only interest then was food and upon enquiry I found that breakfast was ready. Too good to be true – this was the only time in the army I have known anything to be prepared and, dirty as we were from our train journey, we tucked into a hearty breakfast without wasting any further time. We started off with oranges and paw-paw, went on to some excellent porridge and cornflakes, then bacon and eggs and finally toast and marmalade.

The mess was then being run by contractors and a very good job they made of it too. Both the food and service were excellent. After breakfast we took a stroll around the mess area consisting of the central building, where we ate, and several bungalows dotted around, which formed our sleeping quarters. These bungalows consisted of four rooms apiece and were furnished up to a point. However, we were soon able to get more chairs from the garrison engineer and we made the place quite comfortable. Tufton, Fitz and I shared one bungalow and by occupying one room each as a bedroom, used the fourth as a sitting-room. The rest of the day was spent getting our equipment unloaded and generally settling in. We were to spend little over a fortnight in Ahmednagar and during that time there was very little to do at Div HQ. It appeared that the Division was just finding its shore legs once more before we moved on to our ultimate destination. This was still as unknown a quantity as before and we still did not know whether it would be further East or back West to the Middle East, our original destination, or indeed up the Persian Gulf. I managed to play a certain amount of tennis at the local club, typical of its kind and full of very Indian army types who, even then, looked as though they were just stretching themselves after a long sleep, having vaguely heard someone mumbling something about a war. Tufton and I went down to this club with some of the others on New Year's Eve as we saw there was to be a dance. Dance was hardly the word for it, as there were two or three hundred officers, mostly from the Division, and some eight women, who were the rather frowsty wives of people stationed in Ahmednagar. After a drink or two I went to bed, feeling fed up with the atmosphere and the artificiality of it all.

The days slowly went by, eating, drinking and playing tennis in the evenings. I was not attracted by India, at least not the small corner of it that we saw. We wondered more and more what would happen and we then heard that the American convoy was still in Bombay. That gave us a clue. Particularly when we heard that an advance party had to go down to Bombay on 13 January. We finally left on 15 January at 11.00 in the morning.

I have said little about Ahmednagar because although it was heaven compared to this frightful existence, I was glad to see the back of it. So we retraced our steps across the very uninteresting countryside, passing through Poona in the early evening and arriving in Bombay at 4.00 am - not a nice time to arrive anywhere. When daylight came, we were able to see the Wakefield and West Point out in the harbour and we were to embark by tender. We sat around on the quayside from 4.00 am until past 8.00 am. Eventually two small steam-boats of the Indian Navy arrived on the scene, extremely badly handled by officers, who looked as though they had barely completed their training. Eventually after half an hour's labour and much shoving, a gangway was put across and we went on board. Half an hour later we were alongside the enormous bulk of the Wakefield. We had never thought for one moment we should ever see the ship again but, by the time we were back in our same old cabins, we felt as if we had never left them and that Ahmednagar was only a place we had visited in our dreams the night before. Loading by lighter was obviously going to take some little time so we prepared ourselves for several days sitting in the harbour. We actually spent from 15 to 19 January in Bombay harbour before the convoy was ready to sail. The other ships were the Empress of Japan, the Duchess of Bedford, carrying Indian Army reinforcements, the Empire Star, a cargo vessel of 10,000 tons, carrying transport and guns, the West Point and the Wakefield. The West Point was carrying 55 Brigade and 54 Brigade was on the Wakefield as before. 53 Brigade was still out in the blue, but we heard rumours that they had gone direct to Singapore from Mombasa.

Some units of the Division had been left behind at Deolali and Ahmednagar, including our Divisional Reconnaissance Battalion and the 125th Anti-Tank Regiment. These were to follow us after a few days. By the time our convoy had reached the end of the channel, through the mine-fields, there was much discussion as to whether we would turn left or right. Left meant the Far East, and could only mean Singapore, right meant the Middle East. We turned left and realized immediately that we would be fighting Japanese and not Germans. So much for my job as Divisional Intelligence Officer, which, so far as language was concerned, had largely disappeared into thin air. It was not my intention to start learning Japanese at this stage of the proceedings. We still did not know our exact destination. The fighting in Malaya was obviously not going at all well and we wondered whether we were last minute reinforcements for Singapore. Others said that Batavia was a safe bet. We asked the crew but either they did not know or they would not tell us. The days continued warm and pleasant. We were keeping so far south that it soon became apparent that whether Batavia or Singapore were to be our destination we were certainly making for the Sunda Strait, between Java and Sumatra. Our escort ships increased in number day by day until we had three or four destroyers and the cruisers: Durball, Dragon, Dorsetshire, Exeter and Cornwall.

As we entered the Sunda Strait, we had a marvellous view of that famous volcanic island Krakatoa. Although now well covered with vegetation, effects of the eruption are still plainly visible. The island was originally a steep cone shape but half of it has fallen in to the sea and the whole appearance is now one of lop-sidedness. Channels, where the lava must have flowed down, are plainly visible. Soon after passing Krakatoa, we ran into a storm and were unable to see land at all. A strict watch was kept for submarines and particularly for aircraft. Looking back on things now, it seems fairly evident that the bad weather saved us whilst going through the Straits. It was about now that we were finally told that Singapore was indeed our destination. To go from the Sunda Strait or Batavia, to Singapore, ships have to go through a very narrow channel, the Bangka Strait, between Sumatra and the island of Bangka, where an enormous amount of tin is produced. Our convoy was therefore forced to sail in line ahead. It was now 28 January and we were due to arrive in Singapore about mid-day on the 29th.

It was a grey morning with high cloud but, at about 10 am, the sun was nearly successful in breaking through. The cruiser Exeter was leading the convoy and we were roughly in the middle. Suddenly the drone of an aircraft was heard; but it was only a reconnaissance aircraft. Soon afterwards I decided to take a book up onto the sun deck and I proceeded to make myself comfortable for the morning. I sat back and for some time watched the shore of Sumatra. The island at this part is flat, with thick jungle and mangrove swamp extending far up the numerous creeks and inlets. Here and there, one could pick out native huts built out over the water on piles.

The general opinion on board was that we could well be in action against the Japs within a week or so of our arrival. I found that my own attitude towards war had changed considerably in the last day or so. Before, it had been something impersonal and far away, but I realised now that it would affect me very directly. I tried to picture the fighting going on, even then only 50 or 60 miles from Singapore and wondered what the Japs would prove to be like. Ruthless and first class soldiers I already knew them to be. My thoughts became morbid and I wondered what percentage of all those thousands of souls on board the ships in the convoy would ever see home again. I found myself, nevertheless, regarding everything in a particularly detached manner as I felt sure, as I always had been, that I should come through unharmed. Somehow I was convinced that my fate was not to be killed in war, so convinced that right from the beginning I had always taken it for granted. I turned my eyes away from the coastline and read my book, the title of which I have now forgotten. My mind was again pleasantly far away from the war upon which we were so shortly to embark.

Suddenly, far above, I heard an aircraft engine droning and in a few seconds all hell was let loose. The ship was covered in ack-ack guns of all types and we ourselves had mounted over 60 bren-guns. Most of the heavier stuff appeared to be let loose and one or two brens, although the plane was far too high for machine guns. The alarm-bells clanged all over the ship and I started to hurry down to my cabin. The firing stopped as suddenly as it had begun and all we could hear were the alarm bells. I had reached the boat deck and was on my way aft, when the cruiser bringing up the rear of the convoy suddenly pulled out to port and simultaneously three columns of water splashed up, two on one side and one on the other. A split second or two later came the explosions but by then I was already rushing down to A deck. I reached my cabin, where I was supposed to be, and all seemed to be quiet. After about 20 minutes, the order 'secure from general quarters' was given and the incident was over. The machine was obviously a reccy plane and I wondered how long it would take for it to get back to base and for an attacking force to be sent out to deal with us. We decided, while having lunch, that it could easily be done that afternoon as the plane had been over us at about 12.30 pm. Whether or not it was the intention of the Japs to attack us then and there, nothing happened. This could perhaps be explained by the fact that at the time of the attack we were only travelling at about 9 knots. Immediately afterwards the convoy split up and the faster half pushed on at top speed. The Wakefield shuddered as we got up to 22 knots. This we kept up the whole night and by early morning, we were already in Singapore harbour. Later on that morning we heard the air-raid warnings ashore and a force of 37 bombers could be seen going straight out to sea. It seemed that they intended to catch the convoy as it came into the harbour, the reconnaissance plane having estimated our speed at 9 or 10 knots, thus implying that there was time enough to catch us. Our sudden spurt, therefore, had possibly saved us. By about 10.00 am we were tied up alongside.

The scene ashore looked attractive and everything was much greener than India, but I had a feeling that I would not have any opportunity to see much of the town of Singapore. Within minutes of our arrival we had news that 53 Brigade had arrived about ten days before us. They had gone up country the day after their arrival and were in action against the Japs within 48 hours of their setting foot in Malaya. The Japs, at the time of our arrival, were only 35 miles from Johore Bahru and things were going badly for us. After the usual waiting about, we disembarked and finally left the quay by lorry. Transport was supplied by the AIF. We did not go through the town of Singapore itself but skirted it to the northward going through some of the most attractive residential areas. After some 20 minutes or so we arrived at our initial destination, Tanglin barracks, which is just north of Singapore and in one of the residential areas. The barracks themselves were very palatial.

Most of the day was spent in settling in and getting the Div HQ office opened up. This was left chiefly to Tufton. Our senior officers spent most of their time elsewhere. Their tempers on the following day were foul. During the two days we spent in Tanglin, we were cursed up hill and down dale all day. However, where would senior officers be if they had no junior officers to swear at? We fed during this short period in the mess of the Manchester Regiment, which had been one of the regular regiments out in Singapore prior to the outbreak of war. This particular unit was a machine gun battalion. The mess was a palatial building and it gave one a good idea of how the army lived in Singapore before the war. Within 24 hours of our arrival at Tanglin, orders came through that the mainland was to be evacuated completely and that only the island of Singapore was henceforth to be defended. This meant that 53 Brigade would come back under our command, which it did a day later. I saw Brigadier

Duke, known as Bulger – I never discovered why – and have never seen a man so changed so quickly. He had obviously been through an extremely unpleasant time.

Another of the first people I saw on arrival was Stanley Lemin, our Field Security Officer, who had travelled with 53 Brigade on the Mount Vernon. From him I gleaned quite a lot of news. He told me that Greville Kerrison, Intelligence Officer at HQ 53 Brigade, had been killed. This was my first shock as I had known him well in England. He had been sent out to contact one of the battalions, which was believed to have been cut off by a road block. The truck he was travelling in with a fellow officer was subjected to machine gun fire from a bridge and after turning round to come back, Greville was found to have been wounded in the shoulder. He was having it dressed by the officer in the truck with him, when they came under mortar fire, one shell bursting just behind the truck and killing both of them. The driver brought both bodies back to Brigade HQ. Stanley also told us of the trouble he had had over security matters with Malaya Command. Security was quite obviously unheard of in Singapore and, indeed, Stanley was chiefly responsible for getting the thing under way. In fact my initial impression of Malaya Command, although based on what I had gleaned from other people, was one of inefficiency and complete failure to cope adequately with the situation.

Our stay at Tanglin was one of intense anticipation. We had arrived on 29 January and on the 31st, the Division received orders to take up the defence of the north-eastern coast of the island. Divisional HQ moved out from Tanglin barracks to Paya Lebar, where we took over from the 9th Indian Division. This division had been fighting the whole way down the mainland and was pretty worn out after seven weeks of it. Div HQ was situated in a small school building next door to a church. I was amazed when I saw it; we were not 100 yards from two important road junctions. Not content with that, our senior officers then proceeded to cover all the road junctions in the vicinity with military police, who were made to wear red caps. We were staggered. Had this bloody army learned nothing? Singapore was full of Japanese agents and fifth columnists. There had been absolutely no control of the civilians of whom there are just under a million on the island. Had France taught us nothing? If the Japs landed on the island, I could foresee the most God-Almighty chaos arising out of the complete lack of control.

The administrative arrangements at Div. HQ were initially bad. 'A' mess was pleasantly ensconced in a house not 50 yards from HQ, 'C' mess was over 1 mile away in a rubber plantation; a good position, where I thought Div HQ ought to have been put in the first place. It took our Staff officers from 31 January to 3 February to wake up to the fact that Paya Lebar village was a bad bet. I think Tufton was chiefly instrumental in getting anything done in this direction. It was eventually decided that Div HQ should move into the rubber plantation, where 'C' mess had been on 3 February. For some unknown reason, however, we did not move until dark and it was hell's own job getting settled in. It was a good spot, right away from any main road and approached by two tracks. During our drive out from Tanglin to Paya Lebar, we saw for the first time what indescribable chaos there was on the island. Troops were retreating from the mainland in a continual stream over the causeway. Ditched lorries and crashes were frequent. Civilians, even then, were also filling the roads as they trekked in the direction of Singapore. Many of the troops, returning from Johore, did not appear to know where to go. One could see at a glance that we had far too much transport on the island and it only helped to increase the chaos.

And what of the Japs during this time? They were steadily advancing southwards through Johore and a day or two later they were reported to have reached Johore Bahru itself. This was just after we arrived in the rubber plantation at Paya Lebar. The last of our troops, that is to say the last of the troops, who had any hope of getting back (many were already cut off) had arrived on the island and the causeway was then blown up. We gradually settled in amongst the rubber trees and we wondered how long it would be before the Japs attempted a landing. Tufton and I discussed it for hours one evening. We seriously considered then that with the number of troops on the island we had every hope of holding on until help could arrive. By now, the navy had evacuated the naval base some days before and the RAF only had 40 Brewster Buffaloes left, everything else having been evacuated to Java or Sumatra. The morale amongst the AIF and the Indians was bad. They were dog tired and had been fighting for seven weeks and, what is worse, retreating the whole time. Other troops very soon became infected by it. The Japanese air force had now, for some time past, been systematically bombing the island. Where were those wonderful anti-aircraft defences we had read so much about in England?

A dream like everything else about Singapore. An 'impregnable fortress', which was, in reality a vast bubble into which money had been poured for years with no effect. Little did we know then how soon this bubble would be pricked. The only coastal defences were on the south of the island, against a seaborne attack from the south, the most unlikely form of approach. In the north there was nothing, absolutely nothing; no wire, no field gun positions with cleared fields of fire. A mixture of jungle, rubber plantations or mangrove swamp through which visibility was practically nil. Not the slightest attempt had been made to anticipate an attack from the mainland.

We had arrived in the rubber on 3 February and from now on we were kept pretty busy. Things were now running smoothly. The mess staff were doing excellent work, cooking under the greatest difficulties, particularly in the evenings, when no lights whatever could be shown. The meals they produced were first class. Our mess had now increased in size, as we had a liaison officer from 11 Indian Division living with us, an officer commanding a machine-gun platoon from the Northumberland Fusiliers, who were guarding Div HQ and another officer who commanded a tank squadron. The tanks in this outfit were extremely old, all obsolete, but they were the only tanks we had on the island. Although they were later to put up a brave show, they were quite obviously not up to the task. A steep hill in the road was later to prove too great an obstacle for some of them.

We had not been in our rubber plantation 48 hours before the Japs started shelling us. They had been pretty quick in getting their artillery up the other side of the straits and it soon became quite apparent that they had plenty of it. From various cross bearings we were able to get from flashes, etc, we were able to build up a fairly accurate picture of what their gun dispositions were. From now on, things became more and more intense. Our gunners did very good work from the start and were soon letting the Japs have as many shells as we were receiving from them. We had sent out numerous patrols across the creek to the mainland but there was no sign of any infantry. During the day small parties were visible from time to time on the opposite beach, but our gunners were able to disperse these very quickly. During these first few days, I went up to Malaya Command several times. Singapore itself had an air of gloom about it and military vehicles made up the only traffic on the road. My time at Command was spent in trying to get the Survey Department to cough up a few hundred more maps. This was easier said than done, as it appeared that the bulk of the maps had either been destroyed or evacuated to Java. What use maps of Singapore could have been in Java was beyond me. However, after going up three times to Command, I was able to return with a few hundred more.

It was now the 7th February and shelling on both sides had gone on with increasing intensity. It was then that shells started to land unpleasantly close to Div HQ and I was only too glad to dive into the slit trench. Shells whined and whistled over our heads most of the day. This was my 'Feuertaufe', as it was for most of us, but we tried to take it lightly. By now it became increasingly evident that wherever the Japs were going to try to effect a landing, it was unlikely to be up our end of the island. It was true that there was a fair amount of artillery opposite our front, but so far there had been absolutely no sign of any concentration of landing craft and very little sign of infantry. During all this the navy had completed its evacuation except for a motor launch or two used for patrol work in the Strait. The RAF were not far behind the navy in clearing out and from now on it was obvious that we could count on little or no air support.

8 February dawned. The heavy black smoke from the oil tanks in the naval base, which had been bombed and set on fire a day or so before, hung heavily in the morning sky. I shaved leisurely outside my tent after being on duty from 4.00 am to 8.00 am, always the most unpleasant night-shift. All was quiet in the rubber plantation, one almost thought that it was another exercise and not a war that we were fighting. I wandered up to the mess tent to breakfast and had just finished a plate of porridge, when there was a whistle overhead and we all dived to the ground. The first shell landed about a hundred yards away and was quickly followed by two more

which were closer. We had heard this particular gun before and could always hear it firing and were therefore able to start taking cover before hearing the first scream of the shell overhead. We waited and listened and as nothing more could be heard we returned to the breakfast table. The next salvo came over when I had just reached the office tent. Fitz was already there and I had just pulled up the flap to go in when I heard our old friend popping off from the other side of the Strait. Down I went and down Fitz went. Then the scream followed by three ear-splitting explosions and that little lot was over. We could hear the shell splinters hitting the trees, one piece going straight through our tent, making a nice clean hole. The rest of the day was spent in comparative quiet.

Evening came and I went to bed early, but not to sleep. Sleep at night had been well-nigh impossible owing to the counter battery work and harassing fire of our own artillery, which usually started at about 8.00 pm and went on intermittently throughout the night. Soon after 9.00 pm, I did manage to doze off but was suddenly woken up by the most terrific artillery barrage which appeared to be coming from the West. It was impossible to tell who was firing, but it was clearly being done for some very definite purpose, judging from the appalling noise. At 4.00 am we received a report that the Japs had landed in force on the Australian front at the other end of the island. Later news stated the Australians were quite happy about the position and hoped to have cleared all the Japs out by that afternoon – that is to say 9 February, the landing having been made during the night of 8/9th. Everyone was reported to be quite happy that the Australians could deal with the situation, until reports made clear that the Japs had advanced sufficiently to make a large bridgehead. Dive bombing by the Japs started the moment daylight came and this we were quite unable to counter as we had little or no airforce. The situation, whilst not yet serious, was not at all encouraging and it soon became apparent that the Australians were unable to hold on.

And what of 18 Division during these last few days? 53 Brigade, which had returned to our command, after it had retreated from the mainland, had by now been taken from us once more and was under command of 11 Indian Division. The latter were on our left flank. 18 Division, by the time of the Jap landing, was reduced to two Infantry Brigades and their gunners. 125 Anti-tank Regiment and the divisional reccy battalion had arrived a day or two before but had lost all their equipment on the Empress of Asia, which had been bombed, set on fire and beached in the approaches to Singapore. Both these units were, therefore, used as infantry. The 9th Northumberland Fusiliers, our machine-gun battalion, had arrived by the same convoy on a French ship, the Felix Roussel. She escaped the attack which sank the Asia. Now with the steady falling back of the Australians, 18 Division had more and more units taken away from it to form special forces each about the strength of a Brigade; one 'Tom' force, under the command of Colonel Thomas of the Northumberland Fusiliers, the other force under Brigadier Massey-Beresford of 55 Brigade.

By the time these two forces had been withdrawn from the Division, we were almost denuded of infantry and our gunners had the task of holding the beaches on our own front. However, I felt in my own mind, that the Japs were still unlikely to land up our end of the island; they were more likely to exploit success at the western end. By 11 February, although things were quiet on our own divisional front, the situation in the West was serious. The enemy had not been held up and was reported to be in Bukit-Timah village. The Australians, holding the front between the causeway and Kranji creek, withdrew and the left flank of 11 Indian Division was exposed. In the evening, the 15 inch coastal defence battery at Changi was ordered to engage the Japs in Bukit-Timah. The first shell came over just after we had sat down to supper and the noise it made as it passed overhead was quite indescribable. But by the time a few more had gone over we began to get used to it. It was rather like an express train passing at speed a few feet over one's head. Once again sleep was well-nigh impossible that night. Our own artillery kept up constant bombardment of the mainland opposite our front.

The following morning we received a visit from General Heath, the Corps Commander, who explained that, in view of the general situation, it had been decided to shorten the front by withdrawing to a perimeter around the city of Singapore itself. When we heard this news Tufton, Fitz and I looked at each other and I remember saying 'Well, that's that', and Tufton remarked that it was the beginning of the end. Later that morning Div HQ moved back to Chancery Lane. Our HQ was actually established for a short time at the police station in Thompson Road and here we were shelled and dive-bombed. The Division took up its new battle positions and so we entered upon what proved to be the final stage of the battle for Singapore.

In the evening of 12 February, I was sent to contact one of our RE Field Companies, which had been pushed into the line as infantry under 53 Brigade. I was machine-gunned by a damn Junkers 87 which then dropped a couple of bombs further up the road where there was some MT. I still had about a mile to go when I was stopped by a group of gunners. They told me that I could not get through as some Jap tanks had been seen in that particular area. What the hell was I to do now? I thought a bit and decided to dismiss the idea of tanks in the vicinity as the figment of somebody's imagination. I started up my motorbike once more and set off round the corner. There was not a soul in sight anywhere and my heart, by now, was pretty well in my mouth. Eventually I came upon the people I was seeking, delivered my message and sped back to Div. HQ. Now looking back, I am certain that no Jap tanks were anywhere near but it was a scary feeling.

When I got back to Div HQ, I found an unmistakable feeling of tension about the place. Tufton told me after dinner that he had been ordered to be ready at midnight with all essential belongings in pack and haversack. Both of us wondered what this meant. However, I turned in early to try and get some sleep but was woken up at about 10.00 pm and told to report to Hutch at once. I went along and received the same orders as Tufton. What the devil did it mean? I returned to the mess and started, with the assistance of my faithful batman, Hipperson to go through all my things and pack what I could into my equipment. I told Hipperson that anything he wanted from my kit, he could take. At about 11.45 pm Tufton and I were ordered to report to Andy Dillon at Div. HQ. There we saw Becky and Hutch. A staff car was waiting and after being shaken by the hand by Becky and Hutch, the three of us got into the car. It was not until now that I fully realised what was to happen. Earlier I had had a premonition that the three of us with Alastair McDonald were possibly leaving that night for Java to set up an HQ for the purpose of a second Dunkirk. About Java I was right, but that was all. Our destination was Batavia but it was a getaway party and no more. Tufton and I wondered why we and none of the others had been chosen to go as the outlook for those remaining behind had by then become distinctly grim. Becky asked me, if we got back to England or India safely, to send a note to his wife, telling her where we had last seen him and how he was.

It was rather a strained meeting and we were glad to be off. We went first to Rear HQ to collect Andy's kit, for he was to come with us. Tufton and I waited for a few minutes in the road while the stuff was being loaded. It was now about 12.45 am and the darkness of the night was frequently broken by the flash of bursting shells and the flaring fires in the dock area and up at the naval base, where the oil tanks were burning. Aggie came out with Andy at last and we clambered in. We sped in the direction of the docks and we could hear above the noise of our engine, the detonation of shells and chatter of machine gun fire, which sounded, as it always did to me, far too close. Now and again, we heard the high pitched whine of our own 25 pounders as they sped over our heads on their way to the Japs. Each whine was followed by a short silence and then a staccato thud as they ended their journey. Suddenly there was a great flare to the north and the whole night was broken by a deafening report as what must have been an ammunition dump went up. For a second or two it was as light as day. Then only the dull red glow remained. After about 20 minutes of driving we reached the centre of Singapore where everything was in chaos.

There were, literally, hundreds if not thousands, of Australian, British and Indian troops – but mostly Australian – everywhere, wandering aimlessly about the streets. Many were drunk. This was something I was to see all around the docks area over the next two days. Very few of these troops had any right whatever to be there. They had simply deserted from their units, were without rifles or equipment and were without officers. This was, perhaps, the most disgraceful aspect, and there were many, of the Singapore fiasco. We drove slowly through this mob and at last reached the dock gates. Here parties from the various formations were assembled and we went through the gates and along one of the dock roads for

73

about a mile. Then we stopped and waited. There was no sign of the two destroyers which were supposed to take us off. We stood in threes while the minutes went by. Then we sat in the road. We sat and waited and waited, while various senior officers endeavoured to find out what had gone wrong. I frankly admit that I began to be not a little worried. Earlier, my thoughts were that I had done nothing to deserve being given the chance to get away, but now my one thought was to get off the island and forget Singapore, which was becoming a worse hell every hour. My thoughts ran on and went round in circles until finally I did not know what to think. It was by now just after 3.00 am and I became increasingly certain, with every minute that went by, that it was too late to get away that night. Suddenly there was an ear-splitting crash about a hundred yards down the road and we all dived for the ditch at the side. I landed straight into some barbed-wire which I had not noticed before and tore my legs. The first shell was quickly followed by about six more and I had just got myself flat by the time the second one landed. Luckily they all exploded at the same point and nobody was hurt but I am quite convinced that a Jap spy in the town must have informed the Japanese artillery of our whereabouts. Singapore was full of Japanese agents many of whom had been living on the island for years. The rest of the night was strained and seemed never ending. At long last dawn came and we started our march back to the dock gates where we had assembled the night before.

We were told there that there would probably be a further opportunity for getting away the following night and this news somewhat revived our flagging spirits. By now the lack of sleep coupled with a night spent mostly in a ditch was beginning to tell, particularly with Alastair McDonald who had been wounded in the leg and arm the day before. We were told to make for the

YMCA building which was about half a mile from the dock entrance and near the centre of Singapore. Here the whole party assembled. We were about 100 officers and 600 NCOs and men. We started on what was to prove to be one of the most nerve-racking days I had spent. The building consisted of three or four floors and with 600 men crowded into it, there was not much room to move. I managed to get a corner under a billiard table in a downstairs room where all the officers had gathered. With me were Stanley Lemin, Alastair McDonald and Tufton. At about 10.00 am, Andy Dillon called everyone together and a 'council of war' was held. There were about sixty of us there. The position was explained as follows: We had received orders to leave the island and make for Batavia. Naval assistance offered the night before had failed and although a wire was sent to Batavia by Malaya Command that morning asking that a destroyer be sent to take us off that evening, the evening of Saturday the 14th, the navy replied that it was not possible.

It was now up to us to get ourselves away, if everybody agreed, in whatever suitable boats were lying in the harbour. We all agreed unanimously that we should try to make it and from then on we were on our own without any assistance from Malaya Command. It was decided that a party should go down to the docks right away and collect as many boats as possible and put their engines in shape ready for a getaway at 10.00 pm that night. Our destination was to be Palembang in Sumatra, where we should all rendezvous on the following day. The boat collecting party went off and Tufton went with them to collect tinned food stocks and load them. Other people were sent off to do different jobs, one of them being to warn the shore defences not to open up on the boats leaving. Another was to see the harbour master and obtain copies of the mine field chart. Stanley and I were left to wait. We waited and waited and I have never known time pass so slowly. Andy went up to Command to get them to release a large tug which had previously been used for taking the OC shore defence artillery around the harbour but Command refused to help and we were consequently unsuccessful in getting some 300 to 400 men away.

The hours dragged by. All day the guns boomed away and occasionally a Jap shell would crash down not far from our building. We had now been out of touch with the situation for 24 hours or so, and whether our line was holding we had little idea. Some of our guns had already taken up what were to prove to be their final positions right in the centre of the city and in the docks. Their muzzles were elevated, in many cases, to the maximum to clear the house tops. Stanley and I went up on to the roof of the YMCA building and looked around. The Malayan General Hospital, with its numerous red crosses, was within half a mile or so and had so far not been touched by the devastating air-raids. These were carried out by the Japs by 'pattern bombing' – aircraft would come over 30 or so at a time in close arrow head formation and when over the desired spot, all bomb releases would be pulled simultaneously. One heard first of all a slight rustling noise, then a noise of an express train getting louder and louder until all hell was let loose. Buildings shook and debris clattered down onto the roof tops and all would be quiet until the next raid which would follow soon after. Our ack-ack fire only improved slightly and was incapable of breaking these formations up.

Stanley and I just stood there and watched it all; the chaos in the streets, fires, which were by now burning in every direction, the thousands of troops who had deserted. The defence perimeter was now held by a pathetically thin line and yet in the town there was, at a rough estimate, the equivalent of a whole division. Nothing was being done to get these men back to their units. Many of them were drunk as a result of raiding abandoned bars and restaurants. Others just lolled in entrances to buildings. With men like these we did not deserve to hold Singapore. I remember feeling very bitter that day. What a ghastly mess it all was. I found myself hating our own men, many of whom by now would not obey an officer's order.

Eventually evening came and Andy Dillon returned. He had got two boats ready for that night and only 140 people would be able to leave. Our hearts went up into our mouths as Stanley and I listened to the lots being drawn and we realised we should not be going. This first party was to leave the YMCA at 7.00 pm and the remainder of us were to leave at half-hourly intervals making our way down to the docks and hope for the best in finding a boat – a forlorn hope, since almost everything that could float had been rendered un-seaworthy, to deny them to the Japs. Stanley and I were to leave at 11.00 pm with 30 others. The first party left at their appointed hour and the rest of us settled down for a further wait. Darkness came down, accompanied by continuing shelling and machine gun fire. By now there were so many fires burning, particularly in the docks, that it is not really correct to refer to the darkness. It was really a red glow which lit up all the clouds of dust and smoke, which hung over the city. We waited and waited until, at last, 10.00 pm came. Only another hour to go and we should be off. I was dozing in the entrance hall of the building with about 20 or 30 others, when suddenly there was an appalling whine and crash. The whole building shook to its foundations and before I could collect my wits the first shell was followed by two more. Then after a short interval the fourth arrived and I knew nothing more for what seemed like several minutes.

I was saved by a miracle. The last shell had come straight into the entrance hall, where I lay, and exploded about 5 yards from me. It caused the most frightful carnage all round me but all I got were a few bits of stone chipped off by the explosion. Several men lay dead and one, who had been lying quite close to me had both his legs blown off. Medical personnel and two medical officers appeared as from nowhere to help. I found myself, utterly dazed, out in the street in the front of the building and sometime later managed to collect one or two of the other officers forming our lorry party. We were a total of 30 of whom we managed to find about 20. We clambered on to the truck and were at last on our way to the docks. We had not gone very far before we got tangled up in some trolley-bus wires, which were lying across the road. It took us quite 15 minutes of careful work to free ourselves. We reached the docks and could find nothing in the way of a boat apart from a very unwieldy looking sampan which we did not think we would be able to manage, and an old ship's lifeboat, full of holes. I met Stanley down on the docks and he and I, together with a number of other officers of our official escape party discussed what we should do next. We were all so dead-beat by now that we decided to sleep the rest of the night in a go-down and start a further search for a boat in the morning.

We awoke early and got to work but did not find much. Watts, Peter Fane and I, having breakfasted off a tin of M & V, decided to go to Command and ask for the tug which was known to be in the harbour and had been refused to Andy on the previous day. It was Sunday, 15 February. By now we had been out of touch with the battle for so long that we did not even know whether we still held the same line. We heard machine gun fire ominously close during the night and consequently wondered whether we had had to retreat further. We managed to find a large six-wheel truck in the docks and with this the three of us drove to Command HQ. We had no luck at Command, who sent us round to Corps HQ, where we fared no better. Here, however, we spent some time and overheard a conversation between General Heath, the Corps Commander and one of his staff officers. I picked up the words "the white flag will go above the Union Jack" and I knew then that we were throwing in our hand. When, I wondered. The Corps Commander came up and spoke to Major Watts, who explained our position. General Heath then told us that the white flag was being taken out and a conference for an armistice was being held at 4.00 pm that afternoon at Japanese H.Q.

It was, by now, about 11.00 am. Heath told us we had better return to our units. This we decided to ignore and at that moment Becky arrived and spoke to us on his way to see Heath. We again explained our situation and with a wink he said he had not seen us. The seeming impossibility of finding a boat, coupled with the fact that we were completely exhausted led us to give up the idea of trying to get away, as we had been ordered to do, and I finally returned to Divisional HQ at about 3.00 pm. I was not only dog tired but exceedingly hungry. I had not shaved for three days, had not been to bed, nor been able to wash properly for ten days, slept only for short periods whenever and wherever I could and was covered in filth and blood. I went off to get various bits of me dealt with at the nearest dressing station, then returned to the Mess, where I enjoyed a delicious meal of bacon and eggs and fried potatoes. I then slept for an hour or two until woken by several shells falling pretty close. These did not worry me very much. By now I felt that nothing could ruffle me anymore. All I wanted was sleep, above all, silence. Most of us found that the constant shelling, mortaring and dive-bombing, which went on unceasingly was beginning to tell on us. We expected the cease-fire to be sounded at 4.00 pm, but owing to the difference between Jap time and our own, we ceased firing at 4.00 pm and the Japs went on firing for another two hours or so. This was almost more than we could stand, but by evening silence reigned. It was unbelievable and felt quite uncanny. We had a large meal and by 9.00 pm I was in bed and sound asleep.

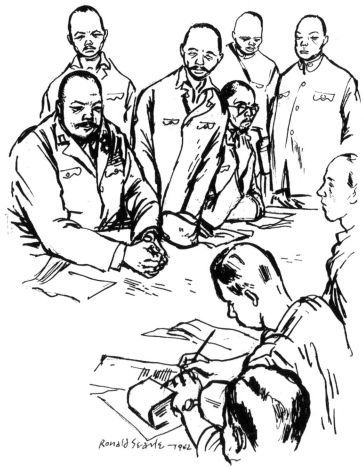

Percival and Yamashito signing Singapore's surrender, February 1942

The following morning I lay in bed for some time wondering why everything was so quiet. Then I realised. The fighting was over and we had capitulated. During the night, both we and the Japs remained, according to the cease fire agreement, in the positions we had occupied at the time of the ceasefire. Now I wondered how long it would be before I saw the first Jap soldier, since hitherto, I had only seen one – a badly wounded prisoner who died shortly after he was brought in. It was a bright sunny morning when Hipperson, my batman, brought me some hot water so that I could shave. I lay in bed a few minutes longer and wondered what our fate would be. It took me some time to realise that the war for me was over and that I was to become a prisoner of war of the Japanese. How did the Japs treat their prisoners and where would we be sent? The answers to these questions would not, I felt, be long in coming.

The whole of Monday we took easily and awaited developments. Eventually we heard that we were to be sent to a prisoner of war camp which would be set up in Changi. Changi, in peace time, was the main barrack area for the garrison stationed in the eastern end of Singapore Island. It lies about 15 miles from the centre of Singapore and I realised that we had a long march ahead of us. We were to move out on Tuesday afternoon. I must now go back to Sunday 15 February and mention that on that morning, during the shelling, Divisional HQ was hit, an unlucky round bursting on the corner of the house, which was inhabited by some of the other ranks of Div. HQ. Brian Barrow, who was standing nearby at the time, was unfortunately hit by shell splinters, nearly severing his right arm just below the shoulder and another entering one of his lungs. All this had occurred before my return to HQ and as far as I could ascertain nobody knew how he was, except that he was very seriously wounded and had been evacuated to Malayan No 1

General Hospital. It was not until after we had been in Changi for some weeks that we learned that Brian had died of his wounds on the day after he had been hit. It seemed hard luck indeed that he should have survived the battle thus far and been killed within a few hours of the ceasefire.

Arrival of Japanese troops in Singapore City, February 1942

Tuesday afternoon came and we set off on our long trek. We had managed to get our mess equipment on to a lorry and we each managed to load our bedding rolls and an odd suitcase on to the same vehicle. The rest of our belongings we carried on our backs. I wondered if I would ever make it. And so we started off on this march which, had anyone been looking on, must have presented a sad sight. That afternoon, 50,000 British troops, marched along two separate roads, accompanied by some of the wounded, who were carried in trucks, making their way into captivity.

It was heart-breaking to see all those men, most of them perfectly fit, and to think that we should have suffered such a ghastly defeat. The reasons for that defeat I do not propose to go into. The whole thing is far too complex and, no doubt, many facts will not be brought to light until after the war. Most of us had our own views on the disaster, but they are very bitter and, no doubt, biased.

By 10.00 pm that night the men had just about had enough, and whilst many of us were willing to go on and get the march over, it was obvious that we should have to call a halt. And so we dossed down for the night in a rubber plantation at the side of the road. We had done just over 10 miles and had about another five to go. We got going again at dawn and arrived at Changi soon after sunrise – very tired, very miserable and very hungry. We were able to organise a scratch breakfast in what was to become our mess and we set to with a will. Breakfast over, we took stock of our position and decided that the batmen being too tired and their feet too blistered to do anything – a fine tribute to their training – we should get down to the job of clearing up and making the place habitable. The house was built as WOs' quarters and consisted of four rooms; two downstairs and two up. B Mess was to amalgamate with C Mess and we were therefore a group of 20. A Mess were to live next door. By lunch time we had the rooms cleared out and had got our kit moved in. John Philips, Richard Sharpe, Fitz Barrington and myself shared the large room upstairs. The large room downstairs was just big enough to make into our living and dining-room combined. Work over, we all went to bed where I slept, off and on, for about 17 hours. One of the most unexpected features of our captivity was that we were to administer ourselves. That is to say that officers were to continue to look after the men and all the Japs would do was to supply us with rations. Beyond that we were to fend for ourselves.

Very little seems to have happened in the course of our first few months of captivity. It was a depressing time. It was a period of re-adjustment to a form of existence, which has since proved quite unreal. I worked in the camp office as Assistant Staff Captain Q and this occupied my time fully during the mornings. There was nothing interesting about the work, which had to be done, but it constituted a routine life and therefore helped to pass those early weeks. Our rations were not good and indeed have, ever since, consisted almost entirely of rice, usually full of maggots, although recently they have improved somewhat. The weather by the beginning of April became very hot and this, combined with the bad food, did not help matters very much.

In the middle of April I went down with the first of frequent bouts of dysentery, which took me to hospital for 10 days or so. I was in bed for about a fortnight in all. One of the most painful things I have yet experienced. This laid me very low. I had lost a lot of weight and when I came out of hospital I was barely able to walk. Going upstairs to bed required the utmost exertion and it was several weeks before I really got over it. When I got out of hospital I gave up working in the office and from this time on, most of my time was spent in reading. I also managed to do a fair amount of Spanish. The days slipped steadily past and by now we were well settled in. We started sending permanent working parties into Singapore to do reconstruction work. This has gone on steadily since and there is only a small proportion of the troops left in Changi. This of course has made for improved living conditions and the number of dysentery cases has gone down, although there are still far too many. Our rations continue to be practically entirely rice, but lately the Japanese have started to supply us with small quantities of meat twice a week.

After the capitulation of Singapore, 15 February 1942

We are lucky in the mess as we have a reserve of such things as bully, margarine, tinned fish and milk powder. But the men and some of the other officers' messes are not so well off. However, things have been greatly eased now by the opening of a canteen and by the issue by the Japs of an 'amenity grant', which in the case of officers, comes to $7.50 per month (Straits Dollars). This enables us to buy such things as soap and tooth-paste and to get extra food for the mess. Included in the latter are eggs, which we can buy for

10 cents each. So now we are sometimes able to have an egg for breakfast with our rice rissoles. So much for food, which provides our one and only interest. For intellectual stimulus, we have been able to start a university within the camp. Southern Area also has one and, between the two, there are some very good lecturers.

Southern Area is lucky as there are a number of the professors and other teaching staff there from Raffles College, which in better days was the Singapore University. One's afternoons can very easily and pleasantly be taken up by lectures. A few weeks ago, we were able to send off postcards but how long they will take to reach England, God knows. This of course has been our greatest worry; to get word home that we are at least alive.

I am now more or less up to date with the accounts of my activities up to June/July 1942. From now on therefore I shall be able to write this up in diary form. I do not intend to write it up every day but every few days when I feel there is really anything of interest to record.

WAR DIARY

August 1942 to April 1943

⌒

5 August 42 Our state of equilibrium has been more than upset by the fact that a party of about 3500, including all Generals and Senior Officers of the rank of Colonel and above, has been ordered to go to Japan. This includes most of our mess. The warning order came through about a fortnight ago and we were due to go about four or five days later. There has, however, been a hitch of some sort as we are still here in Changi, so everybody is very unsettled. Personally I doubt very much if we shall in fact go to Japan. I should like to see it, even as a prisoner of war, although I don't look forward to the journey very much. It would of course provide a welcome change, particularly from this dreadful climate, which is beginning to get me down. Pending any further news we are trying to settle down once more to Changi routine and I have unpacked the few belongings I possess, in anticipation of remaining here.

The second term of the university has now been going for a fortnight and I am attending lectures regularly in a number of subjects. These include 'Nineteenth Century Literature', two hours a week, given by Professor Huff from Southern Area, who was at Raffles College in happier times, 'Drama' also by a man who used to be at Raffles College and 'History and Appreciation of Music' by a man called Rennison, who is said to be a good pianist. He is an excellent lecturer and illustrates his talks by playing on a rather

Street scene: heads of executed Malay 'underground' workers exhibited as a warning, Singapore 1942

managed to obtain a portable gramophone. With these we give classical concerts to the men of HQ and so far we have been able to keep going every Sunday. Mendelssohn's Violin Concerto, Chopin's Second Piano Concerto, Rachmaninov's Variations on a Theme of Paganini, Beethoven's Eroica, his Emperor Concerto and the 7th, 8th & 9th Symphonies, Brahms' and Tchaikovsky's Piano Concertos are some of the things we have been able to enjoy. To return to the university. In the Economics Faculty I go to lectures on Civics, Money, Banking and Commercial Law. Lectures and music make an immeasurable difference to one's existence here.

23 August 42 The month has almost passed and we still find ourselves waiting to go to Japan. The first party of senior officers, including the Generals, left about ten days ago and we now have no officers above the rank of Lt. Col.. Lt. Col. Holmes of the Manchesters is in command of the whole camp. Last Monday, I started a fortnight's tactical and administration course, which I find very dull. The course even includes company drill on the square every morning which, owing to Japanese time, means that I have to get up in the dark every morning. This is actually the second course of its type to be held in the camp. The first having been received with much opposition by the officers ordered to attend. Personally I quite sympathised with them. Psychologically this is a bad time to start militarism in the camp, when everybody wants to try and forget the army and its many lost battles.

The other day I was amazed to find a Shell handbook in the camp which somebody had miraculously picked up in Singapore, when he went in with a working-party. I have been reading it during the last day or two and was shocked to find how much one could forget in three years.

One event stirred the camp considerably last week. We received an issue of tinned soups, jam and vitamin A & B sweets, which had arrived by Red Cross ship from South Africa. We have been told that there may be another vessel on the way. Each man received 1lb 6oz of jam, 18 sweets and 1lb of tinned soup. It made one feel much nearer home when one realised that these things had actually come from the outside world and we felt that, after all, we had not been forgotten. It is astounding how cut off one feels on this island, on only a tip of it at that, where for the last six and a half months I have not moved at any time further than a few hundred yards from our quarters.

By way of entertainment, Southern Area gives concerts regularly. Our own Divisional Signals usually have concerts on Sundays and our latest effort is to start a theatre in the Divisional Area. The first performance was the 'Dover Road' produced by Archie Bevan. The theatre even has electric light fixed up from the engine run by the RAOC. The camp itself, of course has no electric light, although the hospital has now just been hooked up to the main supply from Singapore. Perhaps the rest of the camp will have electric light eventually. It must be a great blessing for the hospital, although by now the worst time is over, as many of the battle casualties have either died or left hospital. The number of graves in the cemetery seems terribly high and funerals, for some time past, have been taking place at the rate of three a day. Now the chief enemies are such things as malaria, dysentery and beriberi. We have been quite busy recently with needlework. Most have been fortunate in procuring a flannel shirt, pullover and a scarf for our expected trip to Japan. The shirts, however, have no collars, so one or two of us have been taking bites out of the tails to make into collars. Some of them have been quite successful. The opportunity of going to Japan is marred by two things. Firstly that it will be damn cold there and secondly that we may be sunk on the way. I do not trust these US Navy submarines, but we may still never go.

27 August 42 Thursday today and our course will be over the day after tomorrow. How glad I shall be! My birthday is also fast approaching. The general procedure whenever one of us has a birthday is to make a cake. For this one has to buy a few raisins and peanuts, with which we make a type of almond icing, eggs and rice flour. Heard today that the Japanese are instituting a card system for everyone in the camp, giving particulars such as nationality, health etc. What the Japs will use these for I do not know; in any case there appears to be more direct control since the Jap General in charge of prisoners of war arrived on the scene. Lieutenant Okasaki is still in immediate command of the camp however. Yesterday I gave my second talk on the oil industry. Another rumour I heard this morning – one hears at least six every day of the week – was to the effect that all those living in buildings, from which one can see the sea, were to be moved. This will be extremely difficult to execute as practically every barrack block in the area overlooks one part of the sea or another. Today General Heath, who has not yet been sent to Japan, and is therefore now the only officer left in the camp above the rank of Colonel, gave the second of his lectures on the Italian-East Africa campaign, in which he took an active part. His first lecture was on Tuesday. It was quite a relief to hear of an action, in which we have been successful, after all the lectures the army commander, Percival, gave us on France and Norway. I am at the moment in the middle of 'Jane Eyre', a book I have not read since leaving school and am enjoying very much indeed.

8 September 42 Time has slipped by and we are well into September. Much has happened since my last entry and I feel as if

I have lived a year during the last week. On Tuesday 1 September, I celebrated my birthday with Berkeley Quill, whose own birthday is on 7 September. We had a terrific feast of sausage rolls, made with bully beef and raisins and various types of imitation tarts and chocolate éclairs. The pastry was made with rice flour with a small percentage of ordinary flour added. It was a great evening as we all played silly games and finally went to bed feeling exceedingly satisfied. This existence certainly teaches one how to enjoy little things to the full.

A few days prior to these birthday celebrations, we had received from the Japs, out of the blue, a large supply of forms, which ran as follows:-

"I hereby solemnly promise, on my honour, not to attempt to escape, while a prisoner of war under the Imperial Japanese Army". The Jap order was to the effect that every officer and man in the camp was to sign two of these forms, one to be sent to Japan, the other to be put in the card index system, which the Japs have started at the gaol. British Army orders, however, do not permit us to accept parole under any circumstances, except of course under duress. Command managed to produce an ACI (Army Council Instruction) to this effect and this was shown to the Japs.

The latter, however, refused to play ball and became nasty. It became apparent that the Japs had received orders from Tokyo to get these forms signed at any cost. On Tuesday 1 September, the Japs, in order to prove that they meant business, took out four men, who had attempted to escape, and shot them. The firing party consisted of Sikhs and it appears that it took 21 shots to finish them off. Two of the men were Australians, who had actually escaped from the island by sea two months ago and had managed to get as far as two hundred miles away, only to be captured and brought back. One of the others was actually in hospital at the time, suffering from malaria, but was nevertheless taken out in his pyjamas and summarily shot.

The next move by the Japs came late on Tuesday night when they told us that, if we did not sign immediately, the whole camp of some 18,000 men would be put into close confinement in Selarang barracks. These are about a mile and a half away from our camp and where the Australians are living. We still refused to sign and on Wednesday afternoon 2 September, we were marched to Selarang, carrying as many of our belongings as we could carry, as we did not know whether it was to be a permanent move or only temporary. The move was to be completed by 6.00 pm. We arrived to find that the area allowed us was only about 200 x 300 yards with perimeter wire on the outside and Jap and Sikh sentries patrolling round. Particularly menacing were the machine guns set up at each corner of the square, in which there were seven barrack blocks each consisting of three floors. These blocks normally take about two companies each i.e. 200 to 250 men in peace time. In similar blocks in our camp we have had up to 850 men, in not unduly unsanitary conditions. Here, however, at Selarang we had to get well over 2000 men into each of the two blocks allotted to the Division. Malaya Command, AIF and 11 Indian Division were no better off. The population per square mile, we worked out, was something in the neighbourhood of 775,000. When we arrived there were no latrine arrangements whatsoever. These had to be dug in the centre of the parade ground and this meant digging through asphalt and laterite. The water had been turned off in all the blocks and we had only one water point per 8000 men. No washing was allowed and all drinking water had to be boiled. We only had enough fuel to last three or four days. When nightfall came, it was apparent that there was not sufficient room to lie down inside the blocks. Many men slept on the roof and out on the square, luckily there was no rain. By the evening the sanitary conditions were already serious. Thursday morning came, and it was a day of bargaining with the Japs, with proposals and counter-proposals on both sides and by the evening, we had more or less reached dead-lock.

The Japs were clearly intending that we should sign the form as it stood. We were trying, in vain, to get it altered to read 'As ordered by the IJA, I promise etc', or words to that effect. The Japs would not play. Numerous conferences were held and it was decided that owing to the untenable conditions – there had already been 60 to 70 new cases of dysentery and several fresh outbreaks of diphtheria – we would have to sign the form as it stood, but try and get the Japs to give a written order to us to sign the form. To this the Japs agreed and on the Friday evening we all signed. At 1.00 pm on Saturday, we started our trek 'home', 'home' being Changi, which we were all very glad to see again.

I had strong personal views about how all this had been handled and a number of us felt the same, but general opinion seemed to be different. Personally, I thought that we should never have moved in the first place.

Well over half the men in the Division are sick, suffering from skin diseases, recovering from war wounds or have recently had dysentery, malaria, beriberi or dengue fever. It was quite clear that to be concentrated in an area as small as Selarang Barracks would lead very quickly to further outbreaks of disease. What was the point, therefore, in subjecting men to these dreadful conditions over a very doubtful point of honour. It seemed clear from the start that we should have to sign sooner or later and the whole thing appeared to me to be ridiculous. However, there is perhaps something wrong with my sense of honour. We are now back home in Changi again and life has returned to normal. Tomorrow, the University re-opens. Yesterday evening I was particularly fed up and felt it was time we all went home. These feelings come and go every few weeks. If only one could get word from the outside world, even a post-card would be better than nothing. The three letters I received from Diana soon after arriving in Singapore, I read through regularly, but the world from which they came is receding further and further into the haze. One day I suppose we shall return to it, but this seems more unreal with every month that passes.

10 September 42 The University opened again yesterday. I went to lectures on Music and on 19th Century Literature. I have just started reading 'Vanity Fair', having finished 'Jane Eyre' and am also in the middle of another book on Russia by Bernard Pairs, first published in 1871. Several of us in the mess are growing moustaches. We started them when we were at Selarang and could not shave. Mine will soon come off, I feel.

23 September 42 Nearing the end of another month and what has happened? First of all, a new play has started and a party of us from the mess went to the first night of 'I Killed the Count', which I remember seeing in London. It was very well produced and a great success. Last Sunday we went to a classical concert in the theatre. Rennison played the Chopin A flat Polonaise and the Moonlight Sonata. This was followed by two songs by Handel, sung by Gunner Wall, who has quite a good bass baritone voice. He was followed by East, a violinist with the London Philharmonic before the war, who played two Kreisler pieces, one in the style of Tartini, the other Paganini. He also played some unaccompanied Bach and this was followed by Foster-Hague, known as 'The Barrel' because of his figure, singing two songs by Handel. About a week ago we had a party of 700 RAF, AIF and other British troops thrust upon us from Java, where it appears they had not been having a pleasant time. About 200 of them, all RAF, are now living in 18 Division area. The day before yesterday 8 men were brought in from Changi Gaol by the Japs. They had been attempting to escape, whither God knows. Under the circumstances, I think they are lucky not to have been shot, as the other four sadly were, when we went to Selarang.

24 September 42 We have had news that more Red Cross comforts arrived on the Tatuta Maru, one of the Japanese repatriation ships. A Swiss Red Cross representative is reported to have arrived on this ship and to have stated that there is some mail on two repatriation ships due in at the end of the month. I had to interrogate a Greek brought up from Singapore, where he had been living with a Chinese girl for seven months. This Greek was with Fortress Signals up to the time of the capitulation in February and he appears to have been leading a pleasant existence. I have been given a new job, Roll-call Officer. This means I have to walk to Command every morning with our daily strength returns, which are then sent on to Lieut. Okasaki at Changi gaol. This is where the Japanese General Fukuyi, in charge of POW camps, has his HQ. I do not mind the walk every day, but my boots will not last long. We are now completely out of 'grindery' (pieces of leather for boot repairs) and no more boots can be repaired. Perhaps the Japs will give us some more in due course. Other news is that officers are to be paid and not receive an amenity grant as the men do. This sounds all right, but could well mean that our pay at home will be monkeyed around with. 'On verra'.

3 October 42 We have just finished supper, having spent most of the afternoon bathing at Beti Koosa. We walk down to the beach, ostensibly to collect salt water to make salt, and although we met a Jap patrol the other day, they did not seem to worry very much that we were there. I am still walking to Command every day in my capacity of Roll-call Officer. This is certainly a thankless task. Yesterday I spent four hours up at Command HQ after the Japs had found an error, which ultimately proved to be Command's fault.

Hut interior, India Lines, Changi, 1942

The prisoners from Java, who were due to arrive at the end of last month, did not appear until later on. When they did eventually arrive, Fitz and I had to go down to Changi gaol to meet 200 RAF men, who are now in our divisional camp. They had to march up from the docks, a distance of 17 miles, and were due to reach the gaol at 1.30 am. They finally arrived at 3.30 am and we did not get to bed until 6.00 am. The two Java parties are due to continue their travels on 7 October to Japan, it is thought. This evening 300 men arrived from Kuala Lumpur, most of them looking very ill and some of them unable to stand up. A large number of them have gone into hospital already. They have obviously been having a bad time up country. No sign of officers' pay yet.

14 October 42 All the officers were paraded yesterday for a pay check by the Japs; we hope to see some of it soon. Two more parties of prisoners have arrived from Java and the first two parties, between 2000 and 3000, have now left the island. A third party consists of some 1900 Americans, some from the cruiser Houston, sunk in the battle of the Macassar Straits and two hundred British and Dutch. The fourth party arrived yesterday, numbering 1500 Army, Navy and AAF, all Australian. The Japs seem to be clearing Java steadily and we are wondering whether we shall be the next to move. Some Red Cross comforts have arrived and we are having a second issue today. Each issue consists of 2 to 3 tins of bully, 2 tins of M & V, a litre of sweetened condensed milk, 3 biscuits, and a small quantity of cornflour, ghee and sugar per man. We hope there is more to come! Yesterday we were able to have a meal without having to look at any rice. All these supplies were brought by the repatriation ships, Tatuta and Kanakura Maru. It is rumoured that some mail has been unloaded, but this can probably be explained by the fact that some people received parcels from relations in South Africa and these arrived in mail bags.

16 October 42 Another 1500 men arrived from Java today. There are indications that the remaining prisoners in Java, said to be some 8000, will pass through here shortly. It is becoming increasingly evident that Singapore will be the next area to be cleared. River Valley and Adam Road camps in the city are now empty. The troops, some 5500, are going up country by train. The Japan A party has not been cancelled, according to the Japs, so we may be off ourselves before long. I have just finished reading 'Vanity Fair' and have also read a Penguin book on Opera by Professor Dent. I am now half way through a book on Manchuria published in 1932 and quite enlightening in view of subsequent events. My shirts are beginning to show signs of wear and my socks are also none too happy. We finally received our first pay the day before yesterday, 20 Straits dollars (Japanese), of which half have gone into Mess funds. I saw Goodman, yesterday at Command HQ. He had been sorting mail from South Africa, about 2000 letters. This is a good sign, as we shall perhaps receive letters from home soon. I am still hoping that we might get some mail before Christmas. In a few days it will be a year since our departure from England and, apart from the three letters from Diana, which I received during the battle, I have heard nothing from anybody, like most of us, since Singapore fell. Meanwhile, we understand that we have been officially reported as 'Missing, believed prisoner of war', not much comfort for our families, whilst the Japs have done nothing. Red Cross comforts continue to roll in and this makes a terrific difference to our rations.

12 November 42 Another month is nearly over and I have written nothing, not for lack of news, however, as much has happened in the last few weeks. More and more men have been arriving from Java, mostly Dutch, with a sprinkling of Americans and Australians. We now have some 8000 men from Java in our camp and in the meantime 8000 of our own people have gone up country by train – it is believed to Bangkok. 18 Division has sent 3900 men from Changi and many of the camps in Singapore are now completely cleared. This means we only have 3000 of our own people left, the balance of our camp of 6000 being mainly made up of 2500 Dutch, 300 RAF and the rest Americans. The latter are under a Major Horrigan who was earlier in the Philippines.

Pro-Japanese Sikh guard punishing British officer for failing to salute, Changi 1942

15 November 42 The last few days have been spent in moving house and we are now established in Quadrant Road. Malaya Command moved into our old HQ yesterday. It is very stuffy here as we are at the foot of a hill. Mosquitoes, hitherto fairly uncommon, have now become a positive menace. The woodwork of this house is full of bugs, which John and I attacked yesterday afternoon. We have suffered from bugs quite a lot since our capture but we are now quite immune to them, and take it all as a matter of course. The move has made most of us feel uprooted and I, for one, do not yet feel settled. A few days ago, Richard, Puss and Bill Border left to go with our most recent up-country party of 650. It was a sad day, wishing them farewell but I suppose we can consider ourselves lucky that our mess has hung together for so long, some nine months. Richard could have got out of it for health reasons, had he wanted to, but he was never one to push himself forward and stick up for his own rights.

The journey was expected to take 4 1/2 days and that length of time in a closed metal goods wagon, on a narrow gauge railway, with 30 people per wagon is not ideal for comfortable travel. Our mess is now amalgamated with the remnants of the Signals Mess, consisting of Major Moore, Graham Sankey and Peter Drinkwater. Also Bill Durden, who together with Peter is in hospital with a poisoned leg. Peter will, we hope, be out in a fortnight or so after an unpleasant six weeks of diarrhoea. We also have a Dutchman living in the mess now. He is officially here as a liaison officer but as far as I can make out, is ineffective and altogether a damn nuisance. He goes by the name of Klaus but is known as 'Santa Klaus'. My days continue to be taken up largely by daily strength returns, but owing to the presence of the Dutch, who will not produce correct figures and seem to be incapable of administering themselves, much time is wasted. All the onus has, so far, fallen on the British, who are left to carry the baby. I have calculated that, by now, I have £280 of my pay accumulated at home.

16 November 42 Life has been particularly quiet for the last few days. I feel, as though I have done nothing constructive lately, just drifting aimlessly, letting this monotonous existence carry me along. The days have been unusually warm, but this is probably due to our being down in Quadrant Rd, which is lower than the 'White House'. It is 3.45 pm and the usual sleepy laziness pervades everything. From the balcony I can hear Fitz moving about outside in the garden. He is very busy as the gunners, who had this area before we took over, left nothing but some very unhappy looking pineapple plants. None of them show the slightest sign of ever producing fruit. After eight months effort in our other garden, Fitz managed to produce one pineapple, one of the best I have ever tasted anywhere. Here he is planting maize, chillies, Ceylon spinach and kang-kong, the two last being our greens mainstay. The maize has been highly successful and we have had corn on the cob more than once.

Several Nip staff cars have just gone up the road. From where I am sitting, I can hear the Sikh guards shouting in salute just the other side of the wire. They inhabit the old Changi Post Office. We have just been having another bug hunt. I never realized, until I became a prisoner, what a strong smell of varnish a bug gives off when it is popped. John and I found a huge spider sitting in the basin last night. It disappeared as soon as we tried to kill it, but we caught up with it behind the bath. This afternoon we found another in John's room and again gave chase. Malayan spiders do not play fair. They have a habit of hopping. This one almost defeated us by darting behind a cupboard but by bombing it with a piece of wood, and knocking off one of its legs we encouraged it out into the open.

The second bomb caused the loss of another leg and a half, and after this it was an absolute cinch. With two and a half legs down, his speed was considerably reduced and the coup de grace was easy. Jackie retired to bed with a temperature yesterday and we thought he was in for a bout of fever. However, he seems to be all right today. John saw Peter in hospital yesterday and says he is better. He is now allowed to sit up and his beard has been shaved off and if all goes well, he is to be allowed up on Saturday.

Spent a thoroughly neurotic evening yesterday, listening to some American swing records, which Berkeley had borrowed from the Americans in the Java party. The evening came to a close with Ravel's Bolero. The combination of a full moon, its rays glistening on the palm fronds, under a cool breeze and the regular monotonous rhythm of the music sent us off into an empty sleep.

21 November 42 Yesterday John brought the unbelievable news of Becky's death in Formosa. He died on 11 November of a heart attack, following diphtheria. The Nips have sent us a copy of the Syonan Times, which has a small paragraph on his death. Poor old Becky and his lost Division. We don't seem to have much luck somehow. We are all thinking of his family and how devoted they were to each other. Most of us at Div. HQ had got to know his wife and two daughters in England. He was always popular, but this was particularly so after we were incarcerated in Changi. He always did all in his power to keep everyone cheerful and to help them keep up an interest in life. A memorial service is to be held in India Lines tomorrow. According to the Syonan Times the body was cremated and his ashes buried in a nearby cemetery.

Kerr returned from Southern Area yesterday with several books. Among them 'Music Ho' by Constant Lambert and 'The 18th Century Background' by Basil Willey. Have just finished Elie J Blois on the 'Tragedy of France'. Well written but it makes depressing reading. Mandel appears to have been the only man in the government to have had the courage of his convictions and to have kept to the standards, which he had set himself. He was one of those who, along with Daladier, were accused of treason against the French Republic.

25 November 42 'Time for a little Sleep'. It is half past two and insufferably hot. Two of the Java parties are due to go overseas on Saturday. They had their medical inspection this morning. General Heath is expected to go with them. His wife will, of course, be left behind in the gaol with the rest of the civilians. She has, John says, got aplastic anaemia, following childbirth. I would have thought that producing children on the diet we have, would be impossible. Major Horrigan, US Airforce, is leaving on the next party. They have been told by a Nip that they are to travel on a 30,000 ton warship for 7 days, and they would then work in an aircraft factory.

Came across the following in 'Music Ho': "Pale tunes irresolute, and traceries of old sounds, blown from a rotted flute, mingle with noise of cymbals, rouged with rust". How well this describes some music I can think of. Am steadily working my way through Drinkwater's 'Outline of Literature', which Kerr has borrowed. Went to a lecture by Rennison yesterday on 'Music from the Time of Ancient Greece to JS Bach'. This sounds a long step, but actually there is very little to say of any interest about the first part of the period. This was the first of a series of 16 talks on music to be given during the next 8 weeks.

A minor mutiny among the Dutch yesterday. Some of the half-castes had been put on charge for various misdemeanours and while the charges were being read out to them, they suddenly disappeared in the direction of their tents. They returned a few minutes later with some 40 supporters, carrying knives and sticks. They formed a circle round the officers and one of them shouted "Now let the MPs come and get us". The 'Gottverdommers' were quite unable to cope with the situation and appealed to Andy for help. He gave them until 3.00 pm to calm down, which they proceeded to do. The Nips have to be kept out of any trouble such as this. The three ringleaders were put in the detention compound and there was no more trouble. Some months ago some men of an 11 Div unit refused to obey orders given to them by their officers, and the men responsible were arrested and given sentences ranging from 2 to 10 years, to be carried out after the war. I wonder whether they ever will.

29 November 42 Terrific flap the day before yesterday. The Nips found two Dutchmen on Pulau Ubin and ordered all the Dutch in the camp to be counted. We got 2000 of them paraded by 10.00 pm and checked by 11.30 pm; not bad since these things always have to be done in the dark without torches. The result was 5 absentees. The Nips were, surprisingly, not very worried about this and their sole comment was "Find them by the morning", which to my great surprise we did. I have now embarked on 'Henry Esmond', which I have never yet read. Saw Peter May, Ione's brother, the other day, in a much better frame of mind as he had received letters from Cape Town.

He also helps to look after the 'Gottverdommers' in transit. He had received a letter from his father, which he gave me to read. It was odd to see something from the outside world. Fitz, Jackie and I have started having Italian lessons, the second one taking place today. Kerr is the Professor. He has managed to get some Linguaphone records from somewhere. Several of us had started to take up Japanese but most of us have let this lapse owing to the unpleasant associations it has for most of us.

1 December 42 A bad day yesterday, all of us becoming very depressed. By evening tempers were frayed and life became almost intolerable. 10 months have now passed since our capture and all we can see ahead of us is an endless procession of days, weeks and months stretching away into a hopeless future. It would be so much easier if we could be given a sentence of so many years. We could then settle down accordingly and watch the months bring us ever nearer freedom. We often say how wonderful it must be in Dartmoor: we would know how long we were going to be there, we would receive plenty to eat at regular times and we would have nothing to do for ourselves, except plan for when we were to get out. Here, I can't. The world outside just does not exist anymore for us.

Attended Rennison's second lecture. The subject was the Oratorio Form, illustrated by records, including Dora Lebette and Harold Williams, singing recitatives and arias from the Messiah and the St. Mathew Passion. The records are old and worn and the gramophone is very indifferent but it sounds all right to us and is quite as satisfying as if we were sitting in the Queen's Hall. Another very bad night, all of us very depressed. These fits of depression come and go without any reason. One night I feel that there is no future ahead of me and that there is no point in struggling any further. The next night I feel that I have got everything to look forward to. And this will go on for month after month until one day, I suppose, we shall wake up to find we are free once more. Never did I think it possible to live on this earth and yet be less a part of it.

8 December 42 Peter out of hospital after six weeks, looking very pale, but better than I expected. Dickie Durden also out, after being operated on for an ulcer. It has been raining hard for three days and nights. People say the monsoon has begun, but I always thought that Singapore was outside the monsoon zone. More rumours today about the Red Cross ship, which is said to be on its way.

11 December 42 More Dutch are due to go overseas. I think we shall be glad to see the last of them. They appear to have very little organisation and as the Nips have made us responsible for them, it is not an enviable task looking after them. John and I have just put in our canteen order for Christmas, which includes such things as peanut toffee, dates and bananas. The food has deteriorated recently, as we have very nearly run out of Red Cross food, which we were able to use for flavouring. The cocoa finished about a fortnight ago and we are now back on issue tea. Breakfast is a particularly tasteless meal, consisting of rice porridge, rice rissoles with perhaps a little fish flavouring and a handful of soya beans.

More face slapping yesterday; three Nip privates, who usually accompany the Nip officer on daily roll call parades, appeared at camp HQ and said they were going to go round the camp. In the afternoon complaints were received from several units that the three Nips had entered officers' messes and troops' living quarters and slapped faces for no apparent reason. The complaints were passed on at the evening roll call by the IJA to the Nip officer. The latter received the complaints quite amicably and said there was too much face slapping, both in the POW camps and in the IJA itself. He said he would deal with the men concerned himself. Nothing more was heard until the afternoon, when the same three Nips paid another visit to the messes and quarters, where the incidents had taken place, and distributed a large number of cigarettes. Fergy has now recovered and we are all hoping he will be allowed to administer the camp area once more. Hutch is being generally bloody minded at present and Bortsch is going slightly mental. Heaven preserve us anyway from some of the so-called senior officers in this camp. If they are not downright dishonest and thoroughly unscrupulous, they are incompetent and sheer bloody fools, and we are all hoping he will be allowed to administer the camp area once more.

15 December 42 A complete nominal roll of all personnel in the camp is required. Several hundred letters from England and South Africa have arrived at the gaol. General air of excitement mingled with a feeling of hope all over the camp. Shall we get letters? Kerr received four from his wife and four others in the mess were lucky. I have drawn a blank and shall have to wait for the next time. Discovered afterwards that only one bag has been received and this contains only 3000 letters. Not many for the best part of 50,000 men, spread out all over Malaya, the NEI and Siam. I think we were almost as delighted to hear all the news from Kerr's wife as we would have been to receive letters from our own relations.

News from home does not remain private property for long here. One has an irrepressible urge to share it with one's friends. I still have Diana's three letters, which I received on my arrival in Singapore last February, and which are my last news from home. These three letters, my only contact with her and the outside world, are becoming sadly dated, being now over a year old. In the batch of mail just received is a card from Becky's wife saying "So glad to hear of you from Tufton". This was the first news we have had of Tufton's successful escape and we were all overjoyed. To think that, had I had better luck, I would also be free, but if anybody deserved to get away safely, Tufton did. He has enormous energy and drive and with his brain should do well in this war and after.

I still continue with my job of checking roll call figures at the main camp HQ, which becomes rather irksome at times, as it seems such a waste of time. But then can one regard anything which helps to kill time in this monotonous existence as being a 'waste of time'?

Have just finished Eric Linklater's 'Magnus Merriman', which has given me a good laugh. Kerr knows most of the originals of the characters. Our Italian lessons continue twice a week under 'il professore' Paxton, but we all find our memories are beginning to go, and a good memory was never one of my attributes.

17 December 42 This morning the general, who has succeeded Fukuye, inspected the camp. All ranks had to parade on the road at 9.15 am. Needless to say the Nips did not arrive until after 11 o'clock. The General drove very slowly in his car, about 5 mph, and the least one can say is that he appeared to be more interested in what he saw than Fukuye ever was. He has been promoted to Lieut. Gen. but we have been unable to discover where he is going. We have been having one of our regular bug strafes. It is quite impossible ever to get rid of them, but at least we can prevent them from multiplying too fast. Peter says they were very bad in hospital and he found that soapy water was always quite effective.

Unfortunately we do not possess sufficient soap to try this method out here, particularly at present, when we have not even got enough to produce soapy water after washing. We had a great time today. Fitz produced some biscuits from somewhere. They were stale, but tasted fine to us. They set us thinking how much we miss wheat flour here. I miss bread more than anything else. With Christmas only eight days away, there is much speculation as to whether the IJA will give us anything extra in the rations. I doubt it. Nobody seems to know whether a Nip has ever heard of Christmas.

22 December 42 It was reported the other day that all Singapore camps are to be cleared out and the men, numbering about 10,000 to return to Changi. The Chinese and the Malays are reported to be complaining that they are unable to get work. 1300 Australians returned yesterday. Today the 'Film Party' returned from Johore Bahru, where they have been taking part in a film of the victorious advance of Nippon troops down Malaya, culminating in the fall of Singapore. We have had a bad blow. Our meat ration, small as it was, has now been stopped altogether. Instead, we are supposed to receive a fish ration of 1oz per man, three times per week. I do not hold out much hope of ever seeing very much fish! First I have never known the IJA to deliver such rations as often as they say they will, and second, a large percentage of the fish we do receive is so bad that it has to be thrown away the moment it arrives. We have now started drinking rice polishings in order to increase our intake of Vitamin B. We used to take these in our rice porridge at breakfast or in the form of biscuits, but these tasted so unpleasant that a less obnoxious method of getting them down had to be evolved. Also so many of us have had worms lately, that we now boil them before drinking. This naturally leads to many arguments as to whether the Vitamin B is being destroyed, and these arguments are by no means confined to the laymen.

We have given up all hope of having a Christmas meat ration. However, we still have some of our South African Red Cross bully left and we may be able to buy a few cockerels. Berkeley hopes to provide some 'hooch'! This is made by the Dutch, who if useless in many ways, are the organisers of a highly expensive black market. He hopes to have 5 or 6 bottles, but I am afraid there is not much hope of 18 of us getting tight on this. Have just finished 'The Good Companions' which I have never yet read, and have just started Colette's 'Le Blé en Herbe'. 'Le Toutounier' is also in the camp somewhere. Our usual recital of records last Sunday evening. We played Chopin's 1st piano concerto. The 2nd we heard a few weeks ago. In both these the orchestra seems to me to be used only as an accompaniment to the piano, and I get the impression that were the piano part to be played alone, it would sound equally complete. Judging from the fact that both these concertos were written before Chopin was 20 years old, it would seem that he was not satisfied with this type of work, since he never wrote any others.

Yesterday we went to see an exhibition of toys made by the men for the children interned in Changi Gaol. These toys are unbelievably good and include such things as scooters, tricycles, dolls houses, games and picture books. Many of these toys are up to the standard of those found in England before the war, and considering how little is available in the way of tools or material, the ingenuity is astounding. It is hoped that the Nips will allow these toys to be sent up to the gaol by Christmas. The Australians have also made between 500 and 600 toys. One of the most beautifully made things there was a double bed, about 10 inches long, made by John Excell. It had a Dunlopillo mattress made from an old car seat, two pillows, sheets, blankets and a blue quilt. John was very irate when I saw him, as he had been accused of trying to give the children the wrong ideas, and had been told that the bed ought to be single. I feel very sorry for these civilians; they are far worse off than we are at present. The women are rarely allowed outside the gaol walls and usually exercise in the exercise yard surrounded by high stone walls.

27 December 42 We have all been very subdued for the last two days, as a result of our overeating on Christmas day. I think the meals we had would have defeated me in normal times, but after nearly a year of Japanese rations it was just too much for me to cope with. There was no roll call parade on Christmas morning so we were able to remain in bed until about 9.00 am when we got up very leisurely. The dining room was decorated with paper streamers made out of highly coloured lavatory paper, different kinds of greenery and flowers. At each of our places was a menu card for the day. Breakfast consisted of mabele porridge, two bully beef rissoles, tinned sausage, 2 eggs and bacon, rice toast, tinned butter and marmalade and coffee. Lunch was rather more modest. Soup, scotch egg, marrow, pineapple fritters, and mince pies. We were then able to sleep until 4.00 pm when we were awakened for tea. We have a very fine gong, made out of an old shell case. When we got downstairs, we were confronted by a vast Christmas cake. After tea, I decided that if I did not take some form of exercise, I would never be able to cope with dinner.

The exercise consisted of strolling rather painfully round to India Lines to watch a soccer match between the Dutch and British. At 6.45 pm we were expected to start up once more, and we endeavoured to go for a 'short, sharp, walk'. Dinner included the following: Hors d'oeuvres, soup, roast chicken, two savouries, bananas, pineapples, dates, peanut toffee and sweets. We drank ginger wine, which had been brewed three months previously from sugar (bought in the canteen) and locally grown ginger.

In addition, Berkeley had succeeded in buying six bottles of arrack from the Dutch at $6 per bottle. There were some abstainers, which enabled John and me to share a bottle. As a result of experiments carried out on Christmas eve, we had found the most satisfactory way of drinking this gut-rot, although some of the braver members of the mess drank theirs neat. We added the juice of half a lime and a little pineapple juice. The result was a drink not unlike a 'white lady'. Only twelve of us were left to deal with this drink, which meant that we each had half a bottle. By 10.00 pm John and I were distinctly happy. Berkeley had succeeded in making the most amazing collection of head gear, the materials he used being banana leaves, flowers and string. A few of the others gave up their hooch and John and I were enabled to go on drinking until we really did not mind whether we were prisoners or not. We turned out for roll call the following morning with the most glorious hangovers. These early morning roll calls are usually rather a farce. Somebody almost always arrives late, or forgets to put on their headgear or, on some occasions, perhaps not even wake up at all. As these parades are never attended by the Nips, there is never any trouble. This particular morning, whether as the result of the hangover I do not know, was the first time I had noticed the procedure adopted by Andy on such occasions. Whether he did it to make things easier or not I have never discovered, but he used regularly to check that we were all present, salute the IJA officer, who would be having his early morning snort up at the end of the parade, and say. "We are all present, Sir, shall I call the roll?" Many people in the camp are convinced that next Christmas will see us out. I am inclined to feel the same. I just cannot think further than 12 months ahead. Some of us prefer to settle down for another two or three years and leave it at that.

31 December 42 New Year's Eve at last. Thank God 1942 is now over. It has been the blackest year in our lives and God willing we shall never experience anything worse. The Nips have presented us with some saki, but the issue is one bottle between 10 men. We have just started rehearsing 'Badger's Green'. The 'Duchess' (Fitz) is playing the doctor's wife. The play is expected to open on 1 Feb in the theatre in the hospital camp area. Have just finished André Maurois' 'The Art of Living' and have now started Mark Twain's 'Innocents Abroad'. The number of men in camp has risen by about

2000 during the past two days, with the return of men from working camps in Singapore. Two evenings ago, Kerr and I played the Emperor concerto up on our balcony, it was a beautiful, quiet evening, and I thought of the last time I had heard this played by Arthur Schnabel at the Queen's Hall in 1937 or 38.

4 January 43 The saki on New Year's Eve was a great success. In its nude state, it was a reddish brown colour and tasted like some very crude Italian Vermouth. However, Berkeley and the Duchess got to work on it and made a very good drink by adding pineapple juice, mint and gula malacca. The evening was quite a success, since Fitz, as PMC, had produced a very good meal consisting of bully, Christmas pudding, and a savoury. At midnight a party of several hundred men, headed by a drummer, came marching and singing along the road. The Nips apparently expected us to make a noise and none of the guards interfered.

8 January 43 We have been busy the last few days with men coming in from the docks. About 3000 Australian and Dutch have arrived from Java. We took 500 Australians into 18 Div. camp area. Most of these were captured in Timor, where they remained until two or three months ago, when they were taken to Java. These men were some of the first Australians to leave the Middle East and were on their way to Australia, when they were diverted to Java. They were then sent on to Timor. They suffered badly from malaria; whilst there only 21 out of the total of about 1500 escaped it. This group was known as 'Sparrow Force' and formed the Timor garrison, 1500 against some 30,000 Nips, not to mention 800 parachute troops. They tell us that Australian troops are still resisting in the central part of the island, which is very mountainous and completely wild. Their tactics are to carry out small surprise raids on the Nips near the coast, shooting them up and laying mines on the roads. They were, certainly until quite recently, in touch with Australia, 7 ton launches being used to bring in supplies under cover of night, and also by air. For some weeks even a destroyer was used to keep the troops supplied, the vessel being based at Port Darwin. Most of the Americans left to go up-country yesterday, and everybody was very sorry to see them go. They were always very cheerful and hardworking. A good grumble this morning with Jackie, in which we almost convinced ourselves that we should never get home again.

14 January 43 The bulk of the Dutch have now gone up-country. Our food situation is none too good. We get no meat and fish only very occasionally. The ration is only 3ozs per man before it is cleaned. We are thus left with rice, some vegetables and a little fruit, such as bananas, which we can sometimes buy at the canteen. The incidence of deficiency diseases is on the up-grade once more. This is chiefly due to lack of vitamins A, B1 and B2. For these we try to eat as much red palm oil, rice polishings, and as many peanuts as we can get hold of. The rice polishings, like the rice, are always full of grubs and weevils. The latter we can sort out, but the grubs are too numerous to cope with, so they have to stay in. I find rice polishings quite disgusting. They resemble nothing I have ever tasted before, but I imagine sour saw-dust would be not dissimilar. Skin complaints are one of the most common manifestations of this vitamin deficiency, but many people are now finding that their eyes are affected. For these eye complaints one can only wear dark glasses and try to keep out of the sun as much as possible – also get all the peanuts, rice polishings and palm oil one can.

The hospital has had to cut down the special foods given to the more serious cases. No mail has yet arrived in any quantity and we are gradually giving up hope of ever seeing any. Kerr was told over a month ago that there was a letter for him at the gaol, but he has not seen it yet. They are said to be censoring them at the rate of 10 – 20 per day. What a hope!

I think we are all getting slightly Russian in our general outlook. "It does not matter. Nothing matters any more. Soon we shall all be dead". Rehearsals for 'Badger's Green' go on every afternoon and the dress rehearsal is fixed for the end of the month.

18 January 43 Another 1500 men are to go up-country at the rate of 650 per day starting next Wednesday. Included in this are the 500 Australians in our camp area. This figure of 650 is becoming more and more frequent in connection with these up-country parties and must refer to train loads. How many to a truck does that make, I wonder? Changi seems to be gradually becoming a transit camp for personnel coming through from Java. Another 1000 Dutch are due to arrive this evening, and have to be housed and fed in 18 Div area. In all, yesterday, 3000 POW from Java arrived in the area and 3200 more are due in today. Not the least difficult job is counting these incoming and outgoing parties, as they invariably move at night.

John and Bill held a joint celebration of their birthdays the other day and we had a terrific feast. They had managed to buy all the necessary ingredients to make sausage rolls (so called), mince pies, chocolate cakes and cocoa. We ate till we were fit to burst. The cocoa was greatly improved by the addition of tinned milk and sugar, neither of which are ever seen in the canteen and I can only suppose they came through the black market. After stuffing ourselves, we played charades and other childish games. The following morning I awoke with a horrible food hangover and John must have been feeling much the same, as he did not get up until lunch time.

27 January 43 Working parties continue to go up-country. As from today another 2400 are to start leaving at the rate of 650 per day. This means that we shall loose the 1000 Dutch at present in our camp area. They are a great improvement on the previous lot we had, and they appear to be much more efficiently organized. They are under the command of a half-caste colonel, but this seems to be an improvement, as the discipline of the men is good. We now have so many of these troops in transit that we have at long last set up an official reception unit. We should have done this weeks ago. I read in the Syonan Times the other day that two Nipponese vessels carrying Dutch prisoners were attacked by 'antiaxis' planes off Tavoy on 18 January. The paper states that "although rescue operations were carried out immediately, 500 prisoners were missing". This is the third time we have read of ships carrying prisoners, being sunk with many prisoners being drowned and, now, we would all rather be sent up-country by rail if we ever have to go.

A paper called the 'Survivor' has been started in the camp and the first number has just been published. It is typed on Nip paper, which is obtained privately, and I doubt if the Nips know that their own paper, which is very scarce, is being used for this particular purpose. The editor is an Indian by the name of Trenchel, who is a medical orderly in the hospital. He has a degree from Oxford, and a degree in Divinity at an American university, after which he entered the church. He later gave up the church and the Spanish Civil War found him fighting for Franco. Ronald Searle is the art editor. I rather think that the future of the paper depends on the supply of raw material from the Nips. Last Saturday we were all locked in for the morning as some high Nip personage was due to drive through the camp. Everybody had to remain indoors and all windows had to be shut. We think it might have been a member of the Imperial family as nobody in Nippon is ever allowed to look down on the Emperor or any member of his family, when they are driving through the streets of a town. We had to remain hidden for three and a half hours. Some say that it was the GOC Southern Region inspecting the camp. If so, I can only say that it is a mighty odd way in which to inspect anything!

1 February 43 Two days ago we were all inoculated against dysentery and typhoid and as a result, I retired to bed for a couple of days and got up today feeling quite fit.

4 February 43 The dress rehearsal of 'Badgers Green' last night. The first and second acts went quite well, but the third was terrible. Perhaps this is a good sign, as the rehearsal was not particularly good. We are due to open this evening to an audience consisting of hospital patients and staff. I am now able to go swimming twice a week and yesterday I went down with Mossy Moore. It was delightful to see and feel the sea again, perfectly smooth with a very high tide. The Nips allow us to bathe on Mondays to Thursdays and usually about two or three hundred are able to take advantage of this. Unfortunately the bulk of the men are employed on camp work, such as gardening for the hospital, wood fatigues etc, and are unable to bathe. We read in the 'Syonan Times' yesterday that 18 large mail bags, containing letters for British POW in the Southern Region had arrived in Japan on 28 January and that these letters will be forwarded to the various camps as soon as possible. I wonder. I expect a good many weeks will elapse before any of us here see anything. But it is good to know that it is on the way, as it gives us something to look forward to at last. One gets tired of living always in the present and trying to make the best of things.

8 February 43 The day before yesterday we spent all day on the gun-park waiting to be 'stuck'. This is a delightful procedure, thought out by the Nips and has become quite a favourite pastime of theirs. It is also known as 'bum-prodding', the chief object of the exercise being to test people for dysentery. The procedure is as follows: at one end of the gun park are some 10 tables, at each of which there are Nip medical orderlies. Opposite each table is a queue of perhaps 100 rather anxious looking prisoners, the degree of anxiety increasing as they move up from the back of the queue towards the front. On reaching the head of the queue, at long last, one has to bend over and while taking a quick, furtive look at the waiting hundreds, the little Nip, with a quick, unpleasant jab, obtains what John would call a 'rectal smear'. This, I find one of the most unpleasant things we have to endure, although the younger amongst us get a certain kick out of watching some of the more unpleasant senior officers undergoing the same treatment. The great disadvantage to this system, at least as carried out by the Nips, is that they invariably get one's personal number muddled up with that on the glass container. However, I have no doubt that it keeps the Nips amused. All men leaving the camp now have to undergo this particular form of indignity and it goes on all day long, sometimes with our own doctors. I only hope that if I have to go through it again, I don't draw John. The first time we were all done was last summer, when we were waiting to be moved to Japan. One gets used to anything and I have no doubt that soon we shall take this sort of thing as being nothing out of the ordinary.

Yesterday, I listened to Cyril Wild talking about Japan and in the course of conversation with him afterwards, I discovered that he was with Shell in Japan before the war. He speaks fluent Japanese and is an outstanding interpreter. In the evening, there being no performance at the theatre, Kerr and I retired to Jacky's balcony and listened to the 2nd Brahms symphony. Since we last played this some months ago, the records have been down to one of the working party camps in Singapore and back, so we are lucky to have them still intact, except for one which is scratched right across, although still playable. Have just finished A G Macdonnel's 'Autobiography of a Cad'.

14 February 43 Have now completed the first week of 'Badger's Green', which has proved to be quite a success. Food is as bad as ever. No meat at all now and very little fish. Our main diet is rice with very limited quantities of soya beans, towgay, bananas and small quantities of vegetables, supplied irregularly. Eggs are difficult to obtain and very expensive. Men just in from Java tell us that they were issued with meat every day of the week except one, that they had large quantities of fruit and vegetables and eggs at 4 1/2 cents each. It is incredible how limited a diet we exist on here, although of course we naturally limit our exertions as far as possible.

It is said that the Nips do not get much more to eat than we do, which is possibly true of their basic ration, but in practice they are always able to add to it considerably, So far, I have kept comparatively fit and my eyes at least do not seem to be affected, as is the case with so many others. If I were unable to read I do not think I would survive. It is extraordinary how cheerful we all are in the mess after a year of captivity. We naturally have our bad days but on the whole, we get over these very well.

Books read include Eric Linklater's 'White Man's Saga', which I found very similar to 'Magnus Merriman', a text book on the 'Renaissance and Reformation' by a woman by the name of Tanner, and Sinclair Lewis's 'Babbit'. This is an incredible hotchpotch of reading but, under the existing conditions, one has to read whatever comes into one's hands. At least the system, or perhaps lack of it, gives one extremely catholic tastes. I find myself reading books, which I would never have thought of reading under normal circumstances, and what is more important, I very often enjoy them and my literary horizon is being gradually extended.

18 February 43 A very dull week. I went swimming on Wednesday, but it was far too hot to be enjoyable. I weighed myself the other day and found that I am still 11 stone 10 lbs. It is mostly rice fat and I have no muscles worth the name. John tells me that I have beriberi. One thing is certain, if I have got it, he certainly has! One of the RAF officers with the party from Java told me today that he knew Denison, when they were on a signals course together at Cranwell in the early days of the war. Most of the gunners in the Java party are from South Wales, as the unit used to be part of the Cardiff AA defences. Jackie has already met two people he knew at home.

I was strolling back from the theatre the other night, thinking what a perfect night it was, when I was suddenly confronted by a corpse being carried across from one of the wards to the mortuary. The body was covered with a thin, white cloth, which made the outlines of the body stand out stark and cold in the bright moonlight. I could see the outline of the legs and feet, the hands folded on the chest and even the rough profile of the face. I wondered who he was, and where he had lived. I thought of his parents, or his wife perhaps, sitting at home, knowing nothing of what was going on. I wondered how many long months or years would pass before they would hear that he had died. He had perhaps been a battle casualty. There are still many of them in hospital keeping up a long, grim, patient struggle for life under the most appalling conditions. Perhaps, in the end, this man had found it too much to continue. His wife will probably never know how he died, or what was going on in his mind. It is just as well. She would never understand, as nobody will ever understand, who has not actually experienced life here.

It seems to be the only existence I have ever had or am ever likely to have. It is the only reality one has in the world and my life at home appears to exist only as a fantastic and intangible dream, in which I never really existed. The hours slip by one by one, becoming days and then weeks. The weeks become months, moving slowly and steadily onwards to further months, which have no end. I often watch the coconut palm opposite our balcony, and every time I look it seems to have put forth another shoot, which steadily ripens and eventually bursts open like some gigantic ear of corn. The tree goes on growing with an almost annoying persistence and a steady, mocking indifference to everything around it. It is as though it says to me "Look, I have a definite purpose in life. Why don't you do something too?".

21 February 43 65 merchant seamen have arrived in the camp, 25 British and the remainder American. They are the survivors from ships sunk by a German raider in the South Atlantic, not far from Cape Town. About half the crew of the British ship, numbering 58, were killed by shell fire from the raider, which loosed off some 50 rounds in 10 minutes. The decks were machine gunned, and she was finally sunk by two torpedoes, fired from two torpedo boats which had been launched by the raider. The German ship cruised around the area for 16 hours looking for survivors, before sailing off. Once on board the raider, the men say, they were well looked after. The ship was equipped with an excellent hospital and the wounded received first class medical attention. These raiders are specially built ships, being heavily armoured and having hidden guns and torpedo tubes. They carry two MTBs, and two seaplanes, are of about 10–12,000 tons displacement and can do 20 knots. On each mast, which is exceptionally high, there is a look-out post, from which men scan the horizon for shipping, being able to see other ships long before they can be spotted themselves.

Peter went up to camp HQ yesterday afternoon to collect postcards. We are to be allowed to send off one more postcard each! This makes the second in just over a year of captivity. We are, once again, limited to 24 words. Of what use are these cards? What more can one say but that "we are very well and the time is passing quickly"? Both these statements are quite untrue but why worry one's family by telling them the truth? I bought some eggs at the canteen yesterday and this morning had two for breakfast. A slightly ostentatious display, but they were worth it. I have been reading Jane Austen's 'Persuasion', which I think is delightful, 'Work of Art' by Sinclair Lewis and 'Rough Justice' by C E Montague.

4 March 43 I finally sent off my postcard, worded as follows:- "Health and spirits good, time passing quickly. No letters received. Regret Bryan Barrow killed. Fondest love to all and Allan & Catherine". Having said that we had received no letters, of course, we have just been told that 40 bags of mail have arrived at the gaol. The chances are that, out of that lot, I shall get one letter and it will then take me another year to let the family know that I have received it. It is officially estimated that there are 5000 letters per bag, which makes a total of 200,000 letters. Am now half way through Turbeville's 'Men and Manners of the 18th Century', which is most interesting reading.

7 March 43 The mail is now being sorted at the gaol. A party of 5000 British troops are to be sent up country on 14 March. We are to send 1400, Southern Area 1100 and the AIF 2500. Luckily, this number does not affect us and we remain put for the time being at least. It is certainly becoming increasingly evident that we shall be off in the near future. Kerr and I had a long talk the other evening about post war reconstruction and similar problems. Rather naturally it is a subject which is much discussed in this camp but it is of course one in which we always feel very much in the dark, since we know absolutely nothing about what is being said or planned in this direction in the outside world, nor along what lines people's minds are being reshaped by the altered circumstances brought about by the war. One thing we both thought was the first essential for any world at peace, and that is the abolition, or at least reduction, of the sovereignty of the individual state. Politically and economically we cannot carry on as separate nations, muddling along in our own particular ways, relying on our own economic and, if necessary, military strength, to get for ourselves a greater share of things that are equally vital to somebody else, and to which fundamentally they are just as much entitled as we. The equal distribution of the world's food and raw materials should be the job of an international group. People must be taught that they have other responsibilities than those to the particular state, in which they happen to have been born, a much nobler and far-reaching responsibility, that to mankind. It must be seldom, indeed, that any ordinary man or woman has wanted to fight and destroy those, whom the men playing the game of power politics have made our 'enemies'. I have never wanted to fight Germans or Japanese. How can anyone like or dislike a whole nation?

This, I think, is well illustrated by the old story of the man who went into a pub one evening and met a friend of his. After some minutes' conversation the two got on to the subject of nationality and the man asked his friend if he liked Americans. Being somewhat pro-American himself he was slightly put out by the other saying that he did not. "Do you like Frenchmen?" he asked. "No", replied the other. "What about the English?" "No" came the reply. "Well, whom do you like?" The other replied quietly, "I like my friends".

9 March 43 I have been told that there is a letter for me at the gaol. At last. We have just been ordered to send another 2800 men up-country on the next batch. This means that we shall be almost entirely cleared out of 'fit' men.

13 March 43 I have just received my first letter since leaving England a year and five months ago. It is dated 9 July 1942 and is the third written by Mother since people at home were informed that they could write to Far East prisoners. This morning I went down to the gaol with the small sorting party. While down there I saw a postcard from Stanley Lemin to say that he and Tufton were at GHQ New Delhi and that they had both been promoted to the rank of Major. There was also a letter for Bryan, which proves what I was afraid of; that the news of his death could not have been sent off before we surrendered. Figures for the up-country party have been reduced and now stand at 1800. I thought this would happen.

Our damn priest has been causing more trouble lately and he is more unpopular than ever. I wish to hell we could unload him on some other mess, although what anybody has done to deserve him, I cannot conceive. Amongst his many other sins, he never takes a bath. Things finally got so bad, particularly when one gets downwind of him, that we approached John as being the senior officer in the mess, and a doctor, and requested him to take some sort of action. John thought that this was taking unfair advantage of his senior rank, but nevertheless said he would speak to him. John has more guts than I thought. Even I am not used to telling a sky pilot to his face that he smells and will he please do something about it.

However John did. He told me afterwards that his opening sentence went something like this. "Padre, I have something rather unpleasant to say to you. I have been asked, as senior officer in the mess, to tell you that you smell". He could hardly have been clearer and I take my hat off to John. Unfortunately, I doubt very much if this will encourage him to adopt more hygienic habits. He is one of the most unpleasant men I have ever come across. Have just finished Shaw's translation of the 'Odyssey', and am now embarking on Thoreau's 'Walden'.

21 March 43 For the past three days, parties have been leaving at the rate of 650 per day. Their destination is unknown but it is thought to be Thailand. Have received two more letters dated 6 and 20 July 1942. From these it appears that the family is now back at Kingswood, but when, why and how I do not know. I thought that I would be satisfied to receive letters but these few merely whet my appetite and give me a very unsettled feeling. It is so unreal to read about what people are doing at home and just does not seem to mean anything here. It is almost as though one had received a letter from someone on the moon. Am still hoping for news from Diana and also Denison. It is now so long since I heard from her, and so much will have happened before I get out of this, that I think she is best forgotten. This is easy to say but not so easy when I remember how much she meant to me at the time, which conjures up such wonderful memories. Jackie has at last heard from his wife and is much happier now that he knows that she got away safely from Singapore.

29 March 43 I have read the following books during the last day or two. 'Seven for a Secret' by Mary Webb, 'Little Madam', a Life of Henrietta Maria, by Janet Mackay and Ernest Hemingway's 'Fifth Column'. We have started a daily news bulletin of news of general interest extracted from men's letters. In this way we are able to glean a little of what is happening at home, although censorship limits this considerably. However, we are able to learn quite a lot about troop movements at home and overseas from the letters from brother Bill to Bert, Bert knowing that his brother is in such and such a unit or division. The camp is now full of the most fantastic rumours concerning up-country parties. There is usually some grain of truth in these and it looks very much as though it is going to be our turn next. The last party numbering 5000 have now all left. Yesterday 40 officers and 1000 men left suddenly by sea and they are said to be going to Borneo. We know that some working parties have already gone there. The camp, rather naturally, has a general air of impermanence now and there is much speculation as to where we shall all be in a few weeks' time.

10 April 43 Have spent the last week or so in bed with headaches and I have begun to think that my eyes may be giving trouble. I had not felt too well for some few days and John finally ordered me to bed for a rest. I had a blood count taken in hospital the other day but found that this was more or less up to standard. At the end of a week in bed, my feet started breaking out into small blisters, which burst after a little and then remain wet and raw. John thought "Ah, shingles!" and sent me round to see the skin specialist. In hospital; John's theory proved to be slightly out and I returned to inform him that I was suffering from 'common epidermophytosis', i.e. tinea of an obscure form. I now spend a large part of my day applying boric acid ointment and spirit to my feet. I got up yesterday for the first time, feeling much better but unfortunately found that I could barely walk.

It has come at last. For a day or two, the air has been full of rumour about more working parties to go up-country, and today we have learned that a party of 7000 has been ordered to leave. The party is to be made up of 3300 AIF, 3150 British, about 400 from the hospital area and the balance from Southern Area. We are practically all going from our mess. The most important exception is the 'Praying Mantis', who, thank God, we are to leave behind to annoy somebody else. The preparations for our departure are already under way, particularly in the department of bureaucracy, where crates are being made to carry typewriters, duplicating machines and masses of stationery and files.

Books read include Flaubert's 'Madame Bovary' and 'Sentimental Education'. 'The Life of Bernadotte' by Dunbar Barton, 'The Power and the Glory' by Graham Greene, 'New Writing'. Now, of course, we are faced with the problem of what books to take with us, when we leave. Kerr, Peter and I are trying to collect as many books of longer term value and interest as we can lay our hands on, which is not easy. Part of the camp library will be going with us, but I shall be very surprised if it ever reaches the same destination as we. I have managed to lay my hands on the 'Oxford Book of English Verse', the 'Oxford Book of Modern Verse' and 'A History of European Literature' by R D Jameson, a lecturer in English at Peking University.

11 April 43 News came through late last night that the force will start leaving next Saturday and that most of our mess are due to leave on Monday on the third train. Tomorrow our rectums are due to be violated by jagged pieces of Nipponese glass rod once again. Well, I suppose the Nips enjoy it. We all had a very good feed of chicken yesterday. We had already decided to kill our share of the chickens and eat them before leaving but it was actually due to an accident that we had them as soon as we did. The corporal, who looks after Stanley's chicken farm, saw two cockerels fighting over a hen, which had inadvertently got amongst them. He dashed in to retrieve the hen and put it back in its own pen. As he did so, however, it flew between his legs, knocking him over backwards and causing him to fall heavily on the wretched bird, which promptly expired. Stanley decided that we had better eat the rest, so two more were killed.

16 April 43 Last Monday we all had our backsides prodded for the third time. Now we are to be inoculated against cholera and plague, and some of us have already had the first dose of serum. Some 20 bags of mail have arrived at the gaol and I have already received two more letters, one from Denison dated end July 42 and one from Father dated 14 August. We understand we are in for a week's train journey but no-one can tell us what happens after that. The popular rumour at present is that we are off to Chieng Mai, which is the terminus of the Thai railway running northwards. It is said to have 500,000 inhabitants and to be in a food producing area. We shall probably go somewhere entirely different.

21 April 43. I have received another 5 letters, one from Diana at last, and the rest from the family. This was wonderful but has unsettled me greatly. These letters are all very well but they only leave one with the feeling that one would like to pack up and go home straight away. I have now been inoculated four times, twice for cholera and twice for plague. I was also vaccinated but it shows no signs of taking yet. Our departure date has been altered several times, but is, at long last, fixed for next Saturday. The trains are leaving Singapore station at 4.00 am. This means getting into lorries at about 1.30 am. The Australians started leaving last Sunday in the middle of a violent tropical storm, which soaked them before they had started. We still have not the slightest inkling as to where we are going, but the favourite now is northern Malaya. We played the Vaughan Williams London Symphony yesterday, but I find it unimpressive. I wonder when we shall hear music again.

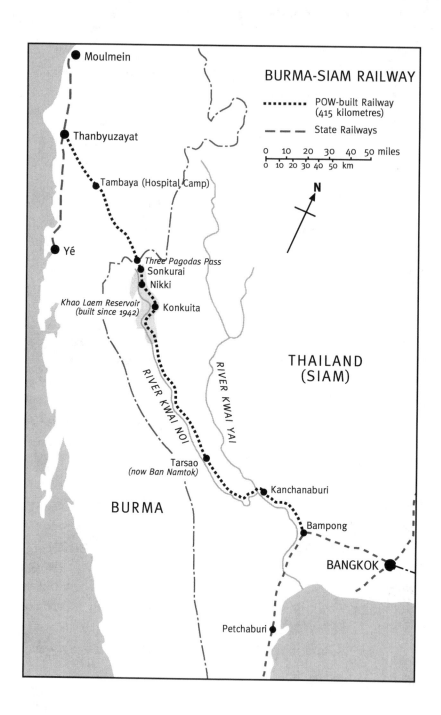

BURMA-SIAM RAILWAY

········· POW-built Railway
(415 kilometres)

– – – State Railways

0   10   20   30   40   50 miles
0 10 20 30 40 50 km

N

Moulmein

Thanbyuzayat

Tambaya (Hospital Camp)

Yé

Three Pagodas Pass
Sonkurai
Nikki

*Khao Laem Reservoir
(built since 1942)*
Konkuita

RIVER KWAI NOI

RIVER KWAI YAI

THAILAND
(SIAM)

Tarsao
(now Ban Namtok)

Kanchanaburi

BURMA

Bampong

BANGKOK

Petchaburi

F FORCE

Forced labour building the Burma-Siam railway

～

Shortly after the last entry in my diary for 21 April, I became one of a trainload of 660 members of F Force. This force had a total strength of 7000, all of whom were sent up to Siam (as it was then called), during the month of April 1943, to build the Burma-Siam railway. It became impossible to keep up my diary until I had returned to Singapore in December 1943.

However, whilst I was still at Kanchanaburi, after the railway had been completed and we were waiting to be sent back to Singapore, I managed to make the following rough notes about my time on the railway on odd scraps of paper.

Conditions on rail journey, Singapore to Siam. Five days and nights, allowed to get out of train for 30 minutes twice a day. No latrine arrangements, we had to urinate and crap out of the wagon door, being held by others as we did so. Most had dysentery and were very weak so that many who could not get up simply defecated where they lay and conditions in wagons were soon revolting. Little or no sleep at night, very hot by day in all-metal box wagons, too many in each to allow all to lie down at the same time. Appalling stench. Occasional food buying at stations; eggs, papayas.

Food indifferent. Staging camp in Bampong, where we spent one night and one day, before marching out the following night on the start of 200 mile march through jungle. Two night marches, fifteen miles each to Kanchanaburi. The sick had to be left at halfway staging camp, a few got lift on lorry with kit. 36 hour halt at

Prisoners cutting into the mountain near Konyu,
Siam-Burma Railway, June 1943

Nightly marches of approximately fifteen miles with 36 hours halt every second march. Reached large British camp at Tarsao, which then the railhead but line still unballasted. Saw Andy Dillon and Colonel Harris. Hope of staying at Tarsao but told we were to go on same night; very tired and very disappointed. Food at staging camps non-existent, just a small amount of bad rice and watery stew. Heard there were at least another ten marches. Cholera camp, where I fell out with bad heel. First meeting with Major Hunt, an outstanding Australian doctor. Met Train 8, under command of Colonel Hingston and Bill Auld. Marched to Nikki where we spent one night. On to Sonkurai camp, one night's march. Monsoon rains had already started in earnest, 24 hours a day. We marched and tried to sleep at staging posts in the rain. No roofing on huts at Sonkurai where we lived in constant pouring rain and work on railway started at once without rest. Went out two days then down with fever. Thought at first to be dengue but after five days of no treatment found to be malaria. Lay in hut for four weeks, unable to move, then out on road again.

Camp disgracefully administered. Developed tropical ulcers on both legs. Cholera rife and men dying at the rate of 20 per day. Conditions in camp ghastly. Camp total strength 1600, of whom 1200 or more are now dead. Stayed at Sonkurai until late August then up to Tambaya in Burma to so-called hospital camp. Warm reception there from Hutch and Whiskers. Also found Fitz and Bill. Peter already there and gravely ill with cardiac beriberi. John at one stage gave Peter only 24 hours to live, but he pulled through after several vitamin B injections, which were John's last. I got dropped feet in both feet from beriberi and couldn't walk, this aggravated by relapses of malaria and dysentery. We had to tie our big toes to our calves with a strip of liana to hold our feet up, so that we could walk. Lost weight badly but have picked up since.

Luckily heart unaffected by beriberi so far. Death rate at Tambaya appallingly high, 800 already dead. Water problems acute due to drying up of streams in vicinity. Final move south to Kanchanaburi towards end of November. Trip took five days and four nights during which we had one derailment. The line in very poor state; travelled down with John, Whiskers and Ken.

A 'beating up' for failing to number in Japanese

Kanchanaburi a tented staging camp. Masses of eggs, tinned meat, milk and fish there. Fed like pigs with consequent bad effect on stomach.

Hutch, Whiskers and John moved into hospital after few days. I went on later owing to yet another bout of malaria, which kept me in bed. Stayed in hospital, ostensibly as staff, until 18 December, when we left for Singapore.

Appalling state of sick, tropical ulcers, cases seen myself of legs bared to the bone from ankle to knee. One man's thighs and scrotum completely rotted away. Indescribable stench, ulcers were scraped with spoons every day, or cleaned with leaches, accompanied by cries of men in their agony.

At night no sleep for the wretched patients, who moaned all night long, their only hope for the morning was to look forward to a repetition of all previous day's agonies and torture. This went on for weeks in many cases.

Men dying horribly. Nothing could be done to alleviate their ghastly suffering.

What hope was there? No man on earth deserves such a death.

How they lasted as long as they did, Christ alone knows. Just a mass of moaning, stinking, decaying, gangrenous flesh. A nightmare none of us will ever forget as long as we live. The stench in the ulcer patients' hut alone was enough to make one vomit. One man had his arm and shoulder muscles bared, with the bone clearly visible. Complete amputation of arm and shoulder joint was carried out but what hope was there of the poor wretch ever living through it? He was dead within an hour. Bodies piled up waiting to be put on the cremation fires. Not enough men to carry the bodies over from the camp, where they had been lying for over two days. How callous one became. The bodies used to sit up in the fire. Others groaned audibly, when the air rushed out of their lungs, the bodies slowly going black, skulls bursting open and the pungent odour all the time. Meanwhile we brewed and sipped tea in the rare intervals of rest, waiting for the next supply of bodies to arrive.

Men went crazy. One man jumped into the river from the bridge and the body was never recovered. The effort made by him to reach the bridge must have been superhuman. He went out at night, pitch black, heavy rain, suffering from cerebral malaria and a temperature of over 106. The river was 1/2 mile from his hut along a very rough jungle track. Another man unable longer to endure the ghastly fate awaiting him preferred death in the peace and freedom of the jungle. In Burma all operations and amputations were made with a sharp table knife and a hand-saw borrowed from the Nips for a couple of hours per day for return, cleaned, afterwards, banana leaves being used for ulcer dressings.

It was just after my return to Changi that I extracted the following notes from the official report, which Andy Dillon had submitted to the Kempeitai, at their request, on the conditions faced by prisoners working on the railway:

F FORCE NOTES

～

Early April 1943, 7000 for a move by train. The following definite information was given by the Nips:

1. The reason for the move was the shortage of food on Singapore Island. Food would be more plentiful up country, where we were going.

2. This was not a working party.

3. In view of the fact that there were not 7000 fit men in Changi camp, 30% unfit to march or work would be taken. There would be 'recreational hills'.

4. It would be only a short distance from the train to the camp at the other end. Transport would be supplied by the IJA for luggage and unfit men.

5. Bands were to be taken.

6. Tools, cooking gear and electric light plant to be taken.

7. Gramophones, blankets, mosquito nets etc would be supplied at the other end.

8. There would be a good canteen available after three weeks. An interim supply of canteen goods was to be taken.

9. The medical party should be 350 with equipment for a 400 bed hospital and medical supplies to last three months.

Each trainload was told, on arrival at Bampong, that it had at least several days' march. Anything, which could not be carried, had to be dumped at Bampong. There were 15 rail trucks of baggage, all of which had to be left. In fact the march lasted 4 weeks, covered 15 stages, all at night over a distance of 200 miles. All torches were confiscated and the way was over rough tracks through jungle. The fit men became casualties through having to carry the sick. There was no overhead cover on the route, or in any of the staging posts. The monsoon rains had started. Food was poor and often consisted of poor quality rice only. Water was short and at Kanchanaburi had to be bought for 5 cents per bucket. There were no arrangements for the sick to be left at the camps and in most cases the sick had to be carried by the fit men. In one case an IJA officer ruled that a chaplain should stay at one of the staging camps as he was too ill to move on. These orders were overruled by a corporal who told the chaplain he must go on the same night. The chaplain died. After all-night marches from 7.00 pm until 7.00 am there were camp fatigues for the men. The only medical supplies available were those carried by hand on the marches after a hasty selection at Bampong. These soon ran out. The men started suffering from dysentery, diarrhoea and ulcerated feet and legs. At Konkoita the POW parties passed through a Thai labour corps camp, which was cholera stricken. On 15 May cholera broke out at Shimo Nieke. Col. Harris suggested that all movement of POW should cease.

The IJA refused and cholera spread to all five F Force camps. Only a very small quantity of drugs could be brought up on the march and 3/4 of our medical supplies had been left behind at Bampong. These were still there when F Force returned in December. The IJA could produce nothing except a small quantity of cholera vaccine (and it was very efficacious) and quinine when required, though Col. Banno gave six tins of milk to the hospital.

End of May There were 5000 men in several camps. The huts were without roofs for several weeks and it rained continuously night and day. Pneumonia started. Work was started straight away and maximum numbers were always asked for by the IJA. Col. Banno quickly stopped Red Cross personnel working on the road. Tools for sanitation purposes were very short, our own tools not having been brought up. The IJA engineers rapidly destroyed their own labour force.

End of June Only 700 men out of 5000 were working north of Nieke. Over 50% were sick and useless for heavy work. The rations were 250gms of rice and a small quantity of beans. The road from the South was impassable and the ration scale consequently fell below that necessary to keep men fit. The hospital ration scale was even lower, presumably to encourage men to go out and work. Sick men were forced to lift loads requiring 100–200% more Thai or Burmese labour. Men were driven with wire whips, bamboo rods and beatings. 14 hours' work per day for months on end, sometimes even 16 and 18 hours. The men never saw their camps in daylight. In some camps the IJA engineers forced the sick out of hospitals.

Sonkurai Camp in May the strength here was over 1600. Now, 1200 are dead and 200 in hospital, of whom many will not recover. At the beginning of August Lieut. Wakabayashi arrived and there were some improvements. July, most of the force without boots, causing poisoned and trench feet. At the end of July the road from Burma was still impassable, but the river was open. Still no medical kit arrived. The morale was now terrible. During the foregoing period men and officers singly or in groups left the camp to escape.

Mid August Some blankets and sacks were issued. More came in November. Clothing issues were negligible. Medical issues were inadequate. For tropical ulcers banana leaf dressings were used. Some bandages were made from legs and arms of shorts and shirts.

As a result there were many amputations, which were unsuccessful under such conditions, practically all proving fatal.

Tambaya hospital in Burma started and 2000 men were sent. 800 men died but it did good, because there were no working parties. From now on conditions at Sonkurai improved but not at Kami Sonkurai, where the engineers were blasting and rocks were falling through the roofs of the hospital, where the death rate was 8 per day, Here the Tamil latrines were 10 yards from a cookhouse, the Tamils being cholera and small pox suspects. Blasting stopped after one man had been killed and others wounded. Infection from skin diseases was 100% since the men slept touching each other.

November The force moved back to Kanchanaburi. 46 died en route and another 180 died at Kanchanaburi hospital in the first three weeks.

In contrast with the engineers, our own guards treated us well. There was face slapping through language difficulties but it was discouraged by the IJA officers, when it was pointed out that it was bad for discipline.

Sometimes the guards prevented the IJA engineers from ill-treating POWs.

7000 left in April. 3000 died. 3000 more in hospital and many more will die.

WAR DIARY

December 1943 to December 1944

～

I was able to take up my diary again in December 1943.

16 December 43 At Kanchanaburi Hospital. We are due to leave the day after tomorrow by rail for Singapore. I am living in the administration hut of the hospital with Hutch, Whiskers and John. Kerr and Bill English left yesterday for Singapore. Fitz is still with us but is in the dysentery ward. He is shockingly thin and looks very ill indeed. He is very depressed and no longer his usual cheerful self but is pinning his faith on an early return to Singapore. We have been told that we are going to Sime Road Camp. I have received seven more letters while up here. To say the least, conditions are odd for receiving mail and the news the letters contain seems fantastically unreal. Out here it does not seem to matter whether so-and so has just been home on leave, or that somebody else has just got engaged or is going to produce an infant. How complicated all the social conventions and traditional modes of behaviour appear to one out here. How I ever tolerated it all I cannot imagine, and yet when, or if, I get back to it all I shall, no doubt, pick it all up again forgetting that I ever regarded it as unnecessary and time-wasting.

A large amount of our time here is spent in cooking and eating. Eggs are plentiful and cheap – 10 to 12 for $1. We eat anything from 12 to 15 per day, when we are not down with another bout of fever. Our digestive systems do not take to this sudden change in intake but that does not worry us very much, since our interior economics have been upset for so long that this aggravation is barely noticed. One can even buy tins of meat at 60 cents a tin and bananas at 1 cent apiece. Gula cakes are 5 cents, pomelos 30 to 40 cents each and excellent fish can be bought down at the river. This place strikes me as being a sort of Shangri-La, where one will never have to worry about anything again as long as one lives. The other day Hutch, Whiskers, John and I put 12 bananas into a washing bowl, mashed them and then beat them with 12 eggs. To this was added a tin of sweetened condensed milk and a tin of strawberry jam. The result was superb and we all decided that this should be tried at home. I was quite surprised that none of us were sick after it.

I have just had another bout of fever, very sharp with a hell of a temperature but fortunately it did not last very long, only 3 to 4 days and my temperature went down and stayed down. I was lying on the ground in a tent but it is wonderful to be able to borrow extra blankets, when a really fierce rigor comes on. Up country we never had enough to cover ourselves during the rigor period and we were always cold. I am putting on weight fast in this camp, which perhaps is not altogether surprising, in spite of one's bowels still functioning 12 to 15 times a day. But it is not healthy, most of the fat being the result of beriberi. All my ulcers have now cleared up. This is a wonderful relief, after having had them for the best part of seven months. Peter has, sadly, had to be left behind. He was still tragically thin when we left Burma and it was obvious that he would never have survived the journey by train. God knows what the conditions will be like up there now. It is expected that the majority of those left behind will die. As for the rest, like everything else in this God-forsaken life, it is entirely dependent on whether the Nips give them enough to eat, allow them to continue resting and give them what drugs they have, which are very few. There seems to be only a 50–50 chance that Peter will pull through. He has now been on his back ever since the end of the march, which was seven and a half months ago. He has been an example to us all, his cheerfulness and patience, lying on bare, bamboo slats for weeks on end and for the last few weeks on a stretcher. I shall always remember him between Philip Jones and Ken, each as pathetically thin as the others. I doubt if all three of them together would have weighed as much as 18 stone.

Our trip down from Burma took five days and nights, and included one derailment of a truck. When Fitz came down, trucks were derailed five times and they passed over one bridge which was burning. What a railway! We were very lucky, as we only had one death on the way down. I shall never forget our arrival at Kanchanaburi, where we detrained at about 7.00 am. The sun was just rising over the hills and the air was cold and beautifully clear. We staggered out of the trucks in our ragged clothes, clutching hold of our precious bundles of personal belongings. We were paraded in the yard by the station. The Nips found we were one short. The interpreter reminded them that one man had died on the train. They insisted that his body be produced to complete the total number we had set out with from Tambaya and we finally paraded; the officers on the left, then the men and, at the far end, a bundle wrapped in sacks. So far as I know the body was buried by the line.

The death rate at the hospital is now between ten and twelve per day. Stanley says that of the total number of Divisional HQ personnel who came up with us on F Force, 75% are already dead. Of the total F Force of 7000 over 3000 have already died and the doctors estimate that the deaths will probably total 50–60%. It is sad to think that so many of the best and most unselfish men have gone. I recall several, who used up all their resistance and energy looking after men in hospital and helping others on the march up through Thailand, never bothering about giving themselves any rest, and who literally killed themselves, working for their less fortunate comrades. What these men did is already forgotten and unappreciated. The majority were 100% selfish, thinking all the time of how they could get more to eat, how they could get more than their ration, even queuing up twice to obtain another helping of rice, with the result that the less greedy, who came at the end of the queue, had to go short or on many occasions had to go without. Personally, I have only on the rarest occasions seen a man offer to share his ration with some wretch who had to go without, and then probably because he was a pal of his. I remember weeping with rage when trying, in vain, to get men to support someone at the end of the column, who could no longer keep up on the march, with the result that the guards insisted that we keep moving and the wretch had to be left on his own in the middle of the jungle track. One could only hope that they were picked up sooner or later. Starvation brings out all that is unpleasant in a human being and he descends lower than the animals. The incredible cunning, which he will use in his endeavour to get more than the other man, whether he be Colonel or Private does not matter. Starvation is a great leveller in behaviour. Whenever I think that I have been issued with a few grains of rice less than the man in front of me in the queue, this prays on my mind to such an extent, that I am not relieved until the next time I get – or think I get – more than the other man did. I am often reminded of those lines of Walt Whitman on the beasts:

144

I think I could turn and live with animals, they are so placid and self-contained,

I stand and look at them long and long.

They do not sweat and whine about their condition,

They do not lie awake in the dark and weep for their sins,

They do not make me sick discussing their duty to God,

Not one is dissatisfied – not one is demented with the mania of owning things,

Not one kneels to another, nor to his kind that lived thousands of years ago,

Not one is respectable or industrious over the whole earth.

18 December 43 We left Kanchanaburi by rail and already the jungle and all its horrors are fading into the limbo of the past. We travelled in open trucks from Kanchanaburi to Bampong. Luckily the weather was fine. Just after passing through Bampong, we were ordered out of the trucks and had to march two kilometres to Nong Pladuk, as there had been a smash on the line. We passed by the tangle of broken lines and piled up trucks, one of the locomotives lying on its side half way down the embankment. Some Nips had been killed so it was not in vain. We reached Nong Pladuk and had the usual long wait before we left at midnight. We were lucky, as we were only nineteen in our truck and by lying on our sides, head to foot, we could all lie on the floor. It would be an exaggeration to say that we were able to sleep but, by our present low standards, we were very comfortable. We arrived at Haggai Junction, where we had another long wait in the middle of the day. We managed to wash at the side of the track, and I got some shaving water from the locomotive, a bit greasy but very hot. Ken and I managed to make ourselves look comparatively respectable and certainly we felt much cleaner, although after a few days cramped up in a box car we were all louse ridden again. This is going to mean a fortnight's hard work at the other end, before we are free of them. I hate lice. They are so difficult to see and their eggs are well-nigh invisible. Bugs are child's play since they are easy to catch, and their eggs are easily destroyed.

We finally pulled out of Haggai at about 2.00 pm, after being told by the Korean guards that there had been another smash on the main line just North of the Thai/Malay border. I began to feel less certain of arriving in Singapore in one piece. We approached the frontier once more, this time to find ourselves on a very high embankment. Ahead we could see a mass of trucks strewn down both sides of the embankment, close to a bridge carrying the track over a small river. A breakdown gang of Nip troops, probably engineers, was at work with a crane. We had to get out of the trucks and carry all our belongings to the other side of the bridge and, as we passed over it in single file, the Koreans counted us. Of course, as always, they got the wrong total. There are many things neither the Nips nor the Koreans are any good at, but I think elementary arithmetic must be one of their weakest points. Having got the wrong total, they made us number. Now this is something that even the best of British troops sometimes fail to do correctly. But make them prisoners of war, tired, half starved, and far from home, they do not concentrate overmuch when asked to number by Korean guards. We had to repeat the performance at least ten times before the little monkeys were satisfied that there were neither too many of us nor too few. By the time we had finished we were all in a bad temper and biting each other's heads off at the slightest provocation.

Soon after darkness had fallen, however, we were amazed to hear the sound of a locomotive in the distance and some minutes later trucks appeared, being pushed by the engine. We had only been waiting about an hour since leaving the other train and, very soon after, we were off once more in the direction of the Thai/Malay border, about 40 miles to the South. This second smash was almost identical to that at Bampong and we began to wonder whether both were the work of Thai guerrillas.

Ken, Stanley and I had managed to stay together in the same truck. With us we had about 16 men of Divisional HQ, so it was quite a merry party. The country, one could see from the train, looked very deserted.

Only one or two of the rubber plantations looked as though they were being tapped, the majority were gradually becoming choked with undergrowth, which will take a lot of clearing away. However, some of the local volunteers think that these plantations will benefit from the rest. At Ipoh only one tin dredger could be seen in operation. Everywhere we stop and are able to get into conversation with Malays or Chinese, we hear the same story. They are being starved by the Nips and everywhere semi starvation is evident. Like us, the Malays and Chinese rely on tap-root (tapioca) to make up their very meagre rice ration, and around every village and kampong one sees tapioca plantations.

At Taiping, we were allowed to get out of the train for about half an hour and, whilst I was sitting on the edge of the platform, a Nip who had been travelling in one of the coaches hitched onto the train, came up and started talking to me in English. He spoke quite fluently and had studied English for three years in Shanghai before the war. He was, he told me, on his way down from Chiang Mai, in the North of Thailand, to Singapore where he was to start an eight month course, before being commissioned. He had been in Saigon, hated army life and the conditions under which the Nip privates were forced to travel. I told him he was lucky compared to us, although the Nip soldier is also packed pretty tightly into rail

147

cars himself. He told me how much he hated the war and thought that it was doubtful if Japan could ever win. She went to war because, as far as he could see, she required 'Lebensraum' for her ever increasing population, which before the war was going up at the rate of close on a million a year. I said that it was time the Nips indulged in a spot of birth control, particularly as they must have been one of the greatest producers of contraceptives. However, this was beyond his knowledge of English, which was perhaps just as well. He was a pleasant looking Nip with quite a western outlook on life.

I saw him again at Kuala Lumpur station and I was presented with some food; one of the advantages one sometimes gets through talking to a Nip. We were given very little to eat on the way down, rice and very watery 'vegetable' stew twice a day. Travelling as a POW is not much fun. Little to eat, dirt, noise, jolting, everybody lice ridden, scratching busily, many with dysentery, malaria or beriberi, the smell of foul, unwashed and sweaty bodies becoming more and more unbearable. All of us becoming increasingly tired, snapping at each other, truckloads of stinking, wasted flesh, no longer human.

Our progress South was unbearably slow until Gemas was reached, where we were hitched onto the back of a passenger train. From now on, until we arrived at Singapore, we travelled much faster and we sometimes wondered how much longer the trucks would remain on the line. The 'thumbs up' sign very much in evidence; the Thais appeared to be much more friendly to us on the way down, compared to 9 months ago. In Johore state, many sentries were stationed along the track and in the vicinity of the stations, making us wonder whether the Chinese guerrillas had been showing activity recently. We finally arrived in Singapore at 7.30

pm, 5 days after leaving Kanchanaburi, all stinking, worn out and thoroughly disgruntled. The usual 'tenko' on the platform, and then into trucks in loads of 25, very few by Nip standards and up to Sime Road Camp. We passed through the residential area of Tanglin and the comfortable looking houses, with their bright lights, the well-kept gardens, seemed strangely unreal and remote from our simple existence. How long would it be before we were to sit in comfortable armchairs and eat off clean tables again?

The majority of H Force were in Sime Road Camp, the remnants of F Force having returned to Changi. I feel rather glad about this as I could do with some new faces and some different people to talk to. We have been told that we shall probably be going to Changi shortly but, as always, we shall probably dig ourselves in for a long stay. If one is always prepared to move at a moment's notice, one will probably never be moved at all. We were given quite a good evening meal, rice and for once, a thick stew and we could even have a second helping. I doubt if this is a taste of things to come, however, since everybody here tells us that the food situation on the island is very bad and that many of the civil population are being encouraged to go up-country to the new settlements such as New Syonan. We have been put into a brick-built building with a tiled roof and a concrete floor. This is absolute luxury. After our meal we went to 'bed', naturally without mattresses, too tired even to wash. I decided to go on smelling until the morning. I was far too tired to notice my own stinking clothing or anyone else's by now and I doubt if they could smell me.

Stanley and I found ourselves in a corner of the room, put our ground sheets on the cement, wrapped ourselves in our blankets (I now had one of my own and no longer had to share one as Peter and I had done up at Sonkurai) and prepared for sleep. At first I found it impossible. I missed the noise and jolting of the railway truck, and the silence and stillness kept me awake for some little time. I lay on my back and pondered over the past 9 months. It seemed incredible that we were back in Singapore, which almost seemed like home again. Here we had roads and houses and could hear traffic; there was electric light in the camp, although not in our building, which none of us had seen for the best part of a year. It all seems so friendly, something which we know and understand. Above all – and this is the most noticeable change of any – we are away from Nips and their ugly, shouting voices, their kicks and their spitting, their own peculiar smell, the calculated brutality of the IJA engineers, with their web-like boots and toad-stool helmets, squatting down at the side of the road, watching through their narrow eye-lids, holding in one hand the bamboo measuring rod; equally effective for measuring off lengths of timber as for beating up their European coolie labourers.

There is a very good canteen in the camp, but, compared to a year ago, very expensive. The Dutch are running a 'Smokey Joe's', where one can buy coffee, ginger cakes, pineapple and banana tarts made of maize and tapioca flour.

26 December 43 Went down with the worst bout of malaria I think I have yet had on Christmas Eve. Stanley told me I talked a lot of nonsense. I am not surprised. I would not have minded if I had ceased breathing, it was unbearable to the point of not really wanting to go on living and yet one does without really knowing why. Yesterday the fever was down and I was able to eat some of the Christmas food, which consisted of rice and tap-root as a basis, helped out with what tinned food we could produce between us. The evening meal was rather spoilt by the Nips deciding to have a practice blackout and we had to finish in the dark.

27 December 43 Have just been told that the nucleus of Div. HQ personnel are to move to Changi today. This includes Andy, Hutch, Whiskers, Cyril Wild, John, Bill Auld, Stanley Davis and me. This is annoying, as my fever is coming up again and all I want is to be left to lie quietly out of the glare of the sun.

3 January 44 We are now in the 'garden and wood area', so called because the men, who used in the early days to work on the camp gardens and wood fatigues, once lived here, but unfortunately we are isolated at present from the main camp area because of one or two cases of smallpox.

However, I went over yesterday to have my teeth looked at and have been told that I shall have to have the nerve removed from one of them. Saw many of the old faces, who have remained in Changi the whole time. They have heard many shocking stories of F Force and are quite staggered by the death rate and the general physical condition of those who have returned. I was stopped by many in the main camp, asking me the fate of people in their units or of their friends. Of those I knew about, at least half were dead. I had food at mid-day with Stevie and afterwards visited Jackie Lewis and Peter May. They all looked comparatively well and I was given a great welcome. It is just like being home again. I shall be very glad when our period of isolation is over. At present one cannot get away from the F Force atmosphere, where morale is still low and there is constant reference to the past, which I want to try and forget.

It will also be a relief to be away from many of the Aussies, with their immature minds, their lack of sense of humour, and their constant references to Australia, which appears to be their only interest in life. Things intellectual or cultural do not seem to exist for many of them and they can be peculiarly childish. In this they resemble many Americans. The Aussies, however, appear to me to work better as a team, and where there is a job to be done, they tackle it far more quickly than our own people. Their individual morale seems to have picked up far more quickly than that of the British troops, who still wander aimlessly about the camp, with hang-dog expressions on their faces, scratching themselves without ceasing. Poor wretches, they are still full of lice.

Most of the men, who have returned from up-country, are easily distinguishable from those who have been fortunate enough to stay in Changi the whole time. This is particularly true when the men are showering. To begin with they are mostly yellow from recurrent bouts of malaria. Viewed from the side, their bodies are 'plank thin', the size of their heads being grossly accentuated, appearing far too large for their bodies. Many of them have large rice bellies, which stick out like balloons. The shape of the pelvis is plainly visible on most of them, and from the small of the back to the back of the thighs, the outline descends in a straight line, there being no flesh on the buttocks whatsoever. All their ribs are plainly visible and the feet look far too long for their matchstick legs. Their shoulders are rounded and the spider-like arms look overlong for the rest of their bodies. Many have the most frightful sores and the majority have scabies with, in many cases, secondary infection. The eyes are completely lifeless as though the fact that they are safely through the past nine months was too much for them. I think most of us find this a little difficult to appreciate. One wonders why it is we who are back, why not those who are dead? One feels a strange guilt that one has survived, but then by the law of averages somebody has got to survive, so why not us?

We are very hungry here. The rice ration is 10ozs per day, soya beans 5ozs and practically nothing else except such things as curry powder and blachang. The officers are now giving $63, out of the

$78 due to them, to the central messing fund for the camp. Prices are now so high in Singapore that this money buys very little. Inflation seems to have started. Bananas are 5 to 10 cents each, sugar $1.10 per pound and peanuts $1 per pound, and all these prices are steadily rising.

It is so wonderful to get back to books again. At present I am reading John Steinbeck's 'Grapes of Wrath', and have just managed to get hold of a book on opera by Gustav Kobbe. The other evening we listened to the first music we had heard for nine months. It was the Beethoven violin concerto and the Tchaikovsky piano concerto. Its effect was overwhelming and brought tears to my eyes. Then the following evening we heard the Beethoven Choral Symphony. It is unbelievable to have this again after nine months without a note of music.

I have got 'dropped foot' again, this time in the left foot only. But it is annoying as it flops when I walk and I can feel absolutely nothing in it. I shall have to tie my big toe to my calf as we did in Siam to hold my foot up. The huts we are living in are full of bugs, but these are easy to deal with after lice. Most of us are clear of lice now, thanks to a lot of hard concentration, and much eye-strain. I find that I have got a strong desire to sleep all day, and I have got no energy at all. 15,000 letters for returned F Force personnel are at the gaol, but these are being held up, pending the despatch of the postcards written before Christmas. Berkeley has just received a letter from his wife in the States, dated August 1943. This must be the fastest yet. Weekly gramophone recitals are now being held in the main camp area, but we are still in quarantine and cannot get across. It is said to be very good now as they have fitted up an amplifier, which enables several hundred people to listen.

8 January 44 I spent yesterday over in the main camp area, as I had a pass to visit the dentist. Had two teeth stopped and the nerve removed from another. Had lunch with Peter May and, in the afternoon, visited Jackie, who lent me Rose Macaulay's 'Minor Pleasures of Life'. In the evening we listened to Tchaikovsky's 'Scheherazade' and tonight we hope to be able to borrow Brahms 2nd Symphony. The general conditions in our camp are steadily improving, and the morale and discipline amongst the men are far better. They have at last regained some of their self-respect, which they had lost completely up-country. This was greatly helped by a small issue of clothing, which included such items as shorts, shirts and some boots. Our isolation period for smallpox is due to expire on 14 January. Our food has improved somewhat in quality although not in quantity. We are able to buy maize flour and rice bread at 20 cents per loaf. The latter is very heavy and indigestible, but it helps to increase the bulk. However, we cannot buy enough to satisfy ourselves every day, as only $6 per month goes into our mess and we are left with $9 per month for buying such things as toothpaste, soap and tobacco, when any comes in. We have just been told that the letters at the gaol are to be handed in for censoring today, so that the first should be up in the camp in a day or two.

18 January 44 Went over to see Eric, who is the medical specialist at the hospital, to have a thorough examination. He found my blood pressure down slightly and me merely 'debilitated' owing to constant diarrhoea. Otherwise I seem to be quite fit. Many of us from up-country are suffering from diarrhoea and the majority of these have had it almost constantly for the past nine months. This, at the rate of once every hour or two, becomes somewhat tedious after a few months. The medical authorities do not know what it is caused by and consequently we hear many theories put forward. However, those doctors on whom I pin my faith, maintain that it is due to malnutrition. Next week, I am to have tests taken for amoebic dysentery.

Recently, I have read Galsworthy's 'Flowering Wilderness', Hemingway's 'To Have and Have Not' and I have now started Fisher's 'History of Europe'. I tried to read Harriet Wilson's Memoirs, but had to give up after about 60 pages. Yesterday evening, went over with Jackie to the 'Officers Club'. This sounds very grand, and is run as part of one of the Australian Officers' messes, where one can buy tea and such things as coconut cakes made with tapioca and sago flour. It is quite a social centre and, of course, the place where the majority of good rumours generate.

Kerr is down with another bout of fever and Fitz has gone to hospital with suspected dysentery again. He thinks it is only worms. The IJA have now allowed us to go and bathe once more, but I doubt if I have got the strength to go as far as the sea, let alone swim. There is to be a general shuffle round in the camp on 18 March and we have hopes of getting into a brick building. There have been some recent additions to our number while we have been away. Several American airmen, some shot down in Burma, others in Indo-China during raids on Saigon, and one or two officers from Wingate Force, captured in Burma. We all find the food very short and are constantly hungry. We cannot get anything like enough to eat and prices in the canteen are steadily rising week by week.

20 January 44 Admitted to hospital yesterday with amoebic dysentery once again, and I have been told that I have an enlarged spleen. This does not surprise me after all the fever I have had. I have quite a pleasant position on the balcony and am well supplied with books, but we are having trouble with bugs. The beds are full of them.

24 January 44 I am still under observation for dysentery and have not started any treatment yet. Meanwhile, I went down with another bout of malaria the day before yesterday. I think this is my thirteenth bout but I am not sure. So now I am on a course of attabrin. Also, my legs seem to be going bad on me, as they are covered in septic sores. I never seem to be able to shake everything off at once and I find that, when one is ill, one usually suffers from more than one complaint at the same time. I have just finished Olive Schreiner's 'Story of an African Farm', which I enjoyed very much. Am now reading C E Montague's 'Disenchantment'.

25 January 44 I have now been informed that, apart from all the other things, I am also suffering from worms. This makes me feel like a spaniel. It is still doubtful if I have amoebic dysentery, but I now have to wait until I have finished the attabrin treatment for malaria before the worms can safely be tackled, although it would be so much easier if they would attack everything at once, dysentery, worms, dropped feet, septic sores and malaria! I heard today that one of the American airmen is convinced that the war will be over in July, so much so that he has taken on bets to the value of $8000. What an optimist! 27 bags of mail have arrived at the gaol, said to contain letters dated August and postcards dated September last year. The numbers working on the aerodrome have been reduced by 500 to enable another 500 to work on the vegetable gardens. The Australian pantomime has opened this week. All the music has been written in the camp and the script is the work of Greener, an Australian newspaper correspondent.

28 January 44 Yesterday, a great day. 13 letters from home, including one from Catherine with news of Allan. It is great to get these letters, but they invariably leave one feeling very unsettled. Many rumours of our being moved to Japan. These have been very persistent now for some weeks. Personally, I doubt whether the Nips will ever bother to move us now. There are so few fit men that we would be almost useless as a working force and I doubt if the Nips have sufficient shipping to take us to Japan.

My stomach is still giving me a lot of pain, but my legs, thank God, are beginning to clear up, although they still have to be kept wrapped up in bandages, making them look much worse than they are. Fitz, I and two others are to go shares in a duck, which should have arrived today. We intend to eat it tomorrow and my mouth is already starting to water at the prospect. Have started re-reading 'The Forsyte Saga' and have also started Maugham's 'Of Human Bondage', which seems to be a typical first novel.

An incredible thing has happened. We have had a small issue of MEAT. This has not occurred for months and months. Something must have slipped up in the IJA supply organisation.

29 January 44 Still in hospital and today I start to be de-wormed. This is not so good as I am not allowed to eat for two days. It is difficult enough to pick up again after even one day without food. I have just started 'Seven Pillars of Wisdom', of which there seem to be several copies in the camp.

2 February 44 Have just finished Steinbeck's 'In Dubious Battle'. It must have been from this that he got the idea of writing a larger work on the same subject which led to 'The Grapes of Wrath'. First attempt at getting rid of worms unsuccessful after two whole days' starvation and I have been told that they will have another attempt in a few days' time, with another kind of drug. There are several Americans in the ward here, all very cheerful and intensely optimistic. They are an amusing crowd and are all airmen shot down in China or Hanoi.

7 February 44 The hospital is now receiving a small daily meat issue, but knowing the Nips, this will not last more than a week or so. I am now on my second period of starvation for de-worming. According to the latest rumour we are all moving to Japan on 15 March. Some of the so-called Changi pensioners (those who have successfully evaded all up- country parties so far) are getting worried. Personally, I am past caring what they do with us next. I feel quite certain nothing could be worse than the past year, since that would mean death and one would have nothing more to worry or care about. I shall not be at all surprised if I see Formosa or Japan or even both before I get out of this. We heard the other day, I forget how, that the senior officers' party, which left here in 1942 was sent first to Korea and later to Manchuria. We now have what is called a 'brownout', which is very nearly as bad as a 'black out', as one cannot see to read. The evenings are therefore spent in idle conversation, Jack Quarrant, one of the U.S. pilots, doing most of the talking. We are all finding that our powers of concentration have gone and that our memories are becoming worse and worse.

9 February 44 Two more letters yesterday. One dated November 42 and the other October 42. They have only taken about 15 months to arrive!

13 February 44 I had my first hot bath for over two years yesterday. This I managed to get as I am, amongst other things, suffering from scabies and have consequently been ordered to have three hot baths as part of the treatment. Scabies is almost worth having. My last bath, I remember, I had on the Reina del Pacifico in October 1941. On the Wakefield, we only had hot showers. As I thought, the meat ration has already been dropped by the Nips. Our diet is now rice, soya beans, and two different kinds of black beans, one of which, in normal times, is not even eaten by animals, but used as a cover crop.

Hungry as I am, I cannot stomach these things. I tried some yesterday but was sick an hour or so after the meal. However, this was probably in part due to the attabrin I still have to take. Bananas are now 6 cents each and are the only thing one can buy in the canteen in any quantity. Reading Evan John's 'King's Masque', the story of Count Fersen and Marie Antoinette. Very good.

22 February 44 Am still in hospital. On Sunday I went down with yet another bout of my old friend 'benign tertiary' (malaria). This, when I had only just finished taking attabrin for the previous bout. Have just heard that another 900 are due down in Changi from Kanchanaburi shortly. We are all hoping that Peter will be amongst them, although I am very doubtful if he has made it. I get frequent visits from John and Hutch and Stevie has been very kind in bringing me eggs from his hens.

27 February 44 Feeling better after 5 days constant fever. This is most unusual as I generally have it on the first and third days only, with possibly another rigor on the 5th day. I am feeling very weak and all I want to do is to lie flat on my back. As this is the second relapse I have had while I have been in hospital, I am now on a fortnight's quinine and plasmaquin course. If this does not have any effect, I doubt if anything will. I feel very deaf and horribly sick, owing chiefly to the quinine, and I don't feel like reading. 320 American Red Cross parcels have arrived in the camp. The Americans have decided that these should be divided between everybody in the camp, but this will not go very far amongst 10,000! I believe the parcels weigh 7lbs each, which gives a total of 2240lbs or about 0.224lbs per head. Saw Peter's name on a list of officers due down from Kanchanaburi with this next party. This is great news. Books read and reading: Ethel Boileau's 'Hippy

Buchan', 'Escape' by Ethel Vance and am now in the middle of Philip Gosse's biography of Charles Waterton, the naturalist, 'The Squire of Walton Hall'.

8 March 44 John came into hospital yesterday with the usual complaint – diarrhoea. I finished my course of quinine yesterday and I am feeling thoroughly dopey. We have each received an issue of 26 Chesterfield or Camel cigarettes from the Red Cross parcels, which finally worked out at one parcel between 7 men. However, the cigarettes are a God-send. There is a greater demand for the Camels, as they are said to last longer. I think this is sheer imagination as it must depend largely on how often one puffs at them! All the food, with the exception of the milk, which has been given to the hospital for the seriously ill, has been put into the messes. Each parcel includes such things as bully beef, bacon and egg, cheese, prunes and jam. General Arimura is reported to have gone to Japan and to have been replaced by a General Shaito. I only hope he does not live up to his name. I have just finished Jules Romain's 'Verdun'. Very moving and have just started Margaret Lane's biography of Edgar Wallace. Yesterday John and I left our beds and had tea with James Bull and Eric. At first, as it is usually, the conversation was mainly medical but we finished up with a long discussion on Post War reconstruction. I forget what we decided but one has so many of these discussions and one finds oneself taking up diametrically opposed viewpoints on exactly the same subject from week to week. It all helps to pass the time pleasantly.

14 March 44 I was discharged from hospital yesterday. On Saturday I went to listen to the new gramophone amplifier, and found it a great improvement on the portable gramophone one usually has to put up with. They played a Mozart Piano Concerto, the Ballet music from Gounod's Faust and finally the Beethoven 4th Piano

Concerto. Both the concertos were recordings by Schnabel. It was a perfect night, listening to music under the most romantic surroundings, lying on the grass under the casuarina trees with a full moon, steadily rising above a bank of low cloud.

John has been placed under open arrest! He is accused of contravening the 'trading regulations' in that he sold a watch to a member of the IJA. This is apparently a measure brought in, while we were up-country, to try to stem the black market. What a hope! So long as food is short and men in this camp have something, which the Nips or Chinese are prepared to buy, trading will continue and I am quite certain that this cannot be stopped by any regulations the POW administration care to introduce. However, John's arrest has caused a terrific stir all over the camp, and people are already taking up sides. John is livid, which is not altogether surprising. The one-time Southern Area provost-marshal came into the ward and searched John's kit publicly, which struck us as being a bit odd, as a result of which John pointed out to the PM (an LPTB bus inspector when he is at home!) that the whole proceedings were a slur on his character and that it might well affect his professional reputation after the war, and warned him that he might bring a civil action against him. This seemed to shake the PM, who from now on seemed to be less sure of his ground. Some of John's kit was removed, but returned 24 hours later. He has now been let out of open arrest. At present, the camp authorities are said to be searching for further evidence prior to Court Martial. I personally doubt very much if anything further will be heard. The whole thing strikes me as being very funny (John cannot see this point of view) and very childish.

Tomorrow we are to be inspected once again. This time it is the new General Shaito, who has taken over from Arimura. The issue of soya beans is to cease in the near future and we are to receive maize in lieu. Hitherto, when we have had maize, it has played havoc with our stomachs and I very much doubt if mine is any better suited to coping with it than it was before. We shall see. The black beans unfortunately continue and very few of us can eat them. Canteen prices are steadily rising: cheroots at 5 cents each, soya sauce 55 cents per pint, green bananas 25 cents a lb.

I am finding it much more difficult to sleep, now I am back in a hut. Up on the balcony in the officers' hospital ward, there was a breeze day and night and sometimes it was even cool enough for a blanket.

21 March 44 Takahashi is reported to have said that officers are to be separated from the men in the near future. This would not surprise me in the least. The only reason they have not done this in the past is, I think, that it is obviously easier for the IJA. There is no doubt, however, that we could administer ourselves far more efficiently and more to our own requirements than the IJA could ever hope to do. One officer, according to this rumour, is to be allowed per 100 men for administration.

At last I am feeling more or less fit again, certainly fitter than I have felt for the past 12 months. I only hope to God that I shall be able to stave off my monthly bouts of malaria this month, which is due any moment now, from the 21st to the 23rd. The only complaint I am suffering from, at present, is a recurrence of beriberi in my feet, the left ankle and foot being particularly swollen and once more I cannot put on my boots and have absolutely no feeling at all. However, the advantage of oedematous beriberi is that it does not make one feel ill.

We have started rehearsing Galsworthy's 'Loyalties'. It is due to go on in a month's time but I doubt if we shall succeed in this. On average 50% of the cast are down with fever at any given moment, which makes things rather difficult. Also we are having trouble with the women, always a hell of a problem in this world without them.

Yesterday evening Kerr and I went over to the main camp area to see Stevie, and we had a long talk with Osmond Daltry, who, minus a leg and an eye, still keeps remarkably cheerful. He is an example to everyone in this camp. We had tea, and bread made of black beans, maize flour and rice. We are now being issued with maize instead of soya beans, so the production of 'tempeh' has come to an end. This was a method of rendering soya beans palatable, which we learned from the Dutch. Very roughly, the beans are split, mixed with yeast and spread out on a table for 36 hours. At the end of the 36 hours, the beans and yeast have formed a sort of cake or biscuit, and are ready for eating. The result is quite good and it has an almost cheesy flavour.

Food is getting steadily worse. A typical day's menu now is: Breakfast: porridge made of rice and maize, with no sugar of course, followed by a very small rice and bean 'rissole' (fried, when we have enough palm oil) and a spoonful of black beans flavoured with curry powder. Midday: 'Soup' made of black beans and green bananas, skin and all, followed by black beans, a small helping of greens, and a maize flour, rice and bean pasty with black beans inside. At 4 o'clock we get a cup of tea, and the evening meal consists of bean and banana soup, followed by black beans, greens (sometimes), bean 'pasty' with maize flour and rice, similar to that at lunch time, and a maize flour and rice 'tart' as a sweet. The latter usually has a few pieces of banana or papaya inside. With this delicious repast we have a cup of tea. Tea we have before or at breakfast, at 11 am with the midday meal, at 4.00 pm, with our evening meal and at 9.00 pm. In the early morning it is reasonably strong but it gets weaker as the day goes on.

There is a continual argument going on, and as far as I can remember it has gone on in all messes throughout the past two years, as to whether it is better to have tea seven times a day, being not over strong to start with and almost pure water by 9.00 pm or to have it less often and stronger.

However it is not even quite as simple as it appears, since, amongst the protagonists of 'the less often' school, constant bickering goes on and has done for the past two years, as to which times in the day the tea should be cut out. Sugar, when obtainable, is now 3.30 dollars per lb, gula malacca $2.85 a lb, onions and garlic $5.00 a lb, 'biscuits' 2 cents each. These are the size of a penny. Sometimes cigarettes are obtainable but are quite disgusting. They are made by the Chinese from papaya leaves. I find I can make a better cigarette myself, if I make it from papaya leaves and chopped up cheroots. The 'Nippon Times', although a little tough, makes quite a satisfactory paper. There is an art even in using this, as it took me some time to discover. The paper should be cut so that the lines of printing run round the rolled cigarette and not lengthways. By doing this the paper, when licked, sticks much more easily than if the paper is cut the other way. It looks as though from the food point of view, we are entering a lean period, which in the event of an allied offensive against Malaya, would be greatly aggravated.

My brain is becoming completely atrophied in this existence, and my powers of concentration are almost nil now. I always hope that the mental effects of these years will only be ephemeral and will disappear when we are freed and are able to enjoy reasonable food once more. Work on the aerodrome continues but it seems to be as far from completion as ever. Air activity over this end of the island seems to be considerable but the machines are all very slow and appear to be out of date, judged by the planes used by the RAF.

Books read: 'An Autobiographical Experiment' by H C Greenwall of the 'Express', very poor, and for the second time 'For Whom the Bell Tolls', also 'Inside Europe'. I am with an amusing crowd in the hut. Donald Wise, whom I first met at Stobbs Camp when we were stationed in Scotland and who, before the war, was on the staff of the 'Mirror' and later the 'Daily Sketch' and 'Bags' Baughan, who was on the Eastern Staff of the Asiatic Petroleum Co (Shell Group) in 1926 and used to live at Lensbury Club, until he was slung out by Engle (a managing director) for some misdemeanour while still a trainee. He then came out to Malaya, where he has been in business for a number of years.

He is now in his early forties, but looks considerably older, and has a great reputation as a consumer of alcohol and, what is more important than almost anything else under these conditions, a truly wonderful sense of humour. Before the war he apparently had a huge stomach and was extremely fat. Now he has lost all this, but still retains a fat man's walk, that is to say that he still leans back as though he had some colossal weight to carry in front. He has a very tanned and weathered face, huge bushy eyebrows, and a mouth and eyes which might be made of rubber, they are so adaptable to his unlimited, caricatural imitations of people both in the camp and more generally. The arguments he has, practically every night, with Donald, keep us amused until far into the morning, the subject of these arguments usually being quite fantastic, varying perhaps from post-war planning to sexual athletics or life in Malaya or whether women like men with moustaches or stomachs. They go on for hours until Donald suddenly drops off to sleep without warning, sometimes in the middle of a sentence. We all talk an incredible amount of nonsense in these after lights-out discussions but perhaps it helps to keep us sane, or at least saner we think than many others in the camp.

Then there is John Olley, an engineer with Borneo Motors Ltd. in normal times, and, I believe, a very good engineer too. He is a member of the Olley family, who founded and ran Olley Airways. He can talk the hind leg off a donkey and usually does, particularly when he gets onto the subject of cars, for which he does not require much encouragement. He is the type of person who, in his own mind, has the whole world weighed up in the palm of his hand, and knows exactly what he intends to do after the war. This, so far as I can make out, is to sell large American cars to the wealthy Chinese of Malaya, who, as he always says, will buy anything flash. Well, I have no doubt he is right. James Mudie is another who lives up at our end of the hut, a quiet and thoughtful man, with a sound knowledge of world affairs, a member of the technical staff of the Malayan Broadcasting Co., who also has to do some announcing, when required, and who received his training with the BBC. Kerr is also with us, and is at present in the middle of writing a short story. His writing has to be done largely in between bouts of fever, which he usually gets about once in every three weeks.

For the first time since our return from up-country, I am beginning to see signs of nerve strain and short tempers. This is inevitable, as the novelty and the initial effects of change of environment begin to wear off, and once more we settle down to another period of blank, dull, hopeless months. We are all very hungry and the meals are now just about enough to whet ones appetite, making one feel more hungry after one has finished than one did when one sat down to it. Under these conditions it is essential to have something to smoke as soon as one has finished eating, to help remove the constant thought "God, I am hungry!". The weather has been insufferably hot – a glaring sun and no rain for about a month. There has been an outbreak of cholera amongst the poultry in the camp. Thank God it is not us this time and that we cannot catch it from the hens.

27 March 44 An order just issued by General Shaito, states that all tents are to be removed from the camp. This affects about 500 men, for whom accommodation will have to be found in already overcrowded buildings.

This is quite typical of the Nips – issuing orders without any regard for their implications. A new scale of rations has been published by the IJA, but already they have stated that they will be unable to adhere to it. Why the hell issue it then? At present our meagre diet is somewhat augmented by the purchase of black beans, which, while they have no value as a vitamin food, do help in increasing bulk, which is very important to us. These beans are purchased through what is known as the Central Messing Fund, the assets of which are supplied almost entirely from officers pay.

Now the IJA have stated that our pay is to be cut and the difference to be credited to an officers' account. This seriously reduces the amount available for the purchase of food for the Central Messing Fund. Thus our 'bulk food' will be reduced to an alarming extent. Soya beans are now unobtainable and it is said that the black beans will cease shortly. This leaves us with a small ration of rice, maize and an irregular supply of vegetables, mostly from our own gardens and certainly not sufficient to keep the whole camp adequately supplied, and a minute fish ration twice a week. As we are now back to starvation level, I can but think that the incidence of deficiency diseases such as beriberi etc. will rise sharply. Meanwhile, malaria is still widespread and shows no sign of abating yet.

I am finding that one of the worst aspects of life here is the impossibility of ever being able to get away on my own. Never, at any time of the day or night, can one be alone, and now that we are living in a hut with only 2 to 3 feet between each bed, the feeling of overcrowding approaches claustrophobia at times. Can one wonder that tempers easily become frayed under such conditions? There was a very good gramophone concert on Saturday evening, which I was unable to hear. They played Beethoven's 3rd Piano Concerto, and the Pastoral Symphony.

We are now nearing the end of another month and a quarter of this year will be behind us. Will it offer us our freedom, however? Three years of this life I think I shall be able to stand, but if it goes on much longer I shall begin to wonder. The physical effects have already made their mark on most of us and many men will have to bear them for the rest of their lives. So far I do not think that the mental effect will be anything more than ephemeral for me, and after a few weeks of good food and restful surroundings at home, this life will quite quickly fade from my mind. However should we have to put up with much more, say four or even five years in all, then I think the effects will be more lasting. Most of all I feel sorry for the men who have lost limbs in the battle. They remain remarkably cheerful, however, and perhaps by the time they reach home they will be almost unaware of their handicap.

I wonder why it is that the Americans in this camp give me the impression of having a more rooted and positive outlook on life? They appear to be more aware of the problems which we all have to face in life. Perhaps it has something to do with their apparently more limited intellectual capacity, which enables them to see everything in terms which are, for me, altogether too simple. Watching men here, it is brought home to me how often we fail to orientate ourselves. We do not know why we do certain things, or what we are striving for. So little time is spent in trying to think things out for ourselves, to try to understand why we behave as we do, be it towards ourselves or to the people with whom we come into contact.

What is our position in and our relationship to the society in which we live? To the country in which we happen to have been born and, more important, the world itself? We must surely have some conception of what we are striving for, beyond the mundane struggle to lead as comfortable an existence as possible, and to be able to interest ourselves in whatever direction our tastes may lead us. It seems to me that if the world remembers that what we want to achieve is 'the greatest happiness for the greatest number', then we shall not go far wrong. In reaching the stage where everybody can be properly fed, and there is proper distribution of food and raw materials, there enters the question of education. This however is rather a vicious circle, as before men can be properly taught, the teachers themselves must be educated and who is to achieve this? I find that in practically every discussion we have in this camp, someone brings it to a close with some such remark as 'Well, I suppose education is the only answer'. On top of all this comes the most difficult problem of all. How can one achieve some sort of faith in oneself. Heaven knows; precious little security is offered in these days. If life is the precious thing we have been led to believe it is, there is little evidence around us of this particular truth. There is no selection in death. I have come to the conclusion over the past two years, that it is essentially the more selfish people, who have the better chance of survival.

30 March 44 The camp received a visit yesterday from an IJA colonel from Tokyo. An itinerary had been prepared for him by the Nips at the gaol and he was not expected to visit this area. However he did, and was able to see for himself what the remnants of F Force look like. He was accompanied by Col. Banno, Lieut. Takahashi, the interpreter Koroasu, and one or two other junior officers. They entered one or two of the huts but did not stay long. The Colonel entered the hut where Col. Hingston was living and he asked him one or two questions. "What is the food like?" Reply: "Not enough. I have lost weight". "How do you expect to be treated?" "According to International Law and the Geneva Convention". Nip reply. "We did not sign the Geneva Convention". To which Hingston replied: "You signed the Hague Agreement in 1923". This was clearly above the Colonel's head, and he merely raised his eyebrows and said: "Anyway, it will do you good not to eat so much. All Anglo-Saxons suffer from over-indulgence. That is why, as a nation, you are so decadent". The Colonel then asked Derek Agnew one or two questions. "How many died in Thailand?" "Three thousand". "Have you any records?" "Yes". "Where are they?" "Here". "I will take these away with me; you can have them back in three or four days". Of course, nothing more was heard.

The drug position in the hospital is worsening steadily. Quinine is becoming very short and as yet the IJA show no signs of replenishing our stocks. During his visit, the Colonel stopped to take a photograph of some of the prisoners. One of the men was a typical up-country skeleton and as he was about to take the photograph, Col. Banno rushed up and pushed the thin fellow behind the others, where his physical condition would not be seen. My beriberi has improved somewhat, but my stomach is still in a hell of a state, running like a tap. When we get free of one thing, we invariably seem to get something else. Many of us, in addition to our other complaints, have now got very unpleasant sores on hands and feet. These start as small blisters, which burst, soon became infected and then start spreading, leaving large open sores. These we have to bathe in warm water four or five times a day, and they must be dressed after each bathe. Donald is in hospital with them and is in a nasty mess, he can barely use his hands. Fitz also has them badly and is being threatened with hospital.

7 April 44 Good Friday; at least I suppose it must be good somewhere. I remember the 'Karfreitag' I spent in Heidelberg seven years ago. A party of us had an early supper and then went into Mannheim to the opera house to hear 'Parsifal', which on this day would be playing in every opera house in Germany. I remember returning to Heidelberg, tired and slightly stunned by 5 hours of concentrated Wagner, the first time I had ever heard 'Parsifal' in its entirety. The next time I heard it was about a year later at the Colon Opera House in Buenos Aires. Last Good Friday we had just heard of our impending departure up-country. Now here we are still in very much the same surroundings, except that there are considerably fewer of us. It is now nearly 9.00 pm and it is almost dark, except for a full moon, which shines out intermittently from behind heavy rain clouds scudding across the sky. There is the eternal, uninterrupted chirping of thousands of crickets, and there is a quiet heaviness in the air as if we were all pausing, tired out, to try and work up enough strength to carry us over the next period of our imprisonment. From one of the huts at the far end of the camp comes the sound of an old piano, hammering out 'When the Lights of London shine again', with a few indifferent voices joining in. Every few minutes we can hear the Korean guards stamping in and out of the guard hut, 50 yards from where we are sitting on the doorstep of our hut.

Our evening meal we finished over two hours ago, and we are all feeling horribly empty. It seems a life time to have to wait until 9 o'clock tomorrow morning before we get anything more. The rice ration has been cut once again and we now get up from our meals

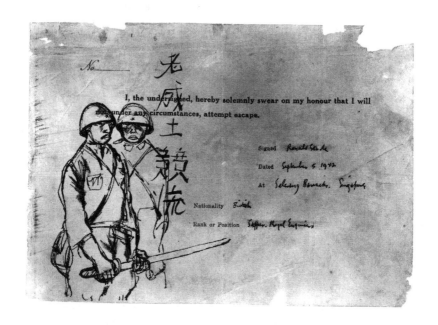

Copy of the undertaking not to attempt to escape issued by the Japanese military authorities and completed by Ronald Searle. To the left of the form is a drawing of two Japanese guards – one appears to be an officer as he is holding a samurai sword. A vertical line of Japanese script runs to the right of the sketch.

Train to Siam, May 1943

Japanese soldier with mongolian ponies on the way to the
Burma Front, Siam 1943

Sick and dying: Cholera. Siam-Burma Railway, 1943

Guards punishing a prisoner, Siam-Burma Railway, 1943

Prisoners going to work along a jungle track during the monsoon, 1943

Sick and dying: Cholera, Siam 1943

The reservoir to the south of the Burma-Siam border, which now covers
the site of Sonkurai, where so many worked and died in 1943.
This is perhaps the most fitting postscript to all the horrors that
so many of us were forced to go through in 1943

feeling as hungry as when we sat down. I suppose this feeling will remain with us until the end. I cannot see any hope of things improving. I am feeling badly depressed, partly due I think to the fact that I have got a constant headache, which I have had now for three days, and it does not let up at night. I thought at first that it must be another bout of fever, but I have had four blood slides taken and they are all negative. Last night I was sick, God knows why.

Have recently finished Ethel Mannin's 'Confessions and Impressions', I was interested in her rather odd views on education:- "apart from technical training, there are probably only two subjects worth knowing anything about; physiology and psychology. All the other subjects are matters of personal taste and interest and to be studied or disregarded accordingly" and "Only that which interests us is ever of any practical use".

The IJA has now set up its camp administration inside the camp, and Lieut. Takahashi now lives inside the camp area. There has been a general tightening up all round and there are more guards, backed by stricter and more direct control. This is taken by most of us as being a good sign. The only fly in the ointment is that I cannot see such measures helping to improve our meagre food. I have heard one or two rather amusing stories recently of squabbles between Lieut. Colonels, living in the main camp area. One was the case of a colonel who gets everybody's back up by booking his place in the queue for the lavatory, (they have these civilised amenities over the other side!) and not waiting his turn like the rest. In another case, somebody used to keep banana skins in an old tin, for what purpose history does not relate. Certain other officers in the mess, seeing this tin, which was lying about the mess every day, used it as an ash tray. Things got to such a pitch that the owner of the banana skins threatened to report the matter to the senior officer in the mess. Whereupon a padre pointed out that the tin in question belonged to him and he did not see why he should not use it as an ash tray. Then there is the story told me by Jackie, of the colonel who used to get up very early in the morning to pick the mushrooms off the grass in front of one of the other messes. There was a showdown when, early one morning, he was surprised by someone from the other mess, who told him that the mushrooms were not his and he was therefore not entitled to pick them. At this rate I shall not be surprised if we are not all certified insane on our release.

Have just re-read John Gunther's 'Inside Europe'. Fitz, Kerr, Stanley, Donald and one or two others have been moved to another hut, and I have now rejoined John.

13 April 44 Much cleaning is going on all over the camp in view of the expected visit by General Shaito. Stanley is down with malaria again and will probably be going to hospital. He has been talking a lot of nonsense for the past 36 hours, but then we all become delirious in turn as we get a relapse! At present we have Donald, Fitz, Bags Baughan, and Col. Hingston in hospital, the last three with malaria and Donald with sores on his hands. A hell of a storm yesterday and the lights and water have been cut off. Books read include Samuel Butler's 'The Way of all Flesh', Seton Merriman's 'Barlasch of the Guard'. Now reading Birkenhead's 'Turning Points in History'. We are all pathetically hungry. Yesterday, however, some sago flour was received by the canteen. On such occasions this is served up hot at 25 cents per pint, a highly exorbitant price, designed presumably to assist in swelling the canteen profits, but even sago and water helps to fill one up although not for long. I have now started sprouting towgay on a wet sack. By keeping it in the dark and watering it lavishly, a tender green shoot can be obtained in about 5 days and it makes a very good salad. It also makes up, to a certain extent, for the lack of green vegetables. The drawback, however, is that it is very expensive to buy in the canteen.

Yesterday I received a letter from Mother dated June 1942, a mere two years after it was written! As there is no news of any mail having arrived, I can only assume that this must have gone astray from some previous batch. How we all wish we could have some more up to date news from home. Our most recent is now fourteen months old. Kerr has just managed to get hold of Daniele Vare's 'The Gate of Happy Sparrows', written, I think, after 'The Maker of Heavenly Trousers'.

17 April 44 Tomorrow I start a week on the aerodrome. This is an entirely supervisory job and entails taking out a working party of 50 men and standing around in the sun all day. It will be quite like old times to be with Nip engineers again. However, I gather that the Air Force engineers are rather more gentlemanly down here. One is less likely to get a crack over the top of the dome with a length of bamboo, than up in Thailand. Also working hours are reasonable, out at 8.30 am and back by 6.00 pm. The men working on the aerodrome receive an extra ration of 2ozs of rice per day.

On Saturday evening I went over to listen to a gramophone recital and heard Tchaikovsky's Piano Concerto and the Beethoven 7th. After wards I went to the hospital to visit Fitz and Donald and whilst there got talking to someone who came from Worcestershire and who knew Diana. He produced an old photograph album from his belongings and actually showed me a photograph of Diana! Also her sister Brenda, whose wedding he attended. Am now reading Aldous Huxley's 'Those Barren Leaves', having just finished Margaret Halsey's 'With Malice Towards Some'. Donald says that shortly after its publication in England he was sent by the

Mirror to interview the people portrayed in it, who lived in or near Exeter, the object of his visit being to stir up the mud and get people's hackles to rise in order to produce a story! I gather he did.

19 April 44 Have just returned from the aerodrome. A rest cure compared to those days in Thailand working on the railway. I get up at 7.30 am, parade at 8.30, march out of the camp at 9.00 am, start work at 10.00 am, break for tea at 11 to 11.15, lunch 12.30 to 1.30, fifteen minutes off for tea at 5.15 pm and return to camp at 6.00 pm. It is admittedly a tiring day, even standing around not working, as there is a terrific glare from the sun, which is reflected from the bright laterite surface of the runways.

It is incredible to think that this was where we lived for fifteen months before we went up-country. Our old 18 Div Area padang and the huts, tents and coconut plantations have given way to a vast earthen waste, dotted here and there with bulldozers, levellers, light railway trains shifting soil. There are also one or two steam shovels. Excavators dig busily at a hillside, fast disappearing, to make way for the main runway, which is to be well over a mile long. Changi camp is at present supplying 850 men for work on the aerodrome, and Chinese and Tamil labour, in addition to Indian POW, are also being used. The Chinese say they receive one pint of rice per day for working on the aerodrome and all the natives bring their wives and children out to work so that they can get enough to live on. Now the IJA has stated that 700 unfit men from Changi are to be sent down to Singapore and are to be replaced by 700 men from Sime Road Camp as they require more men for work on the aerodrome. Another 20 bags of mail have arrived at the gaol. I am very sunburnt after being out on the airfield, and am feeling fitter now than I have done for many months. The trouble is that the extra 2ozs of rice do not make up for the extra energy expended

175

in going out on the aerodrome, and the men must feel this far more than we do, as they not only have to work but they are out every day, whereas the officers can go out alternate weeks.

22 April 44 Returned to camp today feeling as though another bout of fever was due any moment, but nothing happened apart from the fact that I was sick in the middle of the night, but woke up feeling quite all right in the morning. We are all due to move over to the other side of the road tomorrow as the Dutch and Australians are taking over this area. This means that we may get a tiled roof over our heads again. The house we are said to be moving into has a very well-tended garden, but I expect this will be stripped before we get over there. Had slight trouble with the Nips on the aerodrome yesterday. The engineer in charge of the party I was with threatened to bash me, so I said that I would fetch the interpreter.

He walked off then and said no more. I was feeling so bloody annoyed with him that had he tried to hit me, I think I would have had a crack at him. It is sometimes as much as one can do to keep one's hands off these little bastards. Shall have to stop smoking until next pay-day as my money has run out and I cannot face smoking brinjal or papaya leaves neat.

25 April 44 The whole of Sunday was spent in moving across the road. It all looks too good to last. We are in a house again, but today we have been told that the whole camp will be moving, on or about 14 May, to the gaol area. This sounds a most unpleasant prospect. All officers are to be segregated from the troops and are to live in huts to be erected outside the gaol. At present the civilian internees are still living in the gaol, but are to move down to Sime Road Camp by 10 May. According to current rumour, the internees are to be repatriated but I very much doubt this.

176

Nobody is looking forward to this forthcoming period of closer concentration, but most of us, I think, realize that it will have to be gone through sooner or later before we are finally released. The number of men to be employed on the aerodrome is to be increased to between 1400 and 1500 and they are to work in three shifts. Work on this aerodrome is apparently being speeded up considerably. One shift works all day, the second from early morning to midday and the third from midday until late evening. There are hopes of receiving more mail, which is being sorted out at the gaol. The IJA has just issued an order that all officers may now wear full badges of rank. We had to take these off after being captured in 1942 on General Yamashita's orders. The house we are living in was, in happier times, inhabited by an officer and his wife, but we have 50 officers and 12 other ranks in it. It has, until we took over, been inhabited by Dutch officers, who left it in a filthy state. We have had a hard job getting it cleaned up and now it is looking quite good. It is grand to be living in a house once more, but I am afraid it is not going to last very long.

29 April 44 Books read: Daniele Vare's 'The Last of the Empresses', Virginia Wolf's 'To the Lighthouse' and Viscount Morley's 'Biographical Studies". What a collection!

1 May 44 A third of the year is now behind us and soon we shall be entering on the next stage of our incarceration, since the move of material to the new gaol camp area starts today. Let us hope this will be the last move we have to make before we are freed. Many people think that we shall have to do a trip by sea before that day arrives. The move has to be completed before the end of the month, and there is an enormous amount of work to be done in that time. 12,000 men have to be housed and at present there is only cover in the new area for approximately 5000 in the gaol (designed for about 1000 civilian prisoners) and a few hundred in the coolie quarters outside. 40 huts have to be moved from this camp, which means dismantling them, loading and hauling the sections on trailers about two miles to the gaol and then re-erecting them on the new sites. Furthermore, the IJA are only allowing 100 fit men off the aerodrome to assist in the heavier work. Otherwise the work will have to be done entirely by unfit men in the camp. The other ranks are to be allowed a width of one metre each and the officers one and a half metres in the huts. The main hospital is moving to Kranji, near the causeway and is to have 1500 beds. Just outside the gaol there is to be a hospital of 700 beds.

Peter, now back with us, is looking very fit and has put on a lot of weight, although I think a large part of this is attributable to beriberi. He came down from Tambaya in January and has been in Kanchanaburi until they came down to Singapore. Another 96 deaths had occurred in Burma after we left and John tells me that these had been estimated some months ago at 100. Not far out. The majority of our Divisional HQ personnel, who had to be left behind, died, as we expected. They were mostly in a hell of a state when we left. It is all desperately sad and we are all numbed by the news.

Robin Fletcher told me an amusing story about 'I bring', the Burmese who used to bring our canteen goods. He brought some hen's eggs in one day, which were very much smaller than usual. The price he asked was three to the rupee. The Korean guards, who were haggling with him, said he must sell them at five to the rupee. 'I bring' refused to lower his price, whereupon the Koreans threatened to beat him if he did not bring it down. "No good you beat me" replied 'I bring', "I not lay eggs; hens lay eggs. If hens lay small eggs, you beat hens". Robin also told me that the only Nip guard we had up in Tambaya eventually got so fed up living with the Koreans, that he spent more and more time with the POW friends he had made. As he told Robin one evening, "I can understand a little English but I cannot speak a word of Korean".

On Saturday evening Kerr and I went to hear a gramophone recital and were able to enjoy the Brahms 2nd Symphony. This was followed by the Eroica, which I find rather tiring to listen to these days, except for the last movement, which surpasses the others and is worth waiting for. The theme of the second movement I like well enough but Beethoven does not seem to do much with it, with the result that it becomes dull and monotonous. I think it is too long. I am feeling very well now and even have a certain amount of energy, a thing I have not had for months.

3 May 44 Some more letters have arrived in the camp and I received two from Mother dated 18 and 27 March 43 and one from Kinsley dated 16 Feb 43 from East Africa. He gave me the first sad news of the death of our golden retriever, Toy. I had begun to wonder what had happened to him as I found no reference to him in any of the letters from home. It appears that he must have been put to sleep in 1942. In one of Mother's letters there is a reference to some engagement or other. Who has got engaged I cannot quite make out, but it looks as if it must be one of my cousins at South Looe. I am told that there are many more letters to come up from the gaol so am hoping that I might receive news of Diana. So far I only have one letter from her since my capture, received over a year ago.

I think of her every day and night, and wonder how she is and what she is doing. It is now so long since we saw each other last that I wonder whether now, we would still have the same mutual attraction for each other, which we had two and a half years ago. It is not really so far back in time, but out here time is greatly extended by the factors of space and environment, and two and a half years seem like five. In any case it is no use worrying about it. There is nothing I can do, except perhaps hope that one day I shall get a letter from her again. If only the majority of the mail was not over a year old by the time it reaches us. I feel terribly frustrated being unable to write and tell people that I am still alive and well, and what I am doing and what I am thinking about, although I doubt if they would ever understand. Perhaps it is better to be completely cut off from all contact with the outside world, when we are forced to live such a colourless, unemotional existence, with no light and shade, no relief of any kind. Every day and every week are identical and our senses play no part at all. Here, it does not seem to matter what age a man is. Age does not enter into one's relationship with other people, and whether they are 26 or 60 one treats them much the same. They are just fellow prisoners and indeed, the only real grading there is, is physical capacity to do manual labour. Here, of course, many of us younger and fitter men think that many of the older people make the most of their age and do not do their fair share of work. This is undoubtedly true of a considerable number of them, but certainly not as many as we like to make out. This life must be very hard for the man over 60, of whom there are quite a number.

4 May 44 Yesterday I spent pulling trailers to the gaol. Already a very large quantity of building material and general 'junk' are accumulating there, but I shall be very surprised if the new camp is anything like ready by the date fixed by the Nips. This game of hauling trailers is very tiring, and my legs feel quite weak at the end of the day.

11 May 44 Books read: 'The Master Thinkers' (Vignettes in the History of Science) by R J Harvey-Gibson, 'A History of European

Art' by Wilenski, 'Tobacco Road' by Erskine Caldwell, Aldous Huxley's 'Rotunda', in which I thought 'The World of Light' read badly as a play. However, I enjoyed the essays 'Wordsworth in the Tropics' and 'Fashions in Love'. On Saturday we heard the 5th Brandenburg Concerto, the Allegro from the 3rd, this being all we have of the latter, and one of the Preludes and Fugues. It was delightful as this was the first Bach evening we have had. Unfortunately there are very few of his works in the camp.

The survivors of F Force have moved to the gaol and about 400 officers from Sime Road Camp have arrived. They include some twenty Italian officers from three submarines, which were docked in Singapore harbour when Italy capitulated. What a cosmopolitan crowd we are becoming! Three of them came round to see us yesterday evening, a Commander and two Lieutenants. They are great anglophiles and say that Fascism is now finished for good and all. They have been in Singapore since last July, after bringing their three submarines from Bordeaux to Singapore to collect natural rubber for some very special purpose in Germany. They brought out a cargo of mercury and aluminium for the Nips – all this in the torpedo tubes. One of the submarines was for a short time in Kobe, which they describe as being a port of the dead. We finish trailer pulling tomorrow and then go on to hut demolition. Another 20 bags of mail have arrived at the gaol.

15 May 44 Peter has now rejoined us and is living in the same room. Fitz in hospital with another fever relapse. I am re-reading 'Wickford Point'.

A long talk last night with John Morris, who came down from Kanchanaburi with Peter and Kerr. We started off with a long talk from John about astronomy. He is a great authority on the subject. From astronomy the talk turned to material, moral and ethical purpose in life.

A large party of POWs man-haul a wheeled trailer loaded with large tree trunks;
a Japanese guard stands at the front of the trailer holding a rifle

Kerr and I both think that a certain state of nihilism exists. We do not know what our purpose in life is, if indeed there is one, beyond the purely materialistic one of trying to create the greatest happiness for the greatest number of mankind. This cannot surely be an end in itself? There must be something beyond, but it is clearly impossible to get anywhere by applying pure reason alone. There seems to be nothing in life as elusive as the thing we call 'faith'. The interest shown in Christianity seems to become more and more tepid, and Western civilisation appears to have reached a crisis, where it has no belief in anything. People no longer know what to think, and the church is incapable of helping the vast majority of us, chiefly I think, because its teaching is not sufficiently dynamic. It has consistently failed to bring itself into line with modern thought. Science is continually progressing, and will go on doing so. Why not religion? But perhaps we are in error and we ought, as suggested by Huxley, to be more materialistic than we are already and show more interest in this world and less in the possibility of another. After all, as he says "the latter is an invention of man's fancy and shows the limits of its creator". Does it matter whether there is another world or not? How can it affect our behaviour in this world?

We have heard nothing further yet about the move to the gaol, except that all 18 Div. officers are to form a separate group with the MP, RN, Merchant Navy and Americans. This will make a total of about 150, to feed from the same cookhouse. Accommodation is to be kept in the gaol for a senior officer and his ADC. There is great speculation as to who it might be. The majority think it must be someone captured in Burma. All we know is that there is to be no contact between us and him.

19 May 44 The whole of the past week was spent working on hut demolition. This is not a popular job. There are 40 of us in the officers' group, and a lot of 'duck shoving' goes on amongst officers, who consider that it is not work which they should do. The most popular plea is that of being 'unfit to do the job'. If some of the officers in this camp would only get off their backsides occasionally and do some work, they would be a lot better both physically and certainly mentally. On all these unpleasant tasks, one sees the same faces day after day, and out of all the officers in this camp, there are about 50 or 60 of us who do all the heavy work.

Have just finished 'How Green Was my Valley' by Richard Llewellyn. It is certainly a great book. Am now in the middle of Joyce's 'Ulysses'.

From letters received it appears that the British Government, God bless it, is deducting vast sums of money per month from our pay to cover our board and lodgings as guests of the IJA. Well I'll be damned. What next? Heaven knows what is happening to my pay.

The great trek to the gaol starts tomorrow and the first step is to move furniture. The main hospital is moving to Kranji and with it will go all the chronic cases. The rice issue has been increased by 1 1/2ozs per day. Not much but every little helps. I get unbelievably hungry now, as I am out working all day and I find the ration quite inadequate. God knows what it must be like for the men. Smoking is becoming an ever more expensive habit, cheroots now being 14 cents each, when obtainable at the canteen. The continual lack of food is beginning to show its effect on everybody. We all find that tempers quickly become frayed, and tolerance is on the decline. One suddenly loses one's temper over what would normally be regarded as a very unimportant trifle, and I often get up in the morning in a frightful temper and cannot find a good word to say to anybody. I think things will hardly be improved when we are all in much closer quarters in the gaol camp. We have all been badly depressed again during the past few days and we begin to wonder whether we shall ever get out. Life just goes on without end and one wonders if there is any point in continuing.

28 May 44 Tomorrow we move to the new camp area at the gaol. I am to live in a 'coolie quarter' with Kerr, Fitz, and Mark Drinkwater, so I can count myself as being amongst the lucky ones, who are not in a hut. One can just fit four beds into one of these quarters and it will probably be very stuffy at night. There is a persistent rumour that all officers are to be moved shortly to a camp in Johore Bahru. At present Kerr is in hospital again with another fever relapse. The move of the hospital to Kranji has been postponed by the Nips, owing to lack of transport. This is a favourite excuse of the IJA now, when they are unable to carry out their plans. One never sees much sign of any lack of MT, however, as officers ride around in large American cars all day.

A letter from Denison yesterday dated July 1943. He seems to have been enjoying himself at such places as the Lansdowne and the Astor. The latter is a new night club for me. It seems incredible to think that people actually go to these places to dine and dance, while we perhaps are sitting over a bowl of filthy stew and a little rice, suffering from all sorts of diseases, starving, sweating, arguing and swearing in the dirt and heat of this camp. The contrast seems so great as to be beyond comprehension. Well, good luck to all those who can still do it. God knows I could hardly wish my greatest enemy this sort of life.

3 June 44 We have been nearly a week in the gaol camp, having moved last Monday. It has been a very busy time, hauling trailers, carrying pieces of furniture and clearing up the awful mess everywhere. There are now about 900 officers, all concentrated in an area about 100yds by 200yds.

There are 45 to a hut and 4 to a coolie quarter. The huts are very overcrowded, with only 12 to 18 inches between beds, with a gangway down the middle about 12 inches wide. The coolie quarters measure 12ft by 8ft and there is just room for four beds in each. We are, in fact, far more crowded together than we have ever been yet in Changi. Up-country, of course, it was a different story. Donald and I, with a few others from our lines, have volunteered to do a full day's gardening every day. We are not quite sure yet whether we shall make the pace but feel we ought to see how we get on.

After all, we are not much worse physically than many others, and it will be an excellent method of getting out of the crowded conditions of the camp for a few hours each day. The IJA state that bathing will be allowed again so things are going to be better than they have been for a long time past. Educational classes are being started again, but I feel that while one is fit and so long as there is essential work to be done, this should come first. However, I hope to be able to start Italian in the near future.

A library is to be opened and is to have a nucleus of 500 reference books from the old 'Southern Area' library. These include the Encyclopaedia Britannica in its entirety, except for one volume. All officers are to be asked to contribute as many books as possible, which should help to make a very good library as most of us have brought at least two or three books with us from the old area. It is thought that eventually we shall have about 2000 books in all. The most difficult problem at present is to find anywhere to put them, as all available covered space is taken up by living quarters. It is rather like Lilliputian suburbia, living in these coolie lines as each pair of buildings face each other at about 20 yards distance and in the middle there is a narrow roadway. Each quarter is planning to make its own garden and many people are hoping to be able to plant a hedge. In a few months, therefore, all we shall need to make the picture complete will be some little garden gates and a few names such as 'Mon Repos' or 'Bella Vista'. Opposite we have the Australian officers and further along the Italians. At the end of our lines are the Americans, a New Zealander and a Canadian. Ours is quite a cosmopolitan street!

The Italians are extremely pleasant, but of course their presence here causes much argument and unsympathetic comment from many of the more 'English' amongst us. They argue that they let their country down by giving their allegiance to Mussolini, when Italy capitulated and the Nips in Singapore gave them the option of voting to remain loyal to the King or of continuing the fight against the Allies by backing Musso. Most of the ratings chose the latter but the officers unanimously decided that, since they all carried the King's commission, they had no alternative but to remain loyal to the royal family. Not, of course, that any of them were fascists anyhow. For the time being the ratings were allowed to go free, but this did not last long and very shortly afterwards they were all put in the bag. The fact remains that they took a decision that ensured their incarceration by the Nips, and knowing what I do now, I would take off my hat to anybody who voluntarily entered a Nip POW camp. However, the right or wrong of the case does not interest me, since the conclusions one may reach on such matters depend entirely on the particular angle from which they are viewed. There are many people in this camp who will have nothing to do with the Italians, regard them as turncoats, and openly refer to them as those 'bloody dagoes' (naturally they have not got the courage to say it to their faces). This school of thought comes from that class of insular Englishman, who has grown up from his school days – naturally he was educated at the best, or would it be the most expensive, public school – displaying an appalling arrogance, when justification for any feeling of superiority is singularly absent. They make me sick and are just about the most insufferable type of the home product one can possibly come across. They believe that all foreigners are their inferiors.

Cyril Wild told me the other day that he had been at one of the daily conferences, at which the suggestion had been put forward by our people that a hole should be knocked in the South wall of the gaol, so as to facilitate ingress and egress to and from the gaol and the camp area outside. Takahashi said he would consider the matter and nothing more was heard. A few days later, he said that with regard to the knocking of a hole in the wall of the gaol, he had eventually decided against it, as, he thought, the "British Government would be very annoyed to come back and find that holes had been made in the walls of their gaol".

When the Korean guards first took over sentry duties at the main gate of the gaol, they became fascinated by the sliding steel door, which can be raised or lowered by pressing a button. Of course, they all had to take turns at seeing how it worked. After it had been raised and lowered at least a dozen times, it got stuck about two feet from the ground. There it stayed until the following morning and all the working parties leaving the gaol had to crawl out under the door! Takahashi called for the Sgt. of the guard and administered a severe rocket.

Have just finished R R Tawney's 'Religion and the Rise of Capitalism'. It certainly makes dismal reading. Have now got hold of Carrell's 'Man the Unknown'. For some inexplicable reason the rice ration has been increased to 500gms per day, and we now get reasonable bulk, although we still feel a continual hunger.

6 June 44 We are beginning to settle down in this camp and yesterday was, for some of us, the first day on the new gardens. These, in point of fact, are not gardens at all yet, but a large field of very tough lalang grass, situated on a slope, which will entail terracing of beds. It is going to be very tiring work for many weeks as all the lalang has to be cleared by going over the ground with a chungkol. Then it all has to be gone over again, this time as deep as we can go, to get out the deeper parts of the roots. The soil then has to be loosened and raked, made up into beds, terraced and finally the irrigation channels dug. We work from 9.00 am until 12.30 and 2.00 pm until 4.00 pm. Have borrowed Julian Huxley's 'Essays of a Biologist'.

10 June 44 A dull wet morning and we are waiting to go out on the gardens. I have been going out all day since it started and although I get extremely tired, I find I am keeping very fit. At present the whole camp has gone gardening mad. The Australians in 'Scandal Row', opposite, are putting down turf along the side of the road, and on our side people are making little flower gardens. Yesterday, we received a visit from General Shaito and Takahashi, who seemed to be very interested in our gardening activities. The Nip guards have now taken to drilling every afternoon on the padang. I can hardly picture our troops doing this at 3.00 pm under a broiling sun. Today they have been practising bowing and saluting.

Our feeding has been very poor recently. A lot of bulk, but very little taste and large quantities of rice with nothing else. There is to be a mess committee meeting tomorrow, so everybody is hoping for an improvement, although most of us expect the messing officer to do the impossible. This is a most thankless job and when a messing officer resigns, it is often impossible to find anyone willing to take the job on. They get nothing but complaints and never any praise. They are always short of fuel and it has always been a miracle to me how they produce the food they do. A canteen has now been opened in the officers' area, but since this serves over a thousand officers, there is always a long queue. In any case there is seldom much worth buying. Sugar is $3.30 per lb., Gula Malacca $1.80 per lb., coconuts 75 cents each, cheroots 15 cents, cigarettes $1.25 a packet, the latter are Chinese and are quite filthy. They consist mostly of papaya leaves. It is not difficult to understand from the foregoing that one's $20 per month does not buy much.

13 June 44 Have been off gardening for a couple of days owing to a recurrence of my stomach trouble. I only hope to God it is not dysentery. Perhaps it is my old friend ascaris vulgaris again, and all I need is a dose of Bob Martin's powder. This almost constantly recurring sickness is beginning to get me down. There is always an enormous amount of diarrhoea in the camp. It is difficult to keep the flies down under these conditions; in fact they seem to be for ever on the increase. One defecates regularly at the rate of at least 9 or 10 times in 24 hours and providing the medical authorities are satisfied that one has not got dysentery, there is nothing more to be done about it.

Afternoon classes have been started again, and I now have two lessons per week with Cdr. Grapallo. Am in the middle of S Sassoon's 'Complete Memoirs of George Sherston'. The library in the officers' camp is expected to open tomorrow. The days at present are passing fast, now that we have built a routine of gardening, lectures and reading, and I am inclined to think that life might be a lot worse.

21 June 44 We have planted the first vegetables in the gardens and the irrigation system is in full operation. The water for this is fed from the main anti-malarial drain through a series of channels leading to every bed in the garden. Here and there the water can be led into storage 'tanks' about two feet deep, which are simply holes dug into the laterite. At the bottom, a well is to be dug, as here water can be struck only about 10 feet below the surface. Most of my time lately, however, has been spent in de-rooting and levelling. Last night and the night before, the Nips held a practice black-out. The shape of things to come, we hope. Kerr has now rejoined us once more from hospital but the day after he went down with yet another bout of fever, this time only a little more than a fortnight since his last lot. The hospital has now completed its move and John has taken over the dysentery ward. He is very glad to have a doctoring job once more. In this job, his emotions may be given full play by lavish use of the sigmoidoscope. This is now alleged to be the most fashionable form of sexual perversion in the camp.

Last Sunday evening we went down to the hut where Norman Renton lives to hear an evening of ballet music. The loudspeaker instrument has unfortunately packed up and is in any case no longer available to us outside the gaol. We were able to enjoy Scheherezade and the Sylphides music. Only today have I noticed how many amputation cases we have in our street. Opposite amongst the Aussies, there are two men with leg amputations and on our side there is Osmond Daltry, minus a leg and an eye, a little further down is an ordnance officer with a head wound and paralysed down one side of his body and, finally, Gordon Brown, who has lost his right arm, has only three fingers on his remaining hand and a very nasty wound on his right leg. It is wonderful how cheerful these men keep.

They should have been repatriated years ago under the Geneva Convention on the treatment of prisoners of war, but I do not think they will get home much sooner than we shall now. Our Italian classes have now been put up to three times a week and we are beginning to make progress. Cdr. Grapallo is an excellent teacher and seems to have some gift for it. He is also a fluent German speaker, having spent much of his youth in Austria where he has some relations. I am getting through less reading now as I spend so much time on the gardens and the lights are switched off early every evening. However, it is much better to be active. There is always the danger that reading will become a drug and one will then get nothing out of it. We have, after a long fight, succeeded in getting Cpl. Chandler into our cookhouse. He used to be our mess corporal in England and is a wonderful cook. Consequently, we all think that very soon his presence will make itself felt.

26 June 44 Tomorrow, we are to be inspected by the GOC Southern Regions. A rehearsal for this is scheduled to take place today. Yesterday, being Sunday, I spent reading Roger Fry's 'Vision and Design' and started reading Thackeray's 'The Newcomes'. In the evening the usual Sunday gramophone recital, this week a potpourri of operatic music comprising such varied things as 'Armide', 'Don Giovanni', 'Löhengrin', 'The Mastersingers', 'Mignon', 'The Barber of Seville', 'Il Trovatore', 'Tosca', 'Aida', and 'Faust'. We are now reduced to using a small, much battered portable gramophone for our weekly concerts, but it is quite extraordinary how one can still appreciate good music played under the most atrocious conditions, when nothing better is available. The needles are made out of wire and are usually rusty, the records are badly worn and many are cracked right through, but are still considered worth playing. The spring of the gramophone will barely take a twelve inch record and often the machine has to be wound the whole time a record is being played. Nevertheless, there is usually an audience of between 50 and 100 officers.

Today I have had a holiday from the gardens. Although I am now used to being out in the sun all day without a hat and wearing only a pair of shorts and no shoes, it is very pleasant to get away from the constant glare. How I would love to have one really foggy day here, where we all take the sun for granted. I often think of a typical late autumn afternoon at home, everything wet with gentle rain, a ground mist coming up, the smell of damp undergrowth and of bonfires quietly smoking under a pile of wet leaves. I have just been out for a walk before tea, and before going in I take a last look, letting the damp smell fill my nostrils. Inside, the curtains are drawn and I sit down in front of a roaring fire to a good tea. There are times when I feel I never want to see a blue sky again. And yet the prospect of an English winter fills me with loathing.

Lieut. Takahashi has just been round the camp to see if everything is ready for tomorrow's inspection. Everybody is busy 'pansying' up his little plot of ground. Camp HQ are to put up the following points to the General: 1). Better and more nourishing food. 2). More clothing. 3). Better communication with home. 4). More drugs and medical supplies. 5). Repatriation of battle casualties and men permanently unfit. I do not think there is a hope in hell of any of these things being done, but I suppose one must always go on trying.

3 July 44 My stomach has been letting me down again and I am beginning to think it must be dysentery again this time. Am dosing myself with camphoridine twice daily. Have also started scrotal dermatitis again, this time really badly and it looks as though I shall be unable to do any gardening for some considerable time. Fitz has the same complaint in a rather more advanced state and we both spend the day in towels draped round our middles. There is very little that the doctors can give one for this complaint as it is almost entirely due to deficiency in the diet. I also lost my appetite the other day, always a bad thing to do under these circumstances since there is nothing to pick up on. I have been thinking it must be a recurrence of jaundice.

Meanwhile we plod away at our Italian lessons and in a week or so we are faced with an exam to divide the sheep from the goats and form advanced and elementary classes. Grapallo is very conscientious and has unlimited patience with his pupils. It is rather like being back at school with this one essential difference.

At school, being young, one has a certain aptitude for learning but not always a wish to learn. Now, we all have great keenness but the facility for absorbing knowledge has gone. I have been reading much more recently, now that I am confined to a static life. At present I am in the middle of 'The Newcomes', Reinach's 'Apollo' and E. E. Cumming's 'The Enormous Room', which is magnificent. Now the IJA has ordered that all lights will be out by 11.00 hours in the evening instead of 11.30 as hitherto. This is a severe blow as the night is made that much longer. Had a letter from Denison a few days back in which he gave me the impression that my cousin Nancy must have been married a year.

5 July 44 85 bags of mail for British and Australian POW have arrived at the gaol. A few days ago General Shaito inspected a 'Changi Industries' exhibition, held in the gaol. Displayed there was a set of chess men carved out of ivory by Major Horton, from the designs in 'Alice through the Looking Glass'. Shaito was much impressed and expressed a wish to have them. Horton pointed out through the interpreter that he was not willing to part with them. The next day, Takahashi informs camp office that the General is behaving childishly and insists on having the chess men – the pieces are said to remind him of certain Japanese Gods. Major Horton must therefore parade with an interpreter, and there will be a formal presentation! Furthermore if the officer persists in his refusal to hand over the set, the General will order all ranks in the camp to have their hair shaved off. Takahashi was very sympathetic but the chess men had to be handed over.

9 July 44 The scrotal dermatitis is no better – if anything rather worse and I am to be put on a course of Marmite, the curer of all ills in this camp. Have been reading a lot lately and have just finished

'Wuthering Heights' and have now started reading a biography of Leonardo da Vinci by Bax. Our feeding, although under new management, is still bad. It is no fault of the messing authorities; the rations have just got them beat. Kerr and I have recently been experimenting with a new sauce; it contains soya sauce as a base, vinegar, crushed garlic and a small quantity of curry powder. The result is distinctly odd, but it makes the rice taste different if it does nothing else. We are all finding life very trying now we are forced to live at such close quarters. I have never realized until now how lucky we were in the old Changi area, where we could go for long walks without having to go over the same ground twice. The Italian lessons continue three times a week, but we are beginning to find that it is becoming increasingly difficult to concentrate and remember what we have learnt during the previous lesson.

12 July 44 Reading Antoine de St. Exupery's 'Night Flight' and a biography of Stonewall Jackson by an American, Tate. The latter is one of the new American Red Cross books and it is wonderful to feel a new book in one's hands once more, and to smell that lovely odour of new paper and print. Our own books, in spite of the work on them by the gang of book-binders, who are kept permanently employed, are now in a sorry state and cannot possibly last very much longer.

17 July 44 Books: Ring Lardner's Short Stories, Machiavelli's 'Prince'. Our Italian maestros, Commanders Bruti (or Bruti Liberati, to give him his full name) and Grapallo decided they would split up the sheep from the goats, so last Saturday saw me back at school being examined in my scanty knowledge of the Italian language. However I did far better than I expected. Letters are dribbling in from the Nip censor's office, but I have not smelt one yet from the present batch. Perhaps this is just as well. One is dissatisfied if one does not receive one, and even more dissatisfied if one does. The receipt of a letter completely undermines the special sense of values and the basis of existence which one has taken so much pain to set up for oneself, and one begins to hate it. The news contained in letters is so old by the time we receive them here that, with our dulled senses, it makes but little impact on us. From this distance I find it impossible to understand what people do or why they do it. It all seems so pointless, complicated and unnecessary. Life seems so petty with all the stupid social conventions and traditions. Stanley has gone down with a recurrence of beriberi. This time in the face, stomach and legs. His phallus and scrotum are also an immense size and reminiscent of what many of us had up-country.

Received two letters from the family yesterday, giving me news of Nancy's wedding. I was staggered to hear this. I had almost forgotten that people get married, or even that there are women in the outside world. One seems to get on quite well without them and life is all the more simplified by their absence. Before I became a prisoner I could never understand how any man, no matter how deep his religious convictions might be, could renounce the world and shut himself up for life in a monastery. Now I find it no longer so difficult to understand and in future I shall not regard a monk as being so odd!

Have just finished Wells' 'History of Mr Polly', that novel which takes English education as its basic theme. It contains his great description of the state of mind of an English boy at the end of his education in an English school "... (his state of mind was) as if operated on for appendicitis by a well-meaning, boldly enterprising but rather overworked and under-paid butcher-boy, who was superseded towards the climax of the operation by a left-handed clerk of high principles but intemperate habits".

29 July 44 Twelve letters yesterday, dated January to June 43 from the family. The news contained in them is so old that I am left with a feeling of dissatisfaction. I seem to be having a course of H G Wells at the moment as I have just finished 'Mr Bulpington of Blup', which I much enjoyed. At present, I am reading Eugene Lyons 'Assignment in Utopia', one of the best books on Russia of the reportage type, that I have yet read. Am also in the middle of John Drinkwater's study of Cromwell. My scrotal dermatitis is now almost cured and I hope to be able to return to gardening soon. I am getting fed up with not being able to get away from the camp, or take exercise.

Air activity by the Nips seems to be on the increase. Almost every day now, fighters do mock air combat over this end of the island. There are two machines at it now, making a terrific noise as they circle round after each other. It is very reminiscent of the air battles over London in the Battle of Britain days, with the exception that these little monkeys never seem to crash. Every day I hope one of them will fall out of the skies, but they never do. The Nips are to allow bathing again, this time daily. The times are to be fixed according to the tides, which sounds unbelievably sensible. Lieut. Takahashi is to consider the following points: 1). Communication between POW and relations in Java and Singapore, 2). Permission for POW to visit relations in Sime Road Internment Camp, 3). The sending of another postcard. This would be the 4th card in two and a half years. For my part, I firmly hope that if we are to have the privilege of sending another, we shall be home before it reaches its destination. Spent the whole morning today cleaning out our coolie quarters and waging a fierce war on the bugs. We killed them by the hundred, but I doubt if we shall notice the difference owing to their speed of reproduction.

31 July 44 Have been told I am suffering from ova ascaris lumbricoides. In an endeavour to expel these delightful visitors from my digestive system, I have received from my friends in the medical profession, five bright red pills about the size of a marble. They look wicked.

7 August 44 Five more letters from the family, mostly only a year old. Have been bathing three times in the past week. It is a pleasant walk of about twenty minutes down to the beach, through coconut palms, rubber trees and part of our vegetable gardens. Books: H G Wells 'The Shape of Things to Come', Buchan's 'Prester John', Lin Yutang's 'My Country and my People', which I read about two and a half years ago. We now have Hank Moore living two quarters down from us. He is an RAF Group Capt., shot down in Burma and one of the most charming people I have met. Although he is theoretically the senior officer in the whole camp, he would be the last to remind you of it, and considers it a complete joke when the Lieut. Cols., almost all much older than he is, call him 'Sir'. He wears a straw hat to keep the sun off, and this is prevented from being blown off by the wind by a piece of bright blue wool, which he hooks under his chin and behind the large black beard, which he grew whilst in solitary confinement. We have started regular evening roll call parades once more. These were stopped by the IJA shortly before the move to the gaol. The Nips always do this when there is a move on and it is beyond them to keep a check on numbers in camp. They are odd people. If I were running this camp, the one time I would particularly like to have an accurate check on POW would be when movements in and out of the camp are taking place. Listened to an evening of ballet music two days ago. The programme included 'Les Sylphides', 'Le Spectre de la Rose' and the 'Nutcracker Suite'.

12 August 44 Yesterday we were allowed to send off another card. Mine was as follows. "Fourth card. Received sixty letters. Last dated September. Books, music adequate. Love to all. Tell Denison conserve drink for yours optimistically Harold." We have had a slight let up in the continual heat during the past two days during which it has been raining hard. Every evening now on roll call parade, or 'tenko' as we call it, we have read out to us a report of the points and requests put up by camp office to Lieut. Takahashi. Today's contained a reply by Taka. to Col. Newey's query about the non-arrival of Red Cross food. Taka said he wanted it made known that the IJA was not responsible for this. The only possible method of transport was on exchange ships but since seven of these had recently been sunk or damaged, they had met with no success. Col. Newey then asked why Nippon did not make use of a neutral country. To this Taka. replied that there were no neutral countries. "What about Russia?" he was asked. "Ah", replied Taka. "the relations between Russia and Nippon are very finely poised." He went on to refer to various atrocities attributed to U.S. troops, to wit: Sending home to the States the skulls of Nip dead as presents for their girlfriends and making paper knives out of the bones of dead soldiers.

At present am reading a history of the American People by Muzzey. It is one of the Red Cross books received some little time back.

Some Merchant Navy officers have just arrived in the camp, two American, and two British. Three of them were torpedoed on 29 March, 500 miles west of Bombay. They are the only survivors of one American ship carrying coal, and a British tanker (Shell), ex Persian Gulf bound for Australia. After the U.S. ship was sunk, the crew, who had taken to the boats, were shelled and machine-gunned by the submarine. The captain and one of the engineers hid in the water, their heads concealed under a spar projecting over the side of one of the boats. Soon this was the only boat left afloat and the submarine came up alongside and a Nip jumped into the boat which he tried to break up with an axe, without much success since the boat was constructed of steel. The two Americans were discovered and taken on board the submarine, where they spent the next three weeks. True to their reputation, the Nips, after having done their best to kill them in cold blood, treated them well, gave them part of their personal rations of food, chocolate and cigarettes, of which the Nips themselves only have very little, and which is sent to them from Nippon. They were eventually put ashore at Penang, where they were promptly placed in solitary confinement and handcuffed. Later they arrived at Curran Camp near Changi, where they were very badly treated and arrived in this camp, in a very poor physical state.

18 August 44 Books: Maugham's short novel 'Up at the Villa', d'Annunzio's 'Triumph of Death', and a book by Joseph Shearing, the 'Angel of the Assassination', a study of Charlotte Corday, Marat, and Jean Adame Lux. A camp band has been started and is to play weekly. It consists of about 30 players. I have heard it once and it will no doubt be very popular, although for me it smacks a little too much of Margate Pier.

Yesterday I heard the story of the Catholics' altar, which was being dismantled prior to the move up to the gaol. The officers in the Indian Army Mess were anxious to get hold of this altar, but on applying to the padre concerned, were told that it had already been promised to the Dutch. They were also told, however, that if the Dutch did not claim it by the end of the week, the padre saw no reason why they should not have it. The week passed and the Dutch did not show up to claim the altar, so the Indian Army officers sent up a working party with a trailer to collect it. A couple of days later a Dutch officer appeared at the Indian Army Mess and said he had come for the altar of the Roman Catholic Church. "We're extremely sorry", came the reply, "but we have made it into a hen-coop". "Ach, wot a peety", exclaimed the Dutchman, "we wanted it for a duckhouse".

Takahashi has been displaying his sense of humour again. He was out the other day inspecting one of our working parties, which is employed on building a perimeter road round the aerodrome. He went up to the officer in charge of the men and said to him:- "You must get your men to hurry up. I want to be able to hand this road over, completed, to the British". Takahashi is an extraordinary man in many ways; he understands far more English than he speaks or is willing to let on. He has never been to Europe, having learned his English entirely in school. At times he shows a truly English sense of humour, and on more than one occasion has proved himself to be a friend of the camp. This cannot be said with even the wildest stretch of the imagination of any other Nip officer I have come across.

A ship bringing a cargo of POW from Sumatra last June was either torpedoed or hit a mine, which seems more probable and a large number were lost. One British soldier, who was in the hold with the rest when the ship was hit, found himself trapped under some wreckage, which had fallen on him in the darkness of the hold. There was a second explosion shortly after the first and he found himself this time in the water directly under the funnel, which by this time was horizontal and threatened to crash down on top of him at any minute. His life was saved by a Korean Corporal who swam up to him and pulled him clear just before the funnel fell hissing into the water. This same corporal was seen to return to the ship, now right over on her side, three times and each time he brought one of our men to safety. He returned a fourth time but before he could approach the now vertical decks, the ship began to settle down, and as she took the final plunge the Korean was seen to go down with her. An extremely brave man and an action that helps to restore one's faith in the human race. A number of Koreans and Nips were wounded by the explosions, and although a tanker which carried a Nip doctor, picked up the survivors, her doctor took no part in attending to the wounded, either the Nips or the POW. All first aid work was done by the British MO, who had been on the torpedoed ship. Even when the Nip wounded were disembarked in Singapore, our own men had to carry the stretchers, the other Nips showing not the slightest interest, and not lifting a finger to help. They are indeed a very odd people.

20 August 44 Another five letters and two 25 word cards yesterday from the family. The letters are dated from January to June 43. Heard that my card written in February 43 was received in January 44. I hope this life does not go on much longer since I am going to find it difficult to keep up a connected correspondence! Two remarks in this batch of letters, I find incomprehensible and I am beginning to think the family must be working some form of code. The first is "Your peach and apricot trees planted" and the other is "Felicity's Mother very kind". Perhaps this is some new form of esoteric conversation which is current in certain circles frequented by the family but it certainly does not convey anything to me.

A card from Denison dated 23 December contains the following interesting statement:- "Nancy married September, now having infant". With the best will in the world I can only make this four months. Something is obviously not quite 'comme il faut' in the family. Have been reading two of Kerr's short stories, which I thought very good. I shall be surprised if he has very much difficulty in making a success of his pen. He is the best read person I have ever come across and he has a very deep understanding of the psychological problems of life. We have all been inoculated once more against dysentery and typhoid. Unfortunately the dysentery inoculation has no effect at all. According to the doctors there is no adequate insurance against the disease.

3 September 44 Kerr went into hospital again a few days back with a sharp attack of bacillary dysentery of which there is a considerable outbreak at present. I had been back at work on the gardens for about a week when I had to give up once more owing to a recurrence of scrotal dermatitis. I am now being treated by the skin specialist, who is Australian. I find it very difficult and extremely painful to walk about, so I am really chained to the hut. Kerr, at present in hospital and I now live in the hut with Donald and Peter. The move came about owing to the arrival of some more field officers, who of course had to have a coolie quarter to live in. However it does not worry me very much since the huts are much cooler at night although one has much less space. I have Peter on one side of me, our beds are actually touching, and on the other I share a space with Donald about 3 feet wide. Against the wall we have just got room for a small table (we are lucky) and we share a chair. Between our beds and those on the opposite side of the hut there is a gangway about eighteen inches wide. All my possessions I keep in a pack and two haversacks. They consist of the following:

1 pair long trousers

2 pairs shorts. Both very worn and patched

2 shirts, almost in ribbons

2 pairs socks

1 towel, in rags

1 pair boots, soles hanging off

1 pair shoes, ditto
1 blanket
1 mosquito net, with holes
Razor and one blade
Shaving brush
Tooth brush
Mirror
Tin Mug
Rice Bowl
Plate
Knife, fork and spoon
1 piece of soap
Brush and comb

None of the above has been supplied by the Nips and I am one of the lucky ones, being far better off than most. Considering these articles have now been in almost continual use for two and a half years, one can get an idea of their condition. The air is full of rumours – engineers and technicians are to go to Japan, all merchant navy officers are going to Sime Road Camp to join the civilians. All officers are to be moved away from the men. There is once more a general air of impermanence in the camp. The whole atmosphere is unpleasantly like that we experienced a few days before the ill-fated F Force party was sent up to Thailand.

Meanwhile I am much enjoying the change after my move from the coolie quarters. A room shared by three other people and only 8 feet by 10 feet, begins to get on one's nerves after a bit and it was not until I moved away from it that I realized just how irritable I must have become. Peter has become incredibly fat during the past few weeks and we all tell him he must have beriberi again. We have an odd sense of humour here, I suppose, as this disease nearly did for him in Burma. He is consequently known by any one of three pseudonyms. 'Loofah', 'Gummi Frau' or 'Puffin'. Opposite me there is the 'Little Red Tug' or Ross Grey, a short red haired little man in the RAOC. Hank Moore unfortunately left yesterday for Nippon with Brigadier Varley of the AIF. The latter commanded A Force up in Burma. They went by sea to Rangoon at the end of 1942 and started building the railway from Moulmein. They did not fare so badly as the later parties and had comparatively few deaths. They included Dutch, Americans, Australians and British. Rations are to be reduced again. Rice is going down to 16ozs per day, and oil to 10gms. Books: Linklater's 'Poet's Pub' and C K Steit's 'Union Now'. Another 42 bags of mail have been received in the camp and sorting is to start soon. The previous batch of mail has not been cleared yet.

Listened to a very interesting talk by Cdr. Grapallo on the subject of 'Submarine Warfare in the Present War'. I thought it a gallant effort to get up and speak on such a delicate subject. A very large number of officers were present and all felt, I think, that it was a rather unique occasion. A talk in a POW camp by an officer who, not many months earlier, had been trying his hardest to sink our shipping. A man who, until very recently, had been one of our enemies, but who during the past few months has become for many of us a close personal friend. There was an awed silence as he told us of the many weaknesses in the Allied anti-U-boat precautions at the beginning of the war. These weaknesses were, however, gradually overcome and as we became ever more efficient at dealing with the U-boat menace, Axis submarines were driven ever further out into the Atlantic and away from the waters closest to Britain. Grapallo was in command of one of 30 Italian submarines attached to the German Atlantic U-boat fleet. He is believed to have sunk

16 Allied ships. The first six months after the entry of the US into the war was known as the 'Golden Era' in U-boat warfare. The anti-submarine precautions of the American convoys was as bad if not worse than those of the British had been at the beginning of the war. They had apparently learned nothing from the experience of the British convoys and had to learn themselves from bitter experience. However the American/British combination gradually improved their U-boat technique, but at a hell of a price. During the three peak months the Allied Merchant Navies lost 1,200,000, 1,200,000 and 1,400,000 tons of shipping. This was in February, March and April 1942. At last the U-boats were forced out into the open sea and they had to resort to 'Pack-hunting'. The U-boat, Grapallo said, was finally beaten by the aeroplane and the Battle of the Atlantic was won, when the Allies created air bases in Trinidad, Ascension, St Helena and the Azores and brought them into full operation, when virtually the whole of the Atlantic could be patrolled. I discovered the other day that Grapallo was in the Caribbean when we passed through in 1941, but fortunately the speed of the convoy was such that submarines were unable to mount torpedo attacks.

A long discussion with Donald yesterday on our experience gained during the past five years of war. The instability of the human being. The speed (more surprising than the depths to which they can fall) with which men sink to a level lower than the beasts. Their inability to employ themselves in the long hours of mental freedom, which have so unexpectedly been granted them. Their own admission that they would sooner go out and do a day's work than be left to themselves.

Peter has been having his leg pulled unmercifully. He has just received a card from his girlfriend, Sheila, dated 29 February 1944.

It says "Note the date. My last chance for four years. Shame". I tell him he is absolutely sunk. If this is not a proposal I am damned if I know what is. Peter just smiles at all this and says: "No surely not. It can't be". The whole time since I have known him he has always had a photograph of his American girlfriend by the side of his bed. He had it in England, on the way out to Singapore, during the battle and afterwards as a POW. Now I tell him it is time he put her face to the wall. She has not written to him, so I guess that affair is over. In a way I think Peter is rather flattered that anybody should have remembered him all this time. It appeals to his masculine ego. In any case I don't think he was ever serious about this particular girl in England. He always had so many.

4 September 44 My birthday was celebrated yesterday evening. Cpl. Chandler, our old mess cook who is still with us, made a magnificent cake out of the following: 2lbs maize flour, 1lb sago flour, 1 1/2lbs gula malacca, 2 coconuts and a small amount of rice, being added to increase the bulk. We also had sweet coffee. All this cost me $12 or about £1.10s. Any party with sweet coffee is regarded as being really good these days.

The electric light was cut off so we sat outside by the light of two candles, until the moon rose at about 9.00 pm. It was also a celebration of Donald's 5th wedding anniversary. Air activity seems to be on the increase this end of the island. Most of the planes are fighters, flying low. Some, according to our experts, are off carriers and can be seen practising dive bombing over the straits. There is a considerable amount of naval shipping in the naval base, the other day 4 large cruisers with attendant destroyers having been seen to enter the base. Story attributed to Takahashi. He was talking to Col. Newey after one of the daily camp conferences and said to him: "I do not mind your men telling my Korean guards that they will soon be inside the gaol. I do not really mind your men singing the Marseillaise on their way out to work. But I do strongly object to them teaching my troops to sing 'There'll always be an England'.

7 September 44 We heard yesterday that Hank Moore finally left Keppel Harbour two days ago. The ship left in convoy. About 100 merchant ships escorted by nearly 20 naval craft of various types. I only hope they will reach Japan without having to swim for it.

Tomorrow evening we hope to hear the Pastoral Symphony. Life in the hut is getting a bit trying. We seem to be divided into two different groups. Up our end of the hut, we are becoming very unpopular. Chiefly, I think, because we are mostly younger, much more cheerful and far noisier than the people at the other end. This causes much ill feeling; particularly when we talk after lights out. How can one remain silent, jammed up alongside each other in our beds, a hot stifling atmosphere and nobody able to sleep. I sometimes think that those, who take life so seriously, would do better to give vent to their feelings now and again and let themselves go. They would certainly be far easier to live with. I believe that in the long run we shall be the more sane and more human people, even if at times we are accused of behaving childishly and of being mental.

8 September 44 Being admitted to hospital again today with suspected amoebic dysentery. So life goes on, from one damn disease to another. One is never clear for long, even those of us who are regarded as being the healthiest in the camp. I have quite forgotten what it is like to be consistently well and free from disease. Kerr is due out today. Anyway, going into hospital like this is always popular in the hut as it means more space.

If we did not constantly have a large percentage of people in hospital, the crowding in the huts would be insufferable. John, who is now in charge of the dysentery ward, is tickled to death at the prospect of being able to effect a sigmoidoscopy on me. He has been wanting to do this for a long time past but has never had the opportunity. I am now in hospital on a liquid diet. God, I'm hungry. We get half a pint of rice 'pap' 5 times a day. Nothing with it. No sugar to help it go down. My bed is on the balcony giving me a view of Selarang Square, where 17,000 of us were concentrated two years ago, when we refused to sign an undertaking not to try and escape. It is nice to be back in a stone building again, although there are more bugs in the beds. It is a hot, sweltering afternoon. On the padang at the bottom of the gardens, where I used to work, the Nips are parading.

It is the 8th of the month and Imperial Rescript Day. All the troops have to parade once a month on this day to have the Emperor's Rescript read out to them. It is always the same one, in which he declared war on the US and Britain. The 'Red Ball', more frequently referred to as the 'Changi Ball', is having its monthly airing on the gaol flag pole. I can hear the distant strains of a portable gramophone, weak-springed and tired, like everything else round here, playing old records, worn and cracked. Tunes like 'Night and Day' drift into one's ears like some vague, fantastic ghost from remote pre-war life. Did we ever live it? I sometimes wonder. It is all so unreal, so dim and distant.

From my bed I can see the main road leading up to the aerodrome, and my mind is carried back to that day, 17 February 1942 when so many tens of thousands of us trudged round that same corner, worn out, exhausted and depressed as we had never been in our lives, except perhaps last year after returning from Siam and Burma, disillusioned, surprised that we were still alive and relieved that it was all over. We were covered in filth, smelling of sweat and swearing at each other on the slightest pretext. Now, the road, undulating across the balcony panorama, carries innumerable trucks and cars carrying the coolies to and from their work on the aerodrome. From here they resemble toys, with their miniature human freight, packed so tight that if any of them were to faint, they would remain where they were, unable to fall down. Further along 'Half Moon Street', from the buildings occupied by the Nips, occasional hoarse shouts in Japanese.

In the opposite beds to me are two Dutchmen. One, a young doctor, the other about 50, grey and full-bearded, full of interesting tales of the Russian Revolution and its aftermath. He fought in the revolution, having been an officer in the Czarist Navy, escaping through Siberia and, after many wanderings, fetched up in the Netherlands East Indies, where he finally joined the army. Now he is very ill with beriberi and just lives in the past, trying to forget the present, not apparently worrying about the future, which for him is very uncertain. I doubt if he worries as to whether he will live or die. Either way, he has enjoyed his life, a life fuller with rich experience than most of us can ever hope to achieve. He is a man without wife, family, permanent home or ties of any sort: probably without close friends, incredibly alone, taking life as it comes, never worrying. John has just made me come down to earth, by putting his head round the door and gloating over his chances of sigmoidoscoping me.

10 September 44 Books: Michael Arlen's 'Lily Christine', A History of Switzerland, Evan's 'South with Scott'. Was visited yesterday evening by John, Fitz, Kerr, Donald, Peter and Phillip. It is Sunday evening. Just across the road from the balcony is one of the C of E churches and further down the hill is the Roman Catholic Church. It is just beginning to get dark. The C of E congregation is busy singing a hymn and in between the verses, the monotonous chanting of the Catholics is wafted to my ears. The altars of both churches are lit by electric light. In front of each stand the priests, the C of E in black and white, the RC in white. The latter has several acolytes in attendance. Since the Roman Catholics have only one Church, there are always several priests at the services. They draw a large crowd and the stage effects far outdo those of the C of E.

Electric candles are burning in a sort of niche above and behind the altar. Now I can see the priest facing the altar, while the stalls and pit genuflect, some slowly, methodically and conscientiously, the others merely dip in self-conscious hurry. How methodical and pagan it all seems. Just across the road, the heretics have finished singing their hymn and are being harangued by their padre, once a famous cox of the Cambridge University rowing eight. He always gets very excited, almost shouting, floods of words, strings of clichés and platitudes, his excitement carrying him away and making him lose all thread of what he is trying to say, so that the words become a meaningless jumble. His regular attendants sit there, their faces blank, their shoulders hunched. I wonder what they would think of it all if they could come up here with me on the balcony and get a bird's eye view of religious observation? Many quite obviously go out of boredom; because they want to pass the time. One gets a curiously detached feeling, looking at these two groups of people, both equally convinced that theirs is the right way to immortality. One should never, of course, watch other people at their prayers. It makes one horribly cynical of religion, superior almost.

The latest Takahashi bulletin states that, in the event of an Allied landing in Malaya, the IJA will be unable to supply us with vegetables, as no transport will be available for this purpose. I have not noticed that they have ever supplied us with many vegetables in the past. We have mostly eaten those we have grown ourselves. Meanwhile we have enough rice to keep us going until December, palm oil for a month, salt and sugar for two. They do not say whether we shall be allowed to crop the vegetables in our own gardens. Personally, I think that by the time a landing is made on the mainland, we shall all be inside the gaol.

12 September 44 Became a catamite at the end of John's sigmoidoscope yesterday. He told me that I had not got amoebic dysentery yet again, which is a great relief. This means that I should be out in a day or two.

Eric has gone to Kranji for two weeks to have a rest. He always works very hard, considerably harder than the majority of medicos in this camp. At present reading 'Lorna Doone', which I have never read. Am hoping to be able to borrow Daniele Vare's 'Laughing Diplomat'.

14 September 44 Still in hospital. Spent yesterday evening on the balcony at the back of the building. For some unknown reason, nobody else was there and I was able to enjoy the evening on my own. It is seldom that one can get away from other people, even for five minutes. I thought how extraordinary this existence is. Utterly timeless, every month in the year the same, no change in the climate and nothing to work for. The two houses occupied by the officers' ward of the hospital are normally inhabited by European gaolers and their families. They are well built, cheerful and airy and it is wonderful to have a tiled roof over one's head again.

I met a young lieutenant of the Italian Navy yesterday by the name of Jacoangeli. He is actually 20 or 21 but looks about 17. We discussed the possibility of our doing English and Italian conversation when I get out of hospital, which should be in about three or four days now. I am due to see Maj. Clarke again tomorrow. These Italian officers are a very pleasant crowd. It is very noticeable how much fitter they are than we are. They have not yet attained the POW slouch, which the rest of us have got. I have been feeling very impatient these last few days. I hope this is a sign that I am getting better. Am now reading Daniele Vare's 'Laughing Diplomat', having just finished 'Lorna Doone'.

17 September 44 Still In hospital, my Changi balls refuse to clear up. I am getting tired of them. Reading James Joyce's 'Portrait of the Artist as a Young Man'. I have had to miss several Italian lessons. Captain Grapallo amuses us a lot, with his refrains at the end of his lessons "You see it is really wery easy" or "It is not deeficult, I think". This, after some extraordinarily complicated lesson on relative pronouns. When stumped for a word in English, he has a delightful way of shrugging his shoulders. Altogether 'ein sehr sympathischer Kerl', who takes immense trouble over teaching his cosmopolitan class of twenty odd Dutch, Australian and British. The Australians have the most atrocious accents while the Dutch are more at home with pure vowel sounds than the British.

Lying on my bed I can see in the distance many Japanese lorries passing the IJA guardroom on the road from the aerodrome, conveying Chinese and Tamil labour back to Singapore. Food here now is becoming extremely dull. Consisting almost entirely of rice, tapioca root and what little greens we are able to crop from our gardens. The greens are, however, very tough and I am told that the varieties we produce (primarily for quick growing) are normally never grown or eaten by the locals. For about an hour this afternoon, three Nip planes have been practising dive-bombing over the Straits behind Selarang. When will our own planes appear to do some real bombing?

Kerr gave me some of his short stories to read yesterday. Their theme is life in an infantry battalion in wartime Scotland. Good but I don't think the dialogue quite clicks. Donald agrees. Kerr's writing is good and I am amazed how he manages to write at all in this shocking environment. He writes, sitting on the edge of his bed in a hut with fifty other people, talking, arguing, playing cards or just lying on their backs staring into space. On one side the next bed touches his and, opposite, the bed is only three feet away.

19 September 44 A wonderful surprise yesterday as I received four 24 word cards from home, dated February, March, April and the latest 2 May, only 4 1/2 months old. One of them from Denison and another from Mother, saying she had met poor Becky's widow, Honour. It was grand to have such up to date news but as always, whenever I receive mail, I am left completely unsettled and filled with an urgent nostalgia for home. My Changi balls have at last improved and I am now to be put on Violet Ray treatment. This I gather is a kill or cure method. The equipment has been manufactured in the camp from an old searchlight.

24 September 44 I am being discharged from hospital today. Received two more cards dated 1 April. I am enjoying 'Villette' by Charlotte Bronte. This I consider a better work than 'Jane Eyre'. I have also started 'A History of the American Civil War' by Wood and Edmonds. This period of US history is, to me, extremely interesting and there are a number of books on the subject in the camp library. What a ghastly, bloody war it was.

Last night was delightfully cool and I was forced to put my blanket over me. I shall have to cut down on cheroots. I smoke 3 or 4 per day at present and at 18 cents per cheroot they are too expensive on the pay which we receive from the IJA. Ralph Spark is now in the bed opposite me with the same fashionable complaint. He is a pleasant companion to have as he has a good sense of humour. The violet ray treatment seems to be having a good effect and I am to continue with it after I leave hospital. I hope soon to go back to gardening.

27 September 44 A postcard yesterday from Denison dated 27 April saying he is living in a tent near Oxford. The card bears the Abingdon postmark. Monday saw the opening of the new theatre in the gaol. Whilst the sets by Ronald Searle and costumes were good, the material itself was poor and the humour, largely topical, was particularly crude. It is intended that there should be a new show every fortnight with an auditorium seating 900 that will enable about 11,000 to see each show. After the present variety show, 'Autumn Crocus' followed by 'Tonight at 8.30', are to be presented. Quite a few Nips were present last Monday, including Takahashi. On Sunday morning the company had to give a special performance for General Shaito and his staff. I gather things were pretty sticky.

For some time past we have had rumours that POWs have been killed at Nong Pladuk in an air raid. We heard yesterday from an Australian sergeant, who has been admitted to hospital from River Valley Road Camp, that the junction was bombed at 2.00 am one night, when one bomber came over flying very low and dropped two bombs, which straddled the railway sidings. It then bombed the centre of the station area. It then flew off to the north and was shortly followed by about 20 planes which started plastering the sidings. It appears that on the previous day three trains had entered the station and were waiting for some blockage further up the line to be cleared. One was an ammunition train, the second a train carrying petrol and oil and the third a troop train. Direct hits were scored on all three and everything was to all intents and purposes wiped out. Unfortunately one bomb fell on one of the huts in the POW camp near the line

215

and killed 70 prisoners and wounded 80. It is estimated that 300 Nips were killed and 700 wounded. This same sergeant related how the Dutch in the camp panicked, accusing the British pilots of being "fucking murderers". This is said to have led to a fight in which the Australians, backed up later by the British, beat up the Dutch, one of whom was killed. My scrotum has at last cleared up and I am able to walk about again. Today I start doing Italian with Jacoangeli. We hope to be able to do it every afternoon and this way we should get on faster than in a class of twenty.

29 September 44 Working hard at Italian, I spend each morning at it and have a lesson in the afternoon. I am making much greater progress now I can work at it daily. Unfortunately there appear to be no Italian books in the camp. It seems extraordinary that none of the Italians brought any books with them. As it is, we have to rely on an Italian newspaper published in New York. The Italian is bad but better than nothing.

I have been feeling particularly depressed during the last few days. We have all been getting on each other's nerves more and more and this seems to get worse as the interminable weeks slowly pass. I feel I am becoming neurotic and I shall have to fight against it. It is essential to keep my mind occupied with something more solid than reading. If I go at it sufficiently hard, studying Italian will help to fill this need. Unfortunately I am still unable to do any work in the gardens owing to this damn disease of mine. We have been trying hard to get classical records from the gaol. The people responsible for entertainment in the Officers' camp seem to be determined that we shall not have anything worth listening to in the way of music.

Futile arguments and petty bickering become ever more frequent and we seem to have forgotten the tolerance which, I think, we used to have. I daren't think what things will be like if this life is forced on us for another six months or a year. There seems to be no prospect of it ever ending and I often wonder whether people outside will regard us as being sane, when we do finally get out.

I have just bought 1lb of cucumbers at the canteen for $1.50; quite a luxury but at least they will make the rice taste of something else for a change. We are all beginning to look extremely ragged now and few of us possess shirts or shorts, which are not torn and covered in patches. Only some of us have towels and most of these look like very ragged dishcloths. God, how tired I am of all the dirt and filthy conditions, in which we are forced to live. I have heard today that the IJA is to stop issuing soap. Heaven knows the issue has never amounted to very much and has never been enough to enable us to wash ourselves and our clothes. My toothbrush, in constant use now for over 2 1/2 years looks as though it has been under a steamroller. However, we have known nothing better for so long now that things like this do not seem to matter anymore. Flies and mosquitoes seem to be forever on the increase.

5 October 44 I have started gardening again, but at present work in the mornings only. In the afternoons I work at Italian. It is wonderful to be able to get outside the camp again and breathe new air. I go out on the gardens at 10.00 am and return in time for the midday rice. I have just finished Kay Boyle's 'The Death of a Man', which deals with the early days of the Nazi movement in Austria. I have now started 'South' by Shackleton, his account of the 1914–17 Antarctic Expedition. The Italian is going well and I feel I am making good progress. I now have an hour every day with Jacoangeli and attend Cdr. Grapallo's classes 3 times a week. Mentally I am feeling much better now I can get out and take exercise. I find that a morning's work enables me to concentrate much more easily on my reading.

8 October 44 Imperial Rescript Day. I wonder what the Emperor has found to say this month. The IJA must, I feel, get very tired of hearing the same thing read out to them month after month without their being any nearer to victory. We now have a permanent 'brownout' throughout the camp and the huts are very gloomy. For a hut of 45 officers we only have three bulbs, covered by a cylindrical shade, which throws the light straight onto the floor. This evening Donald is sitting opposite writing another short story; Stanley, Roy and Kerr are busy discussing a much-loved topic – the trip home. Seven or eight others, including myself, are endeavouring to read. All of us are sitting in a space approximately 12ft square in an attempt to get a bit of light.

Over at the Coconut Grove Theatre the ORs of the officers' camp are rehearsing for a variety show they are to put on next week. Above all this there is the eternal, monotonous chirping of grasshoppers and crickets. And last, but certainly not least, hammering. Hammering seems to go on all day and all night, month after month, and we seem to have had it constantly for over two and a half years. There is hammering when a hut is being erected or dismantled, hammering from the various workshops, hammering by officers debugging their beds, hammering even by people flattening tobacco stalks, which can be bought at the canteen. Hammering, hammering, hammering, until I wonder if I am not going crazy.

11 October 44 Camp bulletin No 9 stated: "News. The Representative Officer has again requested that an IJA bulletin might be given to the camp. The reply given was that it was not considered to be necessary as there was always P Party. (This is the working party which goes into Singapore every day from the gaol. They naturally pick up quite a lot of news, and of course many rumours, from the Chinese and Eurasians in the town). The

Representative Officer said that the rumours brought in by P Party were mostly in the realm of fantasy, and one did not know what to believe. The conversation then terminated". This bulletin also stated that a fishing pagar is to be built for the supply of fresh fish for hospital patients. Yesterday I started all-day gardening again and I have already got quite brown. I imagine that even the palest of us must be very dark compared to anyone at home. Indeed, the majority of the POWs are considerably darker than the average Nip.

I have been up to the hospital again today and was told finally that nothing can be done for my stomach. I can only assume that it is quite incapable of dealing with the food it has to digest. Meanwhile the diarrhoea continues at the rate of 8 to 10 motions per day. Most of these occur during the night, and since the bore- holes are about 100 yards from the hut I spend a considerable part of the night taking enforced exercise. Luckily I have had it for so long now, I am quite resigned to it. At least I keep fitter than most men in the camp and as long as I am able to go out gardening, I have nothing to worry about.

13 October 44 Busy on the gardens this morning. I am becoming more and more native as the days go by. It is extraordinary how one can quite easily work all day under a tropical sun with no hat on one's head, no shoes on one's feet and wearing only a small pair of patched shorts. Manual labour under such conditions, I am convinced, not only keeps one physically fit but is also good for one's mental stability. If ever in later years, I find myself in a city, white and pasty and mentally stagnant, I know the answer.

Two days ago a man in Hut E3 found an old mortar bomb lying on the ground. He picked it up and, throwing it over his head, remarked "Wouldn't it be funny if it went off"? His words were cut short by a violent explosion, the bomb fortunately bursting in a drain. One of the RA officers was cut by a flying splinter but luckily only slightly hurt. A pity the man who threw the bomb did not blow himself up. A buggery case reported from the gaol. Two Australians involved, the scene of action being one of the gaol courtyards. It is surprising that this is the first case – at least to become public – and that there is not more of it. The answer probably lies in the serious lack of vitamin E in our present diet.

'Autumn Crocus' opens on Saturday. We are all looking forward to seeing another straight play. 10.45 pm According to the latest IJA order, all entertainments are to stop. The reason given is that General Shaito had heard the British National Anthem being "sung frivolously". The order prohibiting shows starts: "For the alleged ribald singing of the National Anthem on the night 12/13 October." This means, amongst other things, that Italian lessons will have to stop.

14 October 44 Gave myself a holiday from the gardens this morning and went bathing. Very pleasant, deep blue water, the surface broken only by the smallest ripples. The peaceful scene being marred by aircraft, fighters and dive bombers, roaring overhead as they climbed up from the aerodrome only a mile or two away. After taking off they circled round, gaining height and finally sped out seawards. Further out in the direction of Pengarang the planes were practising dive-bombing. The latest news on the gaol buggery case is that both the pederast and the catamite are to receive three months each. This strikes me as being an unduly hard sentence.

Why stop the men's only fun? The catamite's defence is said to be as follows. "I was bending down undoing my boots when I took a step backwards and walked right onto it". The cessation of entertainments is only for one week. The ban now appears to be due to some of the Indians singing the National Anthem in the gaolers quarters just outside the wire.

Starting tomorrow we are to receive an issue of Soya beans at the rate of 80gms per day. Towgay and rowgay are now both unobtainable.

18 October 44 Weighed myself this morning – 11 stone 5lbs. Today I heard the story of the Nip with Changi balls who went to see Major Clarke, the skin specialist. Major Clarke asked him to take down his shorts and looking at the man's undercarriage enquired. "Itchy?" The Nip immediately shook his head and with a bewildered look on his face answered: "Ni, ni", at the same time holding up two fingers. The Japanese for one is 'ichi' and for two 'ni'.

We have just finished a 48-hour A.R.P. exercise and for the past two evenings we have been blacked out. It was attended by General Shaito and Lieut. Takahashi. As part of the exercise a bomb was supposed to fall in the vicinity of our lines. For this purpose two ORs had to climb onto the roof of the coolie quarters at a given signal, throw down a large sheet of corrugated iron, at the same time blowing a whistle to imitate the noise of the falling bomb.

21 October 44 An air-raid warning last night while I was spending an hour of German conversation with Commander Grapallo. Grapallo speaks German as well as he does Italian having spent much of his youth in Austria. We hope to have these German conversations regularly. We went gardening as usual this morning but at approximately midday the sirens sounded again and we are beginning to wonder what justification there is for these warnings. Have just finished 'Kitty Foyle', an excellent book, which I found very sad and it left quite a lump in my throat.

Jacoangelli has just come round to tell me that Takahashi has ordered all the Italians to move inside the Gaol. Damn it! This means an end to Italian and German lessons. Takahashi came round to inspect the brownout today and afterwards complained that he was not saluted. We thought this was the reason for the Italians being moved inside the gaol as they were amongst the offenders, but we were informed later that they were being moved for their own safety!

22 October 44 Sunday. Until further notice the Italians are to be confined to their quarters and they are not allowed to speak to anyone outside. This smacks very much of punishment to me. All entertainment has been curtailed and no assembly of more than 25 people is allowed.

The Nips seem to be getting jumpy about something. Performances are allowed twice weekly in the gaol theatre and, in fact, the Nips have ordered a 'Command Performance' of 'Autumn Crocus'. I cannot somehow imagine an audience of Nips making head or tail of it. Am rereading Alexander Woollcott's 'While Rome Burns'.

This morning I was amongst those harnessed to the urine cart. This consists, like all the other trailers, of an old army truck chassis with a tank from an old petrol tanker. Urine is now very valuable for the soil. We use it diluted 50% with water.

The whole camp is becoming more and more ARP conscious, we should rejoice at the possibility that something will soon start happening here, but in fact we resent it for disturbing our daily routine. ARP officers are being appointed for each hut and a so-called dispersal area has been allotted to us just outside the wire. 'Dispersal' is hardly the right name for it, since practically the entire officers' area has to concentrate there in the event of an air raid. It is depressing to think that I have, throughout this war, always been on the receiving end of air attacks. First of all the Luftwaffe in England in those far off and, in retrospect, pleasant days of 1940, then later the Nip Air force during the fighting in Singapore and now the combined British and American air forces. One can only hope that our intelligence is better than one imagines, since there would be the most ghastly slaughter if the gaol were ever hit.

25 October 44 Some more mail has arrived and I have received a card from home dated 17 May 44. This is very quick. Some people even received photographs. There was trouble on P Party yesterday and two Australians were brought back in handcuffs. I suppose they had been stealing. I am now reading Negley Farson's 'Behind God's Back'.

27 October 44 Donald and I paid a visit to John Olley, Bags Baughan and James Moody yesterday evening. Rumour of a move to Johore has reared its head again. Another 70 bags of mail have arrived at the gaol.

29 October 44 Reading H G Wells 'Mr Britling sees it Through', and three plays by Eugene O'Neill, 'The Emperor Jones', 'Anna Christie' and the 'Hairy Ape', I must try and get hold of his others to read: 'Strange Interlude', 'Days Without End' and 'Gold Beyond the Horizon'. Several cables have been received in the camp. One dated last Tuesday only five days old. Sunday morning was spent, as usual, hauling the urine tank wagon to the gardens. The officers' gardens only receive this valuable load once per week. The remainder of the time it goes to the main OR's gardens. In the afternoon I rested and read O'Neill, as I only had a loan of it for the afternoon.

31 October 44 It rained heavily this morning and we were unable to work in the gardens. We were out this afternoon, however, but it was very hot and sticky. Kerr in bed with bronchitis. He is having rather a bad time and spends about three hours every night, sitting up on his bunk, trying to get enough air. I seem to be very much better these days and must be more tolerable to live with. Donald extremely depressed last night. He hits the depths more deeply than any of us. During our 'tea breaks' on the gardens we often have very interesting discussions. Bruno Brown, a Ghurkha officer and in peace time a tea planter in Assam, Major Standish of the 22nd Mountain Regt., Rawl Knox, son of the editor of 'Punch', Terry Wright, Ken Archer, Donald and myself. Ken is always cheerful and ready to laugh and is consequently a great asset. He is secretary of the Selangor Turf Club in happier days. We sit round an empty compost pit, smoking dried papaya leaves and drinking black, heavily smoked tea and it is the time of day I enjoy most. It creates the pleasant feeling that one has accomplished something constructive and one can sit down and rest before continuing. This afternoon, the Nips have been doing machine gun drill on the padang. Am re-reading 'For Whom the Bell Tolls'. I find it very important that one's reading should be stimulating and not just anodyne, but this depends very much on what books are available.

1 November 44 Two Australians caught flogging rice over the wire at 10 dollars a pound. The Australians excel at crime here. Out of 20 men undergoing sentence, 18 are members of the AIF. We are all steadily becoming more neurotic as the days go by. People tend to fly off the handle on the slightest provocation. Futile arguments and petty bickering are rife and it becomes increasingly evident that we are losing our sense of proportion.

2 November 44 Postcard from Denison with news of various mutual friends in the services and it is good to hear that they are all right, although the news is more than a year old now. No word of Diana. I often think of her with her lovely golden hair and her happy laugh. I dream of the evenings when we used to drive down through Worcester to Shuthonger Manor and dine and dance together until dawn bade us return, she home before starting work on the farm and I to 18 Div HQ at Ribbesford House and the cold discomfort of an English wartime officers' mess and having to sleep in Nissen Huts with very little heating.

I wonder if she ever thinks of me any longer and how she is coping with farm work, which even when I first knew her was very tough, particularly as she has a very petite figure and is not all cut out for hard physical work. Probably she has forgotten my existence, human memory is short and I fear that my own recollection of her is becoming dimmed by distance and time.

5 November 44 Guy Fawkes Day. A dull morning with high stratus cloud, giving way to occasional bright patches of sky. The brownout siren sounded on the gaol at 9.45 am and in the distance we could hear the bark of an AA gun. There was another and another and the shell bursts could be picked out quite easily as the puffs of smoke began to be dispersed by a light wind. Then somebody at the door of the hut shouted that there was a plane appearing from amongst the bursts of AA fire. We all crowded round the door of the hut and, almost as an afterthought on the part of the Nips, they sounded the 'raiders overhead' siren. A second and then a third plane appeared suddenly from behind a thick cloud. AA fire increased in intensity but from the position of those watching on the ground, the bursts appeared to be too low and some distance behind the plane. We estimated that the latter must be flying at over 20,000 ft. As the firing eased off for a moment, a close formation of eight planes broke into view following exactly the same course as the first aircraft. It was some time before we realised that this was no longer a practice but our first full scale air raid.

This was the moment we had all been waiting for for the best part of three years and it seemed incredible that it had arrived at last. In all we counted 45 four-engine planes, all of which came in from the direction of the naval base and then turned North, following the same course, like a game of follow-my-leader. They flew over in groups of four or six and only three turned south in the direction of Keppel Harbour. As they came over the camp we could plainly see their staggered wings and four engines, the noise of their motors hardly reaching us. Off to the north we could hear cannon fire and we presumed that Nip fighters had gone up to the attack. The planes appeared to be searching for shipping but, if any bombs were dropped on the Naval Base or Keppel Harbour, we did not hear them. An AA shell fell in the dysentery ward, crashing through a green metal locker between two beds and burying itself ten feet under the ground. It fortunately did not explode and the two men on the beds on either side had a narrow escape. Assuming there were ten men in each plane, there must have been between 400 and 500 men several miles above us, who this evening will be back at their base, discussing their first raid over Singapore over a well-earned drink. At long last we felt some contact with the outside world. Takahashi's sole comment: "It was only practice". For a Nip he has a very keen sense of humour and knows how to talk with his tongue in his cheek. For the rest of the day the excitement throughout the camp was intense.

12 November 44 Armistice Day yesterday. Somehow I find this a little out of date and wonder what will be done after this war? I suppose we shall have one bigger and better Armistice Day for Wars 1 and 2. None of our own bugle calls were allowed but the Nips allowed us to blow the Temple Call from the roof of the gaol. This was quite effective. I do not see that it matters whose call is played so long as it sounds good, which it did, as it was played four times, to the North, South, East and West.

Today, Sunday, there was a combined service for all denominations except, of course, for the Catholics, who remained aloof. We have been working hard on the gardens during the last few days. Out at 9.30 in the morning and back at 4.30 pm, a long day under present conditions.

Donald and I now take out our midday rations regularly to avoid a long walk to the camp and back. Lunch is not a very edifying meal these days and is usually eaten in strained and oppressive silence. The evening rice is eaten in slightly more cheerful circumstances as by then we have usually had the 'Canary' or 'Pipe' as the radio news is called, and this naturally stimulates a lot of interest although the war, from our point of view, could hardly be going more slowly. However there is the feeling that yet another day is over and we are another 24 hours nearer freedom. To return to the gardens. Donald and I are given a couple of small rice rissoles each, over which have been waved for a second or two the rotting remains of a Malayan fish. This imparts, as Shakespeare said in another context, to the rissole "a very ancient and fishlike smell", which by the time we get down to our midday meal has also become slightly sour. With these two doubtful looking objects we have a finger-full of rice and a few raw leaves of Ceylon spinach, picked from the garden. This we regard as being quite a high class lunch. The fact that we have leaves with our midday rice has got back to the camp and is already the subject of much caustic comment in certain quarters, from which one has long since expected it to come. After lunch we have 3/4 hour of peaceful, uninterrupted reading before starting work once more. A very sore throat three days ago and now a heavy cold has broken out and I am completely 'bunged up'. Have just finished Maugham's collection of short stories, 'The Cosmopolitans'.

13 November 44 Yesterday evening a party of Dutch arrived at the hospital from River Valley Camp. They had been removing detonators from the island to Johore and one case blew up killing several Chinese working with them. One Dutchman arrived dead and another died within a few minutes of arrival. The Nips seldom seem to take proper precautions either when dynamite is to be used, or weapons are to be cleared, to ensure the safety of POWs with the result that such deaths are completely unnecessary. It is all incredibly sad. The Camp is to take in 300 sick Dutch civilians, who have been working on some small island not far from Singapore. This particular party (this sort of thing is getting rather monotonous now) started off 1100 strong and now there are only 80 men fit to do any work. The first batch of 55 sick arrived yesterday in quite original style. They were brought to within a few yards of the shore in a launch and were then told to get out and wade ashore. It is said that there are two Norwegians in the party, so the camp is becoming more and more cosmopolitan.

The first issue of the new paper 'Here Today' will be in circulation in a day or two. It consists of articles, short stories and book reviews and promises to be the best camp periodical by a long way. It's editorial staff consists of Jackie Lewis, Kerr, Donald, Charles Charlton (on the editorial staff of the 'Times of' India), and Rawl Knox. The latter once told us how his father, as editor of Punch, would not allow him, for reasons that are fairly obvious, to write articles for the journal. Rawl refused to be beaten by this and submitted articles under a 'nom de plume'. Every now and again, his Father would recognise his son's style, and he was forced to adopt a fresh 'nom de plume'. A short while ago we received an issue of English tobacco from Singapore. It amounted to about 450 lbs. The Sgt in charge of the tobacco factory promptly thieved 50lbs of it. Every damn thing in this camp is crooked. Almost without exception those in responsible positions take advantage of it. Fortunately the Sgt was caught and given 90 days in the detention compound. Here we have a prison within a prison! Have been reading Ambrose Bierce's short stories, 'In the Midst of Life' and am now embarking on Heinrich Mann's 'Berlin'. Have also got hold of a 'History of Europe during the Revolutionary and Napoleonic Eras' by Grant and Temperley.

15 November 44 Two letters yesterday, one from Mother dated 30 Aug 1943 when I was at Sonkurai in Siam (what a contrast) and one from Nina Archer Thomson, both over a year old. Half-day only on the gardens today. Spent the time collecting human manure from the 'farm' for the new brinjal bed. A delightful occupation. The farm consists of a septic tank, where the raw shit undergoes some sort of treatment and is then passed into a tank. Here it rests on the top of large stones, which allows the moisture to drain away. The more valuable part is left and dries into a fibrous looking cake. For our purposes, however, we require something pretty rich. We therefore collect it, when it is still in a fairly raw state, when it is dark green in colour and has a smell to match. As it gets lower in the tank, we are forced to give up using a chungkol from the edge and have to get down into it – in our bare feet, of course – and pass it up in cans.

This took quite a bit of doing at first, but we have soon got used to it and, surprisingly, there developed, in time, fierce competition to do the dirtiest and most stinking job. The only times we used to rebel was when we returned to camp to find that the water had been turned off! This manure was, needless to say, the most valuable thing we had for the garden. Every week and every day are again becoming increasingly difficult. Short tempers, lack of any sense of proportion, futile arguments, intolerance of each other, until I wonder how much longer we can continue. The tolerance which we all learnt in the early days, and came to value so highly, has now been forgotten. Some of us still have our sense of humour, though I have no doubt this is very diminished. During the past few days I have known the deepest and blackest depression since our days in Siam. Up country, we were confronted with a sense of complete and utter hopelessness, so intense that our senses were completely numbed to the point where whether we lived or died no longer had any significance and, at times, death seemed to be preferable. It is impossible to keep up any degree of continual anticipation of eventual freedom; it wells up within one from time to time only to recede again, leaving one in complete dejection. Out with Kerr and Donald to the gardens and we discussed at length how infinitely adaptable the human body is, providing there is the necessary positive mental outlook. I am convinced the two go hand in hand. This is amply borne out in this camp. Whilst it is obviously not by any means a generalisation, in most cases fit minds equal fit bodies. I have just finished reading Heinrich Mann's 'Berlin'.

19 November 44 Air-raid warning, brownout, sounded shortly after 10.00 am. today. The all-clear sounded about an hour later but there was no sign of any activity. Nip fighters patrolling very far up in clear blue sky.

Am much enjoying Prince Lieven's 'The Birth of the Ballet Russe'. Now that I have read it, I feel I have missed a lot by not paying more attention to ballet before the war and I hope I shall be able to make up for it when I get back. I am still very nervy and am beginning to suffer from claustrophobia in the hut. Four feet three inches space including the width of one's bed is beginning to tell on all of us. One constantly lives in other people's pockets. I am greatly helped by spending from 9.30 am to 5.00 pm out on the gardens, where I can obtain a sense of relative freedom.

For the first time since a canteen was started in Changi in 1942 we are completely without smoking material, which does not help our mental stability. It looks as though we may have a smokeless Christmas, which is going to be pretty dim. In any case, the meals we are getting now I could eat three times over without the slightest difficulty. Bulk has gone down even further owing to a reduction in the amount of tapioca root coming into the camp. Also soya beans are due to finish at the end of this month and then we shall have no more tempeh.

22 November 44 Have finished Lieven's book and am now reading Santayana's 'The Last Puritan'. He is a new name to me. Kerr tells me that he is a professor at Harvard and is of Spanish extraction, as his name suggests. A lone B29 appeared over the camp, flying in from the North and circling over this end of the island, leisurely, impudent. It turned to Keppel Harbour, then in the midst of sporadic AA fire slowly headed southward and disappeared against the evening sun. The four engines and long staggered wings stood out clearly against the early evening sky. As on the two previous occasions, on which planes have appeared, we first heard the AA fire followed by the noise of the engines and finally the sound of the sirens coming in as a bad third. There were no fighters in the air at the time. It is very noticeable now that, whenever an allied plane is heard, there is an excited buzz of conversation throughout the camp, heads crowding gaol windows behind the bars accompanied by light-hearted cheering when the siren eventually sounds. This makes the Korean guards livid with rage.

I have now been appointed to the exalted – and ridiculous – position of 'Hut Commander'. This does not entail any arduous duties and as far as I can see merely consists of trying to settle the many childish squabbles of one's fellow officers. We are still intensely busy on the gardens and during the last fortnight our officers' gardens have produced over 3 1/2 tons of vegetables, chiefly bayam, Ceylon spinach, and red amarynth. It is now months since I heard any music and it does not seem likely that we shall get any more. Personal antipathies and domestic squabbles become more and more frequent and all find it increasingly difficult to control their frayed tempers, slanging matches being heard every day all over the camp. Senior officers are certainly no exception.

26 November 44 Sunday and the end of yet another insufferable week. Gardening every day. Without this physical exercise I would surely have qualified for a mental home long ago. Books read. 'The Last Puritan' and 'The Life and Letters of Sir Edmund Gosse', the latter by Evan Charteris. I came across a depressing definition of love in Santayana's book, put into the mouth of the character Jim Darnley; "What is love-making but a recurring decimal, always identical in form and always diminishing in value".

Two battleships, one cruiser and seven destroyers have entered the Naval Base during the last few days. What a target; where are the B29s?

Donald and I spent the whole of yesterday collecting excreta from the septic tank in 'Shit Farm'. The tank consists of a concrete container approximately 20ft long by 12ft wide, into which the excreta is pumped. Here they are allowed to settle while the moisture is drained out beneath. The shit is from 2 to 4ft beneath the top of the concrete tank, has the consistency of oily mud and has a powerful smell. Donald says it is an acquired smell, but I don't agree. We shovel the excreta into cans which are then either carried directly onto the gardens or their contents are decanted into a wheel barrow. One is lucky if one finishes up a day's 'shit shovelling' with only a few splashes on one's legs and arms.

Preparations for Christmas. Cake for twelve of us: Ingredients 4lbs maize flour, 1lb sago flour for binding purposes, (for binding the cake not, I trust, ourselves), 2lbs gula malacca, 2 coconuts, and some rice to increase bulk. This is going to cost us a total of about $36, or $3 per head.

Prices keep going up and there is very little to buy. The rations steadily decline and the word 'bulk' looms larger in our lives than ever before. Our hut is now infested with rats. They live in the atap roof and we hear them scampering about, squealing, during the night, they even nibble our soap, so I assume they must be as hungry as we are. To the Dutch half-castes a rat is worth $1. I think they are the only ones in the camp who are prepared to eat them. Letters very slow in coming out of the gaol. They are said to be held up by Takahashi who was recently on the bottle again.

Donald and I are wondering how we can get booze for Christmas; I'd give anything to get drunk one evening and forget everything for a few hours. Some people, who have flogged watches and cashed cheques with black marketers are distilling alcohol from gula malacca, at present $5 per pound. The present rate of exchange is said to be one dollar to the pound and now is said to have dropped to 85 cents. This will buy one part of a coconut or just two cheroots. We are very badly off for smoking materials and it looks as though we may have a smokeless Christmas. It is not until one has to go without something that one realises what a slave to it one has become. Strong rumours again that a Red Cross ship is due in shortly. One ship-load would solve all our troubles until our release.

27 November 44 Brownout sounded at 12.30 today. Blackout sounded about one hour later and lasted about one and a half hours. No allied bombers seen but Nip fighter patrolling over the end of the island throughout the period of the alert. A bright sunny day, blue sky broken up by regular shaped lumps of cumulus. Rain somewhere up-country perhaps. Visited Eric Cruikshank yesterday evening and spent a very pleasant two or three hours discussing many topics. Smoked my first cheroot for quite a long time. We are still pretty well smokeless. Story of men in gaol having made so much money on P Party and on black-market that they can afford to employ other POW to work for them and even go out and represent them on working parties. Feeling very hungry these days.

Have just got Lin Yutang's 'Moment in Peking' out of the library. Unfortunately one of those local editions printed on very cheap paper and very tiring to read. However, it is often a case of 'faute de mieux'.

29 November 44 Another month has nearly passed. It is a hot sultry afternoon. Am sitting outside the hut, having just received our November pay, all of which is likely to be spent on a great endeavour to end Christmas Day with a replete belly. Not an easy thing to do since we are expecting nothing extra from the IJA and today the soya been issue ceases, and bulk is reduced once more. This is a great blow since the tempeh produced from the soya beans is about the only thing we have that has any flavour. It was always sufficient to give us one good tempeh pasty every day. There will be nothing to replace it. Last two days in gardens spent in 'bunding', one of the dullest forms of manual labour yet to come my way. This particular form of torture entails building small dams at intervals of ten to twenty feet depending on the contours of the ground between the rows of tapioca beds. These have to be remade whenever the heavy rains wash them away.

Another case of flogging drugs has occurred, the second in recent weeks. The culprit has received ninety days in the detention cells. Personally, I would willingly shoot anyone trafficking in medical supplies, as they are at least guilty of manslaughter, and it is for me quite the worst offence that can be committed under the circumstances here. Selling drugs may well – and up-country certainly has – led to the needless deaths of many. My Christmas budget is as follows: $4 for a Christmas cake for 12, $4 for 1lb of taogay, $6.40 for monthly mess, $8.50 for monthly contribution to women and children at Sime Road camp, $1 for 1/8lb of sugar for porridge for Christmas morning, $1.25 for 1/2lb gula malacca, $2.60 for five cheroots (very small), $1 towards batman's Christmas present. Total – $25.25. Our pay for the month is $30. The balance not already allotted will go on things such as coffee on Christmas morning and some more cheroots if available. The latter we rarely smoke as such in these difficult times. We cut them up and roll cigarettes from them. I think that it is going to be a lean Christmas this year, our third in captivity and I sincerely hope our last in prison. Just received a letter from Mother, dated 3 October 1943.

3 December 44 Rumours that all field officers are to move inside the gaol. I would not be surprised if we all have to move in eventually. The Italian officers are now allowed out once more, five at a time, for gardening during the day, or in the evenings until 10.00 pm. Pantomime opened at gaol theatre – said to be good. Col. Hutch has invited me to spend a fortnight with him when Harwood Harrison goes to Changi next month.

Harwood is a Suffolk MP. The change will do me good, particularly as I get on very well with old Hutch nowadays. Better than ever before.

Rumour that rice ration is to be cut by 2ozs per day, but no confirmation.

Several people are finding that their ankles are swelling up. Medical theory is that this is due to starvation and not to beriberi this time and it is therefore useless to give such cases rice polishings. What a Christmas we are going to have! Lin Yutang's 'Moment in Peking' was very enjoyable.

4 December 44 The 'senior naval officer's dog is suffering from beriberi and now has pneumonia; it cannot stand up and has to be carried around. Have got tinea in my crotch once again and so have to lay off gardening. Several serious cases in officers' wards. One beriberi case from whom 2 gallons of liquid have to be pumped at regular intervals of 2 or 3 days. One young man of 28 or so with cancer of the stomach, now only has a few days to live and knows it. I knew him in Changi in 1942. Very sad as he has got so far. Spent yesterday evening with Eric, discussed religion, novels, medicine after the war etc. We always cover a wide variety of subjects on these Sunday evenings.

5 December 44 Yesterday evening received four letters. Two from Mother dated 20 July and 6 August. One from Father dated 18 August and one from Denison dated 22. All 1943, written after receipt of my first postcard, sent on 20 June 1942. It has taken 2 1/2 years for me to receive acknowledgement of the receipt of a card. However it is better to have full-length letters than more up to date but less informative 25 word messages.

Reading F D Omany's 'South Latitude', being his account of the voyage of Discovery 11 to the Antarctic and the rescue of Elsworth. Have also taken out of the library Joseph Heigersheimer's 'The Limestone Tree'. Since receiving these four letters, one from each member of the family, I have indescribable nostalgia and yearning for home. I weighed myself again yesterday, still 159lbs the same as on 18 October and must be full of liquid still. The following from

Omany's 'South Latitude' is very applicable – "It is personal idiosyncrasies, the little mannerisms and habits that people have, their nervous ticks which drive one almost to insanity. It is not so much the hardship or lack of comfort, or a pain in the foot, or hope deferred making the heart sink. It is listening to the other man or even the Archangel Gabriel puffing at his pipe, or listening to him sniff, or rattle the pages of an old newspaper, or move restlessly about the tiny room. And there is something maddening about the way other people go to bed. Nothing is so individual or expressive as the nightly routine with which a man prepares himself for rest. It is a wonder that no one has ever been shot for the way he cleans his teeth. The silences are filled with irritating and antagonistic sounds. The trivial sounds of someone else doing something for the 100th time". This is an admirable summing up of what really annoys me about the way others behave and indeed I could almost shoot some of my fellow POWs for the way they get up in the mornings.

8 December 44 The third anniversary of the outbreak of the Japanese war. Everybody expects there to be a raid today but I think we shall be disappointed; nothing will ever happen here. I am quite prepared to spend Christmas 1945 in Changi. Current reading; 'The Nine Days' Queen' by Richard Davey about Lady Jane Grey and her times. Very good. I was struck by the following, repeated by Katharine Parr at her wedding to Henry VIII: "To be bonny and buxom in bed and at board till death us do part'. I think I shall have that put in when I am married, if the marriage is to take place in a church. It would cause such a stir and relieve the general boredom of the service. Much enjoyed Heigersheimer's 'The Limestone Tree'. A novel woven into the political history of Kentucky up to the years following the civil war. Interruption by several people, including Donald and Kerr, who had saved a couple of pasties from the evening meal until 10.00 pm; an anti-social habit and thoroughly unpleasant for everybody within smelling distance. One is quite hungry enough without being reminded of it in this fashion. Also, as I have already said, I could almost kill a man for the way he gets into bed and the way he brushes his hair, or looks at himself in the mirror. But we are all guilty of these faults.

9 December 44 Captain Clibourne died yesterday and the funeral takes place today. Large crowd of officers. Full compliments paid by IJA guards and sentries and Takahashi was present. He took off his hat and, advancing to the grave bowed and said a few words in Japanese. Rumours have it that we are to get 4oz extra rice, 40gms soya beans, some oil and salt. This will not do much more than increase that all important thing called bulk; quantity is more important than quality here.

24 December 44 Christmas Eve. Great excitement, not over Christmas but because we are at last to be allowed to send a 25 word cable. The first batch is due to go off today and I hope to send mine the day after tomorrow. Not a bad effort. It has taken the Red Cross three years to fix this up.

25 December 44 Christmas Day. Greeted at 9.00 am by a breakfast consisting of a pint of porridge, and sweet coconut sauce, angel on horseback (fried fish on a biscuit) and soya bean bread with lime jam, 1/2 pint of coffee and tea. Everybody in great form with much coming and going with people wishing each other a happy Christmas, particularly on the opposite side, where the Australians are, with their habit of shaking hands.

This was imitated ad lib by everybody over on our side. At 10.00 am Fitz, Peter, Kerr and I went into the gaol, which was open to the officers all day today, to see the Divisional HQ men. We found quite a few of them – Ludman, Simkins, Clark, Blench (our SSM) etc, joined later by Hutch and Whiskers. Morale in the gaol is terrific; if the troops could have been given rifles and bayonets, they would not have been stopped by anybody and would have reached Burma. I have certainly never seen our troops in better form. What a comparison with last year. We next visited the Italians, who were extraordinarily cheerful and very hospitable, showering cups of tea and cakes on us. We did not get back home until nearly 1.00 pm to find a savoury bun waiting for us. Saw Eric and Colonel Pratley, amongst others. Lunch consisted of taogay soup, sweet potato pie, adzuki bean pasty, vegetable pie, savoury tart, cheese savoury and a sweet. The cheese, almost running, had been issued by the Nips quite unexpectedly, half an ounce per man. The IJA also came across with 6 cheroots per man. At tea we had a large slab of Christmas cake. The interval between lunch and tea filled up by a visit to John, Eric and Webby for coffee, with which we had santan.

After tea I took half an hour off to conserve my strength for the evening meal. At 6.30 pm dinner consisting of taogay soup, fried whitebait, fried soya bean, sautéed sweet potatoes, greens, savoury cutlet. Followed by fish rissoles and tempeh pie, an excellent duff and sweet sauce with a lime jam tart. Coffee. A terrific meal, I was quite defeated. Hutch very merry all day. In the evening drank coffee and had mince pie, extraordinarily well made with taogay, lime peel etc. To bed for a very disturbed night. At about 12.00 midnight, a Christmas Eve visit by Peter May.

26 December 44 I sent in my 25 word cable which runs as follows:- "Mail to July. Letters Katherine, Nina received. Health spirits good. Occupied gardening, swimming. Any news Diana? Her last letter August 1942. Fondest love, thoughts, Harold".

WAR DIARY

January 1945 to September 1945

∽

2 January 45 Another year over, thank God! Yesterday, New Year's Day – a holiday. An extra rissole and some lime jam for breakfast. A normal, dull lunch, dinner very similar to that eaten on Christmas Day. All this extra food was a complete surprise. We also had a savoury turn-over in the evening. New Year's Eve, John, Whiskers, Fitz and Stevie came round.

Hutch and I produced coffee and a cake, excellently made by Cpl Chandler. As a matter of interest the cake recipe was as follows;- 1lb maize flour, 1 1/2lbs sago flour, 1 coconut, grated and squeezed into a santan, 1/2 a marmite jar of oil, 1 1/2lbs of gula malacca. Result highly successful. The previous night sat up to watch partial eclipse of the moon at 00.15 hours. We did not see much. Yesterday had tea with Eric and Webby. John came in later having been busy with sigmoidoscopies – 31, he said, that afternoon. He and Major Hunt, AAMC, have to test everybody known to have had amoebic dysentery. Cyril Wild returned yesterday afternoon from 'I' lines, while Eric Hinde came down for 3 weeks from the hut, during the time that Harwood Harrison is at Kranji. So we are now four instead of two which Hutch and I had enjoyed for two or three days. Basketball game yesterday pm. United States versus Australians. The latter won; much barracking from AIF supporters.

Gardening again this morning. Delightful weather, bright sunshine and a really cool breeze. Unfortunately very rare for this Changi climate. Koreans said to have received comfort parcels, each consisting of a yo-yo, one Chinese lantern and candle, a jig-saw puzzle .The latter very crude, unpainted and when assembled represented a tank. One Korean said to have been seen stamping on his lantern in a furious temper. I almost feel sorry for the Koreans; they do not really have much of a life with their Nip masters.

4 January 45 Brownout sounded Tuesday pm on aerodrome. Gaol siren not sounded. Busy on garden digging up sweet potatoes – very poor yield. General Shaito and Lieut. Takahashi's drivers said to be chief fences in camp black market activities. Have been spending evening talking German with Captain Grapallo, who was telling us about the Allied landings (aborted after two days' fighting) at Bordeaux. There were actually two landings, one at La Palisse and one at the mouth of the Gironde. He also mentioned that the occasion of the allied raid on Dieppe, where at that time the Germans had a very small garrison, marked the first and last time that Frenchmen assisted the German army in pushing the allied troops back into the sea. For the active assistance, which took France by surprise and which quite shocked the country, Hitler freed all French POW from German camps, who belonged to the Dieppe area. A great reception was held for them in Paris, members of the Vichy government, the Mayor of Paris, and numerous high German officers being present.

We also heard about the so called 'Blitzmaedchen', attached to the German army in France and who were responsible for communications. Grapallo went on to say that the Germans only had approximately 400 AFVs in the whole of France in 1942, some Landwehr battalions and only two regiments in the Bordeaux area. Practically the whole of the German army was then concentrated in Russia and the Balkans. Von Reichenau and von Brauchitsch regarded as Germany's two finest Generals. One of the Blitzmaedchen on the German staff in Bordeaux was blonde, 18 and beautiful and had been the German woman tennis champion. Altogether rather a bizarre conversation when time, place and our peculiar circumstances are taken into account. Cyril Wild leaving quarters tomorrow to join 'Daddy Heath' (Lieut Gen Heath, Corps Commander) permanently in Formosa.

6 January 45 Listened to Major Withers-Paine's first lecture of a series of six on 'Heraldry'. Rather an esoteric subject, but having a certain fascination. No gardening in morning as Nips turned us all back. Appears that they were firing light automatics on the padang.

7 January 45 Spent morning cooking. Eric Hinde, Hutch and I decided to make ourselves a pie for lunch. For this purpose we used about 1lb of taogay, 1lb sweet-potatoes – two dollars per pound from the canteen. The taogay we flavoured with two bulbs of garlic, three chillies and some curry powder. Potatoes were mashed up with a small amount of taproot and these we spread over the taogay mixed with one pint of breakfast porridge to form a crust. The result after twenty minutes baking was successful.

The latter half of the morning Donald and I spent coffee drinking with Peter Coope, Charles Charleton, and Jacky Lewis in the Indian Army lines. It was pleasant to taste coffee made from canteen purchased coffee beans at $8 a pound instead of the usual burnt rice, sweetened with gula malacca. We all sat under a large jack-fruit tree at the end of their hut.

8 January 45 Made garden stew in the morning. This should have been for Christmas, but was a little 'en retard' due to prolonged efforts, eventually not in vain, to obtain official sanction from the

OC Officers group, Camp Office and Lieut. Takahashi. A very good stew it was too. It consisted of sweet potatoes, brinjals, byam, Ceylon spinach, artichokes, ginger, coconut beans, chillies, and taproot. It worked out at roughly a pint per man and one of the most delicious things we've had for a considerable time. Sitting down to lunch we were greeted by the joyful sound of ack-ack fire and sirens combined. Shortly afterwards a solitary plane, far away towards the northwest, appeared out of the cloud flying NNE. Rumours today of the camp splitting up with the AIF staying here, which perhaps is not surprising, since the camp originated with the antipodeans. The Dutch are said to be going to Kotatingi and the British to Kuala Lumpur.

10.00 pm; went to a musical show in the gaol theatre. First part consisted of a swing band and the second, Mitchel and his Serenaders, playing Hungarian, Viennese and Spanish music. Ecoma, a Javanese half- caste and a professional, danced a tango and a waltz extremely well. He has now established himself as the leading 'female' dancer in the camp. He certainly has an outstanding technique and is amazingly graceful. The show was very well staged and directed. 'Tonight at 8.30' opens next week and after that comes a musical called 'Music through the Years' produced by Flight Sgt. Bill Williams. I have just returned Rose Macaulay's 'Dangerous Ages' and Bullitt's 'Uncensored Diary' to the library. For some reason I did not finish either. I am now reading Churchill's 'Into Battle' and Brown-Davies' 'The Anointed'.

10 January 45 I was working in the gardens this morning when the quiet was suddenly disturbed by a burst of ack-ack fire. We then picked out a plane flying eastwards and, when well out to sea, it banked steeply and headed off in the direction of Singapore. We saw the four engines and staggered wing of a B29. As the plane approached Singapore it was met by intense ack-ack fire, most of it low and far behind the target, as far as we could see. Shortly afterwards the sirens sounded a black-out.

Subsequently there has been a report from P Party to the effect that Monday's plane dropped three bombs near an aircraft carrier in the naval base hitting some lorries and killing some Indians there. One of the Nip guards on the gardens this morning, who speaks some English, told us he was homesick and we did not feel inclined to disagree with him. A Nip civilian visited the Americans the day before yesterday and it appears that he spent 22 years in Honolulu and the US, when at the outbreak of war he was interned in the Midwest. The area of the internment camp was ten miles in diameter and was wired in. He had excellent rations and was allowed a weekly visit on parole to the local town. He had his own drinks supply, long-wave radio and says he was much better off as an internee for 18 months than as a civilian attached to the Imperial Japanese Army. He apparently received between 50 and 60 US Dollars per month and was well treated throughout. He was repatriated in 1943.

One of the stories going the rounds today is that of the Assistant Chaplain General who is alleged to have sold his gold cigarette case for $1200, then cashed cheques to the value of £100 at the rate of $3 to the £. This caused so much adverse criticism that he has now torn the cheques up. It would appear that, perhaps at last, his conscience is catching up with him. Those signing the cheques were, apparently, made to add a statement on the back covering the amount in the event of their death.

11 January 45 The brownout sounded shortly after we arrived in the gardens this morning and, just after returning to camp, which we have to do now in the event of a brownout, the blackout sounded. This was followed by ack-ack fire and the appearance of two B29s flying in from the north. Several Nip aircraft could be seen circling low down, presumably to avoid being bombed on the ground. The weather conditions were ideal for any attacking force. High stratus cloud, with broken puffs of dark cloud well beneath, making fighter interception difficult. The first two bombers were followed at irregular intervals by others flying in twos and threes from different points of the northern sky. The majority headed in the direction of the naval base, some for Keppel harbour whilst one or two after flying over this end of the island turned back towards the north west, possibly looking for shipping. We estimate that upwards of fifty planes must have been employed in the raid. It was the most spectacular we have yet had. The bombers leisurely making their way across the sky, the white and black puffs of the ack-ack bursts looking like large parachutes hanging in the sky, while the angry buzz of the fighters, of which there were not many, could be plainly heard above the bursting ack-ack.

Occasionally, bursts of machine gun fire broke into the general din and now and again a loud explosion from the direction of the naval base, heavier than the ack-ack, suggested that bombs were falling. There was a general buzz of excited conversation from everybody standing in groups in front of their quarters, fingers pointing every time another bomber was sighted. These visits by allied planes have a very cheering effect on us all, but for my part I find them unsettling too. I think of all the men above, about 500 this morning I suppose, all returning to India or Ceylon or wherever their bases may be, taking off their flying kits on landing and having made their reports, walking over to the mess for a drink and a meal. Many, I do not doubt, have dates with their girlfriends this evening and as I sit reading in a hard uncomfortable chair with the silent stars overhead, wondering when it will all be over, they will be eating, dancing and drinking under the same stars, stars which to them must seem infinitely friendly. The most important thing is to control one's imagination and not to allow it to run away with one.

Yesterday evening we went to see Peter's production of 'Three Men on a Horse' with an all American cast including Joe Menella, Bagett, Callagher, and various others. Callagher has an accent that could be cut with a blunt knife. It was a great success and caused great amusement. I was thinking to myself, yesterday, what an incredibly restricted and damaging life this has been. Three years without any responsibility whatsoever, nothing that can possibly help one in post-war life. All the days, weeks, months, and years with nothing to think about or consider but myself. How disgustingly egotistical we shall all seem. Nothing but this constant concentration on the 'I', the 'Me', the only person of real importance in the community. None of the men who die here, none of the thousands of dead left behind up-country mean a damn thing to me anymore. I am the only one who matters at all and I seem to matter a hell of a lot. It means everything that I should get enough to eat, that I should keep fit, if I can, and that I should return safely.

Thursday evening; one B29 is reported to have been shot down and between three and five Nip fighters destroyed.

12 January 45 Two Australians were brought in to camp with bomb splinter wounds suffered in yesterday's raid. They are from Hamilton Force. Reports from P Party indicate that one B29 and at least one Nip fighter were seen to have been shot down. The B29 received what appeared to be a direct hit from 'flaming onions' over Johore. The fuselage broke away from the wings with the engines catching fire. The fighter on his tail must also have been hit as he plunged earthwards, crashing about a mile from where a truckload of Q Party were sheltering in a drain by the side of the main road north of

Johore. We find ourselves suffering from quite a reaction to yesterday's raid. The effect of such raids is very marked. They lift one up to such a pitch of excitement and anticipation that one half expects somebody to come along and release us. Twenty-four hours later, one returns to the same uninterrupted vista of the dull routine of life as a POW. Am much enjoying D H Lawrence's short stories, though I shall have to rush in order to get through them in the time allotted. I am becoming rather tired of the inescapable bridge and poker conversations – the post-mortems on the former being particularly annoying. Thank God I don't play cards. Bridge is played by a large proportion of the camp, afternoon, evening and night, and in some cases in the morning also. I regard cards at the moment as an invention of the devil.

16 January 45 What appeared to be a plane on reconnaissance came over the camp at 11.30 am on Sunday, The brownout and blackout sirens followed in quick succession and we thought we heard bombs drop but could not be sure. The plane was at an immense height, with its vapour trails plainly visible way up in the sky. We spent last Saturday afternoon making a sambal with the following recipe: 1lb of blachang, 4 bulbs garlic, 3/4oz chillies. I first pounded the chillies into a fine powder then cut the garlic up and crushed it, fried the garlic in palm oil, enough to cover the bottom of a pan, then added blachang and chilli powder.

Fried until well mixed and stored in Marmite jars; the result was not at all bad. Sunday morning I again spent cooking, this time making a pie consisting of 2lbs of taproot, boiled and mashed, about 4oz of taogay, boiled for 3/4 of an hour, then poured off the water, used as soup for the evening meal, and added 1 pint of breakfast rice porridge with garlic and a couple of chillies. This was put into a baking dish and covered with taproot to form a crust. This I had mixed with a little palm oil after mashing. It was baked in the oven for 20 minutes with very good results. Needless to say all this food is not bought by me since I have no money but by Eric Hinde, who cashed a cheque a week or two ago. I am, in fact, broke and have been for a week now and expect, as a result, to be smokeless until the end of the month. What a life! Although the canteen's cheroots and cigarettes are barely worth smoking, it is hell to be without them and one feels much hungrier, when one cannot take the edge off one's appetite by smoking.

The Nips seem to have been having a form of ARP exercise during the past few days; transport in dispersal bays camouflaged with palm fronds. Staff cars have been seen going to and from the aerodrome, also with camouflage nets over their windscreens with branches etc. They seem to be expecting something. The Nips have apparently picked up a note in Half Moon Street written by somebody in the camp to a Chinese on the subject of the exchange of a thousand Dutch Guilder note for Singapore Dollars.

Lt. Takahashi stated this evening that unless the man, who wrote the note, owns up the whole camp will be punished and the canteen will be closed down. This is typical of the IJA. Punish 10,000 men for the misdeed of one. The closing of the canteen will in any case not affect me – not until the end of the month. Have just finished D H Lawrence's 'St Manier' and 'The Captain's Doll'. Both very good. He is certainly a master of the short story, although both these are more like short novels, each being over a hundred pages in length. We are all wondering if any more mail will arrive and I am still living in hopes that I will receive a reply to the cable written a week or two ago. Perhaps ours have not even left Singapore yet.

19 January 45 I was weighed again today and have lost six pounds since 4 December, now being 153lbs, which suggests that I am successfully losing some of the excess fluid caused by beriberi. Both yesterday and today we have been busy putting compost on the vegetables, although our work was pleasantly interrupted by the presence of Donald Wise, Peter Coope and Bruno Brown, since we spent most of the time sitting around the edge of the compost pit talking. There was trouble the day before yesterday with the Nips. Firstly a man on the aerodrome was kept out late as the Nip in charge of his party was dissatisfied with his output, and secondly an OR belonging to the Argyles has been missing for the past two days. Furthermore P Party returned with more than 1400 dollars' worth of cheroots and all buying in Singapore has now been stopped. The trouble over the 1000 Dutch Guilder note, referred to three days ago, was apparently caused by an Australian Major. Fortunately it seems to have blown over. Two evenings ago the gaol show was stopped half way through for no obvious reason, but it may have something to do with the report that the daughter (or is it wife?) of General Shaito's driver is said to have an Australian bun-in-the-oven. It is said that she is going around proudly patting her stomach and saying "Australian number one". This is said to be particularly galling to Shaito, who has been trying to 'make' the woman for the past year and has been beaten to it by a POW. Not bad going.

We have heard that a new wiring party started work some three days ago and are working two miles south of here, where the coast road enters a cutting, the work is said to have been ordered by Wakabayashi, who is the officer in charge of civilian internees at Sime Road. Nobody seems to know what the wire is for. Perhaps the civilians are to be moved back to this part of the Island? A twin-engine Nip fighter is reported to have crashed on the aerodrome a few days ago and we have also heard that a lot of shipping arrived in the harbour yesterday and that a very large battleship is at present in the naval base. Where are those B29s?

21 January 45 Reading Conrad's 'Under Western Eyes' and William Hazlitt's 'Essays and Characters'. Yesterday afternoon I attended the third lecture on heraldry. The subjects including 'sub ordinaries' and 'charges'. I have learned that there are no fewer than 358 different types of cross used in heraldry.

23 January 45 Am now reading C Edmond's, T E Lawrence's, and Brett Hart's short stories and have just read a symposium of 12 broadcast talks on science and religion published in 1931 and given by Julian Huxley, J Arthur Thompson, J S Haldane, E W Barnes, Professor B Melanovski, the Dean of Canterbury (Shepherd), Canon B H Streeter, Rev. C W O'Hara, Prof. Sir Arthur Eddington, Prof. S Alexander, Dean Inge, and Doctor L P Jacks. I found that Melanovksi's definition of agnosticism fits my case very closely. Today's camp gossip has it that an AIF officer tried to bribe a sentry, prior to pinching wood. He was caught and dealt with by Blackjack. The Argyle OR who disappeared has been recaptured in the vicinity of the mental hospital north of Paya Lebar. He is now in a cell in gaol. 'Tonight at 8.30' opened on Saturday evening. Oswald Daltry had done the production and I am hoping to see it on 12 February.

25 January 45 There was a brownout siren at 11.45 pm last night when there was bright moonlight. There was high cloud but unfortunately nothing happened. Planes appeared to be active in the vicinity of the aerodrome up to the time of the warning. Presumably practising night landing as they were flying round in circles. 250 men arrived today from River Valley Road camp.

Expenditure in the canteen for the past three months has exceeded income received by the camp by some 1/4 million dollars, which I suppose is an indication of how good trade has been. Unfortunately the canteen will have to be closed at least for a week or so and monthly purchases by the camp will have to be restricted in order to bring income and expenditure into balance again. All this will no doubt come as a severe blow to the Nips, who are responsible for purchasing from the Chinese traders, since they have no doubt made handsome profits in the well-established Asiatic way. Life continues dull, the weather is hot and we are all becoming very, very tired of each other. Next Thursday will be the 3rd anniversary of our landing on this god-forsaken island – a date to be forgotten as far as possible. Three more weeks and we shall be in the fourth year of this futile and aimless existence. God, when will it end? Surely we have not done anything to deserve very much more?

28 January 45 The blackout sounded at 2.30 am on Friday, We heard planes but it was impossible to say whether they were Nip or Allied. The sirens went again at about 11.45 when two B29s appeared from the North West. One turned towards the naval base and the other flew round this end of the island going off in the direction of Keppel harbour, presumably looking out for targets. Had a long conversation in the gardens during the morning break with Peter Coope, Denis Russell-Roberts, a charming regular army type and Rawl Knox. The Nips held an ARP exercise on Friday and Saturday, when two B29s appeared just before it was due to start. We are all wondering whether the softening up of Malaya, prior to big scale operations, has now started. We received our January pay yesterday but there is nothing to buy in the canteen, only salt at $3.60 per pound and tea. Even tooth-powder and soap have run out, the former never having let us down at all yet.

However, tooth-powder is now being manufactured in the camp out of wood ash. It is, I am told, a dirty grey in colour. There is nothing to smoke at present except cheroots, brought in by P Party which cost 50c each and are very hard to come by. P Party now bring in sugar and salt, usually concealed in their G Strings and arm pits. They have got their smuggling activities down to a fine art. The messing charge has gone up to $10 per month for Captains and above, and to $8 for Subalterns. This leaves us with $20 per month, which does not go far on present prices.

A ship of some 2,000 tons entering the naval base from the direction of Keppel harbour on Friday hit a mine off Pengerang Island. After circling twice in a sinking condition it made for Pengerang and beached itself. As it did so a second explosion occurred and clouds of steam were seen escaping. Rumour has it that mines were dropped by B29s last Thursday night. This would seem to be the only reason for allied planes coming over at night. I cooked another taogay/tap-root pie this morning and it was the best yet. We have received a report from River Valley Road camp that according to a Korean guard, who has recently returned from Thailand, Colonel Toosey of 135 Field Regiment was killed in an air raid on Nong Pladuk camp. We have no confirmation of this. It appears that the remainder of those in River Valley Road camp have gone by sea to Saigon, where they are said to be going to work on aerodrome construction. Am reading Sir Walter Citrine's 'My Finnish Diary' and 'The Great Victorians'. Our old friend the four-engined flying boat has been over again and we are consequently wondering if any more mail will arrive. Many people connect the delivery of mail with the appearance of this lumbering old plane. There is still no evidence that our cables have even left camp yet, let alone Singapore.

30 January 45 Yesterday morning the Korean guards had some sort of parade on the padang. Both Colonel Banno and Lt. Takahashi were present. The latter ordered us all back from the gardens. The Nips cannot stand being watched, at least by POWs, so most of us went down to have a bathe. It was a delightful morning, an overcast sky and pleasantly cool. A lone B29 came over this morning and the brownout sounded again but there was no ack-ack fire. We saw a tanker in the straits while bathing yesterday. Apparently it has been there some six days.

Padre Duckworth's church is being used for black market activities with men hiding behind the altar, whilst haggling over prices of Rolex watches with the Koreans. A typewriter, stolen from one of the offices the other day, was found under the pillow of an Australian in hospital before he had managed to dispose of it. There has been an enormous amount of rain lately and most of my time on the garden has been taken up by weeding. The experts say that it is a good sign, when there are lots of weeds as it indicates an improvement in the condition of the soil. God knows, the earth can certainly do with some improvement; it is very tired at present. Spent Sunday evening with Eric, most of the time being taken up by a long discussion on religion and our attitude to life. Eric's is an unmistakeably materialistic outlook and mine tending very much in that direction, though mixed with the vestiges of idealism from my adolescence, but I feel that little of this is left to me after my experiences of the past 5 years.

Yesterday evening, Cpl Paul Miller came round for a chat. He is in hospital after coming up from River Valley Road camp and used to be in our DIV HQ Cipher section. He was in the lst/5th Forresters having been in France with them in 1939/40.

3 February 45 Last Thursday we had the largest air-raid over Singapore to date and counted 86 planes. They all flew in over the Naval Base leaving in a north-easterly direction. They were a great sight, with the sun glinting on the wings and the four engines being quite visible on several of the planes as they turned and came over our end of the island. The first group consisted of four planes, followed by groups of 11, 10, 19 and 6. Three went over Changi aerodrome and we heard afterwards that they were chasing shipping leaving the Naval Base. The last three groups consisted of 7, 5 and 18 planes. After this there was a slight lull in the proceedings and the brownout sounded at 12.15 pm. The black-out had first been sounded at 11.15 am, so it was a busy hour or so. At 12.25 however, three more B29s suddenly appeared and were met by heavy ack-ack fire from the Naval Base area. The black-out was promptly sounded again and the final brownout was finally heard at 12.35. An exciting morning. Every time the thud of bombs was heard, which must have been anywhere from 10 to 15 miles away in the area of the Naval Base, a restrained but clearly satisfied cheer could be heard from the prisoners concentrated in the bowels of the gaol buildings. The Americans always give a running commentary to the other ranks looking out through the bars at the end of the corridors in the East block on the 2nd, 3rd and 4th floors. These windows have large weather flaps of concrete overhanging them and the wretched men inside cannot see anything above eye level. They, in turn, can be heard transmitting the account to their less fortunate comrades, who cannot get a position at the window. Both yesterday and today a reconnaissance plane has been over and we have now had planes overhead four days running as there was another one over on Wednesday, the day prior to the raid. It is noticeable how they always seem to pick ideal weather for a raid. Good visibility and high cloud.

Yesterday I made some very good pancakes out of breakfast porridge, a spoonful of sago flour, fried in a slightly oiled pan. We ate them at the evening meal with some sugar supplied by Harwood Harrison, who returned from Kranji the day before yesterday. James Bull, the radiologist, who fell into an ARP trench about six weeks ago and temporarily paralysed himself, is much better, although taking things slowly and is now able to sit up in bed and wash himself. He was earlier on the dangerously ill list. It is reported that we can expect the ration scale to be halved. This would mean going down to about 230gms of rice per man per day. Everything seems to point to a deterioration in the food situation in Singapore. I have heard that there is a '1000 Club' for ORs, qualification for membership being that a man has to be able to produce, on demand at any time, $1000 in cash. Now that Harwood is back, I get bridge from early afternoon to late evening and either bridge or sometimes poker after that. God, I am fed up with cards and Harwood is a positive menace as he talks about nothing else. However, I must try to be tolerant.

The wire around the camp is being doubled and it is said that when the whole perimeter has been completed with two lines of wire the whole thing is to be to be doubled again to four rows. Why, I cannot think, since escape is impossible. I have been swimming recently; three times in fact during the past week. Extremely pleasant to be down on the beach and it makes a liberating change from the camp environment. I usually go down with Peter Coope and sometimes Bruno Brown. Yesterday we actually managed to encourage Donald to come with us. 'Pygmalion' is to be performed in the officers' area. Fitz and Peter are in it, the former playing his usual female role! My stomach is giving trouble again, not quite so bad this time. Kerr is in hospital again. They think he may have appendicitis, pyelitis, (inflammation of the urinary tract), renal colic, and possibly food poisoning!

7 February 45 Two B29s over on Monday morning, another said to have flown over at 12.30 am yesterday. No alarms were sounded. Pleasant afternoon bathing on Monday, when I went down with Peter, Bruno, Charles Charleton and Donald. Robin Fletcher, who was also with us, had his right eardrum pierced by a flying fish skimming out to deeper water. Have just finished reading J M Thompson's 'Lectures in Foreign History 1494–1789'. They were given to first year undergraduates at Magdalene College, Oxford between 1921 and 1924. They are excellent, plenty to get one's teeth into and very lucid. They form an excellent basis for further reading, which I must do when I can again lay my hands on more books. I came across the following the other day, which appealed to me; 'Judge a man by his friends and a master by his servants'. John Morris delivered a lecture on Africa in Kranji camp the other day, after which a padre, Daniels by name, was heard saying "What right has that young fellow got to talk about Africa? He has never been there". To which the reply came "Padre, have you ever been to heaven?"

9 February 45 Bathed again yesterday morning. Apparently one of the ORs in the gaol in sending his last card, addressed it to Winston, 10 Downing Street, London, the message reading: "Dear Winnie, please prod Louis". I think that adequately reflects the feelings of all of us here.

I have been told that a motor tyre now fetches $10,000 in Singapore. Members of P Party, who have been issued with sacks to keep their clothes clean, sell the sacks to the Chinese at $2 a time. Eric Hinde went into hospital yesterday with beriberi. He has to go in, in order to qualify for his issue of rice polishings. He will probably be in for a week only.

I am now a complete 'bung', using a bottle, gardening and going around barefoot. I am told, incidentally, that the Pathans use stones and that when they embarked to come out here, they brought a supply of stones with them from the hills and the plumbing staff on board ship were suddenly faced with a rather novel stoppage in the drains. No doubt Pathans are tougher than we are and I trust I shall be free before I go any further down the scale.

Takahashi is threatening to stop us swimming. Whether this has anything to do with Robin Fletcher's ear being pierced when bathing the day before yesterday, is not known. It was apparently a particular species of flying fish, which has a very sharp point on its nose. When he was hit he thought someone had collided with him rather violently and swore at Bruno Brown who happened to be nearest. He was in great pain and bled profusely. The doctors say it will be two to three months before it heals up. Am now reading Malcolm Muggeridge's 'The Thirties' and am disappointed. It is funny at Ramsay MacDonald's expense. Ken Archer is now out of hospital and is at last showing signs of recovering.

11 February 45 A disappointing day since we had hoped for a raid but again we only saw one plane. Yesterday one had come over at midday and was engaged by fighters as it came overhead, machine-gun fire could be plainly heard, followed for the first time by the whiz and thump of spent bullets falling around us in the gardens. We all felt pretty naked, which of course we were in a pair of shorts and nothing else. After a running fight which seemed to last some minutes we saw the B29 flying along leisurely and quite unperturbed in the direction of Keppel harbour. These American planes seem to be more than a match for Nip fighters. Our rations were cut yesterday.

15 February 45 In another half-hour, at 4.00 pm, we shall have started on our fourth year of incarceration with still no sign of release. Comment would be superfluous. B29s are still coming over 4 to 5 times per week in their ones and twos. This morning, however, six appeared just before lunch, coming in from the north-west and heading over Changi out to sea. Shortly afterwards they returned. They flew very wide apart, the central ones directly overhead, the outside ones just visible far out to the north and south, bright silver in the sun against the clear azure sky, suddenly changing to black on a background of high white cloud.

Books read: Balzac's 'Eugenie Grandet' - Kerr Paxton considers it to be one of the best novels he wrote, 'Essays of the Year 1929–30', including Hilaire Belloc on spelling. Have also managed to borrow one of the American Red Cross books which are difficult to get hold of, the 'Epic of America' by James Adams. Only 100 of these books were received but this is certainly an improvement on our own Red Cross, who so far have achieved nothing. This is probably an unfair comment, since no doubt they have been doing their best. Three years is enough of this hopeless, brain-putrefying existence where 90% of the people in camp, when they are not actually playing, are either discussing bridge or poker or reading about the former in a book by that Cuthbertson couple. Harwood Harrison, known as the 'Pons Assinorum' or the 'Adenoidal Half-wit', now talks bridge and poker throughout the day when he is not playing, which, in fact, he does for at least 8 hours per day. Shooting or otherwise doing to death anyone of the calibre of 'Pons Assinorum' should be regarded as justifiable homicide.

17 February 45 Black-out sounded this morning. Took a couple of days off gardens due to stomach misbehaving itself. John Phillips came and had dinner (so called) last Wednesday. Have had a bad day with my stomach. Rained all day, felt thoroughly cold although wearing a sweater. Completed my misery by reading some of my letters from the family. If I am to have a thoroughly depressing day, I may as well do the thing properly and make myself feel completely nostalgic. Went to bed early feeling thoroughly homesick.

There is talk of our having to sign another non- escape form. I will sign anything. It would clearly be done under duress anyway and consequently not binding. This time, I hope we shall do it without a 'Selarang Square' performance. I never did consider that necessary last time.

Conferences are going on between the 'Big Men' of the camp to decide what to do with the camp messing fund, as we are now each paying out $30 per month to help out with the ORs' rations, which are no better than ours. 'Hatchet Smith' was playing his banjo in the garden during a brownout the other day and ran foul of the IJA and was locked up in the gaol for three days. Livingstone, an AIF officer has been sent to live with the Italian officers in the gaol as a punishment. He had been keeping some ducks for one of the Korean guards and supplying him with eggs. After some weeks of this, the Korean, thinking he was getting an unfair deal, decided to move his ducks to his quarters in Half Moon Street. As he was moving them, he was met by Takahashi and the whole story came to light.

Two days ago a most unpleasant thing occurred. Two Australians, finding a Tamil asleep in the vicinity of where they were working on the aerodrome, thought they would go through his belongings to see what they could find. Whilst doing so, the Tamil woke up and let out a shout. Whereupon the Aussies knocked him over the head with a chungkol and made off with 30 Straits dollars. Four hours later the wretched Tamil died. Before doing so, however, he was luckily able to identify the two Australians, who had been caught by the Nips. The Australians are being dealt with by the Japanese civil authorities. The IJA said that had it been a Nip soldier, and not a Tamil, the men would have been shot on the spot. My view is that it is a pity they were not. As it is, I hope they will be suitably put away in Singapore where they have been taken. No doubt the local free Indian press will be able to make great capital out of the incident. It is undoubtedly one of the worst things that has happened yet. So much for the much vaunted superiority of the white man.

People are talking bridge all round me at the moment – Damn them. Latest report from the gaol – two American airmen are on view at the New World Amusement Park in Singapore. They are said to have been shot down in a recent raid and people pay 5 cents to see them. Their eyes are said to have been gouged out, but I do not know that this is really true.

22 February 45 Brownout Monday morning but saw nothing. It is reported that six planes were over on Tuesday and raided Seletar. All we heard here was one explosion. On Wednesday one B29 came over the camp. Takahashi reported to have said that we shall be down to 100gms of rice per day, before we get out of here. I shall not be surprised. Stories of Koreans from Java – 30 arrived here a few weeks ago from a unit in Java. The Koreans attacked Nip officers and NCOs. One officer and 17 NCOs said to have been killed with a light machine gun. The Koreans then made for the hills. Eight were executed and the remainder of the unit were brought here or were sent to Sumatra. This has already had a great effect on the Koreans here. A few days ago two Koreans went to Singapore, passed two Nip NCOs and refused to salute them, as they normally have to do. An argument started and the Koreans knocked the Nips down. The following day the Kempeitai came up here but could not identify the men concerned. Most of the trouble stems from the fact that the Koreans originally signed on for two years' service. Having already done double that in many cases they are becoming pretty fed up and want to return home to Korea, There is certainly no love lost between them and the Nips. Philip Jones in conversation with Takahashi asked him if, in the event of an allied landing on Singapore, and our being liberated, he would have to commit hari-kiri. To which Takahashi replied "No, I do not think so, unless of course I was ordered to". Takahashi said that he would sooner trust some of the POWs here than he would his Korean guards.

24 February 45 Largish raid yesterday on Singapore. We counted 105 B29s. The harbour was attacked and many fires started. One large oil fire was clearly visible from the camp. The planes came in from the South West and left by the North coming over in groups of eights, nines and tens. Some 22 of the planes returned to the target area after turning over the sea. Nip fighters do not appear to close with the bombers and attack them with machine-gun fire, but to dive towards them from above, sometimes in the opposite direction to the bombers, and let off a thermite bomb. These burst in the form of a white mushroom-shaped puff of smoke and look very villainous from the ground. However, they are rarely, if ever, near the bombers which continue quite unperturbed. It is interesting to compare the oil fires in Singapore now with those which greeted us on our arrival in Singapore more than three years ago. At least this time it is their oil and not ours. A truckload of 50 Koreans was rushed off to Singapore, presumably to assist in fire fighting. According to stories from our working parties in Singapore, the bombers dropped mostly incendiaries and only a few high explosive bombs. One party at Alexandra was locked into a go-down during the raid and soon some incendiaries came through the roof and in a very short time the whole building was on fire. The men inside managed to break down the door to find the guard covering the door with a light machine-gun. However, they decided rightly that this was less dangerous than the threat of fire and made for some shelters in the vicinity. In the event the guard took no action.

During the return of one party the truck broke down in the town and the prisoners were nearly mobbed by the Chinese as if they had arranged the raid themselves. Morale amongst the civilians is high and they are just waiting patiently for the day. Work on the gardens today consisted of collecting sludge from the shit farm. Ken Archer is now back on the gardens after three months in hospital. His eye is very much better. Everybody now collecting large reserves of taproot. The only way of keeping it is to bury it and it reminds me very much of the squirrels in Arosa before the war, rushing away to bury the peanuts, which we used to give them against the approaching winter. By the afternoon the smoke from the Singapore fires had formed a thick, heavy pall of dark cloud which much resembled a thunderstorm approaching. Soap is now almost impossible to get. Reading now George Moore's 'Esther Waters', which I have never yet read. Enjoying it immensely and R L S's: 'Kidnapped'.

I have now taken out of the library Lord Frederick Hamilton's 'Vanished Pomps', his memoirs of his experiences as a young attaché at the British Embassies in Berlin, St Petersburg and Vienna.

25 February 45 P Party say the docks two miles westwards from Clifford Pier are a mass of flames. Some of the men returned to camp yesterday evening considerably shaken by their experience in Singapore. They spent 8 hours in a shelter and were not even allowed out by the Nip guards to urinate. The bombing is said to have been extraordinarily accurate, and quite terrifying.

26 February 45 3 B29s over – no anti-aircraft fire and no sirens sounded. Spent yesterday morning on the gardens – and the afternoon too. We now have to take down the urine trailer on Sunday afternoons and put the delicious liquid on the gardens. Excellent for the plants, not so good for us. In fact it has been a particularly pleasant weekend, shovelling sludge all yesterday, urinating on the gardens all Sunday afternoon! Spent Sunday evening as usual with Eric discussing many subjects. Today we brought up two trailer loads of wood for the cookhouse.

28 February 45 Another month over, thank God. The usual B29s. We are getting blasé about them already. Terrific news, a Red Cross ship is due to arrive in two days' time and is to be unloaded in six. Please God, B29s stay away from the docks! Supplies said to be in 14,000 packages and to have come from the United States. What this will mean to us it is quite impossible to say. Apart from the small amount of stuff received early last year, it is the first since the limited South African supplies in

1942. We shall probably receive no more than POWs in Europe are sent every month, but this will not detract from our enjoyment of it. Tins of bully beef, cheese, chocolate, Chesterfield cigarettes are all dancing in front of our eyes already. 80 bags of mail are also reported to have arrived. Heaven knows, it is time we had more mail also. We have been patient enough to deserve anything new – even our freedom.

1 March 45 A big parade of Koreans on the padang this morning. We were turned back from the gardens. General Shaito, Colonel Banno and several other officers were there all looking quite smart, even old Banno, known by most of us as 'Clickety Click' on account of his dentures, which are very loose. He looks more like a rickshaw coolie than an ex-cavalry officer of the great IJA.

Saw 'Pygmalion' yesterday evening. Adequately produced and acted in the Coconut Grove Theatre. Rather spoilt by the first act having to be played in the cold, unfriendly light of day, but this is unfortunately unavoidable as all shows outside the gaol must, according to camp order, be over by 9.00pm. Only the Gaol Theatre may go on until 10.00 pm.

2 March 45 Another great day, 53 B29s, this time in small groups of 4 or 5 attacking the naval base or Seletar aerodrome. We are not certain which it was yet. Heavy ack-ack fire over naval base direction. More fighters up than usual, we counted 14 in the air at the same time, letting off thermite bombs. The raid lasted from 11.00 am until 12.40 pm. We sat and watched planes coming over from the gardens. Some 'overs' from the fighters (explosive bullets) landed in the camp area; four medical orderlies in the hospital being hit, none of them seriously. The worst case was a fellow who had the tendons exposed across the back of his hand. The patients at Kranji only receive 250gms rice per day. Here, by pooling, we manage to give everybody a minimum of 312gms.

3 March 45 A reccy B29 was over yesterday afternoon presumably photographing damage. Red Cross ship now stated to be definitely in. It is to be unloaded by the Nips. We were to have sent a party down ourselves, so heaven knows how much of the stuff will ever reach Changi.

A Nip hospital ship is said to have struck a mine yesterday, while leaving the naval base; unfortunately it only bent a few plates. A twin engined plane crashed while taking off yesterday breaking its under-carriage. Also, the engines fell off. Hutch has been very off colour recently but the news of the arrival of the mail seems to have bucked him up considerably, and our meals are less silent than they have been for some days past. When he is really fed up with life his behaviour is very reminiscent of that of a small boy in need of a good dose of syrup of figs to shake him up. However, we are usually able to exercise our powers of tolerance, thin though they may be at times.

5 March 45 Spent a busy morning yesterday cooking. Made rissoles out of mashed taproot flavoured with towgay, garlic and fried krapok, (flakes of pink coloured prawn dust). Result very good. Donald told me an amusing story of the last raid on Singapore. It appears that part of the cold-storage plant was hit, and a Chinaman, taking advantage of the general shambles, picked up a large fish and, tucking it under his clothing, started to make off with it. Unfortunately he was spotted by a Nip, who noticed the large bulge down one side of his body. On closer examination he saw the rather cod like fish, the head of which was peeping out from the man's shirt collar. He made the Chink take out the fish, seized it, and clouted the poor man over the head with it, knocking him to the ground, unconscious.

A party of 150 prisoners have gone into Singapore to unload the Red Cross stores at St. Andrew's School. It is interesting and perhaps not just coincidence that no B29s have been over since the ship docked about a week ago, A busy day watering on the gardens, but our labours proved in vain as it rained hard all the afternoon.

7 March 45 The camp talks about nothing but Red Cross stores and what we are likely to get. As far as I can make out from Philip Jones, the position is as follows - all the supplies have now been unloaded and are under lock and key under a Korean guard at St. Andrew's School. The stores include packages from the US, Britain and South Africa. There are medical supplies; food in individual packages from the States, similar to the few we received last year; books, mostly of a technical and reference type; gramophones and records and some clothing and boots. It is interesting to note that the amount we received from South Africa in 1942 amounted to 29lbs per man and we made that last over 6 months. There is no news yet of mail but I understand that, in any case, this would have gone direct to the Kempeitai postal organisation. The cigarettes are said to include Camels and Old Gold. The latter has caused a certain amount of trouble as they have the legend 'Freedom is our Heritage' on the packets, which is regarded by the Nips as propaganda and as a result it seems doubtful at present if we shall be allowed to receive them. We had trouble like this before over 'V for Victory' cigarettes, which the Nips refused to give us. There is also a considerable quantity of medical supplies, which have arrived just in time to save the lives of many TB and diabetic patients. That is to say, if any insulin has been received. What a Godsend this must be for these men. It will give them new hope of surviving.

On Monday I went with Fitz and Ralph Spark to see Bill William's show 'Music Through the Years'; good in parts with some quite excellent dancing by Ekoma, the Javanese professional dancer. He would pass off as a woman anywhere. The grace and beauty of his dancing are truly remarkable. The choreography was by Wally Danes and the music by Bill Williams. Costumes and scenery were done entirely in black and white and the whole scene was amazingly effective. It is perhaps interesting that this short ballet went down very well with the troops, many of whom had probably never been in a theatre before, apart perhaps from a music hall.

The only thing which marred an otherwise very good show, were scenes and songs from the last war, which I found atrocious but may well have appealed to the syrupy, sickly sentiment of the average 'digger'. I found them thoroughly embarrassing. The Australians, however, lap up this sort of thing and apparently can take any amount of it. This evening, I hope to listen to a recording of the Beethoven Violin Concerto and the Emperor Concerto, weather permitting, since it is raining at present. This will be the first real music I have heard for several months. I miss music more than most things in this camp. I feel incomplete without it.

I am at present reading J B Priestley's autobiography dealing with his time in the United States, chiefly in California and the West, called 'Midnight on the Desert'. This is the first Priestley I really enjoyed although it descends to a waffle towards the end on such subjects as three dimensional time etc. Have from the library at present an anthology edited by William Beach Thomas called 'The Squirrel's Granary ('A Countryman's Anthology)' which I find fascinating.

9 March 45 Bad news. As from Saturday we are to suffer another cut in the rice ration. This time we come down to 220gms, or just over 7oz per day. This represents 1 3/4 pints of loosely packed boiled rice. So we steadily approach the starvation level again. The men on heavy duty rations suffer worse this time as they come down from 460gms to 270gms. The IJA rations have also been cut from 600gms to 400gms per man. Not that it is much of a consolation to us to know that the Koreans are getting less to eat also. This news is being received very philosophically by everybody at present, but of course their stomachs will not feel the full effects for some days yet. It is something most of us have been expecting for some time past. 18ct gold is now fetching $2000 per fine ounce. A gold sovereign was sold the other day by an officer for $500.

Whilst on the subject of money, one of the other ranks is in possession of £1500 Australian and over £1000 in cheques as a result of black marketing activities. A party of 50 other ranks of the forestry group has gone down to St. Andrew's School to sort out and make an inventory of the Red Cross stores. They are expected to take 7 to 10 days over the job. The Nips have ordered 1 1/2 tons of extra root and vegetables to be produced from the gardens per day to help make up for the cut in rice. This is all very fine, but the taproot has always been regarded as our emergency reserve. What will happen when this has gone? We cannot keep up 1 1/2 tons per day for more than a week or two – if we are not freed soon we shall be in a very serious situation. For some inexplicable reason the theatre shows have been stopped. Yesterday the Nips even threatened to have the theatre pulled down, but this order has been rescinded. The Nips appear to be worried about something. Reading 'Through French Windows' by David Horner. Not very impressed. On Wednesday, in spite of a few drops of rain, I listened to the Beethoven Violin and Emperor concertos. What a glorious evening it was; the first music for a long time.

Reproduction was much better as the gramophone has been re-built since it was last used. Have now taken out of the library Lawrence's 'Oriental Assembly' and a small book of English Essayists edited by V H Collins 'Three Centuries of English Essays'. It is a wet day, showers accompanied by a gusty wind, which reminds me rather of weather at home.

11 March 45 The camp is in the throes of signing non-escape forms once again. This time without any show of opposition as on the first occasion, when some 18,000 of us were concentrated in Selarang barracks in 1942. Now the mere knowledge that one will be shot if attempting to escape is sufficient to represent duress. The exact reason for this signing is not clear to me, except that last time we all put our signatures to a standard form, some of us using rather indelicate 'noms de plume'. This time I understand the forms already have our names and units printed on them, according to the camp nominal rolls. This morning Lieut. Wakabayashi, of up-country fame, visited Osmond Daltry next door together with about four other Nips and interrogated him about the show which had just been banned in the gaol, 'Music Through the Years'. After searching the quarter for subversive papers or other possibly dangerous documents, they all went off to the gaol-theatre where the three ballets and the final scene of a ship leaving the dockside had to be played through in the presence of the IJA representatives. The final scenes, I admit, must appear to any Nip to be allegorical to say the least – the defeat of the Nips, our final liberation and departure for home. However, it would appear that such was not the intention. The new reduced rice rations are as follows:- heavy duty 270gms, light duty 225gms and no duty 180gms.

Yesterday was our first experience of these new rations and the day's meals consisted of the following: Breakfast 1 pint of rice porridge, midday 1 pint greens soup and 1 fried rice and greens rissole. Evening 1 pint thin soup, 3 medium sized doovers. Needless to say we all retired to bed at the end of the day feeling very empty. The full effect of this light diet will not of course be felt for a week or two. Apart from losing weight, we shall get accustomed to it as we have done to everything else during the past three years. This morning I made the usual Sunday morning pie of taproot and grated coconut. Taproot is now $2 per lb and coconuts have now gone up to $2.40 apiece. The peacetime price was 2 cents. We have now had four days almost continual rain and it has been cold enough to wear a sweater. We have consequently been able to do only a limited amount of gardening.

Kerr is not at all well again; stomach pains and vomiting, He was given an unknown variety of laxative last night, which sent him to sleep in two minutes flat and he woke up this morning feeling better, but light headed and as though he was slightly drunk. I went up to see him after breakfast and he was sitting up suggesting that it would be a good thing if he were to have another dose as it had such a delightful effect. Am reading R L S's 'Essays of Travel' having just finished T E Lawrence's 'Oriental Assembly'. The former is excellent reading and includes 'The Amateur Emigrant', the account of his trip to New York. He has a delightfully easy style in these essays, better I think than in his novels. He shows his remarkable powers of description and drawing of character, which makes the people he is describing come wonderfully to life.

To return to more mundane affairs, one of the goats – five were received for the hospital – has just 'pupped', or more accurately 'goated'. There is a story circulating that the first of the Red Cross stores are to be delivered tomorrow. Came across the following in 'The Amateur Emigrant': "An aim in life is the only fortune worth the finding; and it is not to be found in foreign lands but in the heart itself". Our garden in front and at the back of our coolie quarter now contains 6 young brinjal plants, 3 tomato plants and 6 Ceylon spinach plants, not much more than seedlings.

15 March 45 Last Monday a grey overcast day, the brownout sounded at 10.30am and about half an hour later was followed by the blackout. From the gardens we saw 9 B29s in the far distance but only for a minute or two before they disappeared again into the clouds. P Party say they saw 20 planes in all. Two Nip planes crashed on the aerodrome last Saturday, unfortunately without fatal results. These 'whiners' – so-called owing to the peculiar noise made by their propellers – are, according to the Americans, a type of fighter bomber having two engines and four gun turrets in the nose, tail and two blisters on either side of the fuselage. To my untrained eye they look villainous, but I am told they are very out of date. One of the two crashed while landing on one wheel, the other while taking off.

Sunday evening Fitz and I spent with John and Eric. Cyril Wild was there and told us a lot about life in Japan, where he had worked before the war for Shell. On Monday we heard that Ludman, who had been one of my draughtsmen at Div. HQ was in hospital with cerebral malaria – usually fatal – and was on the 'D.I.' list. This came as a hell of a shock to me as I had received a visit from him only a few days before. He had been admitted to hospital at the end of last week with a 4+ infection of malign tertiary. He luckily came under Eric in the hospital and he was able to keep me posted as to his progress. After reacting favourably to quinine, he appeared to be much better by Sunday evening, but he suddenly collapsed in the night. Eric was called and administered quinine and toxin injections and gave him oxygen as his respiration had almost ceased and his pulse was negligible. He rallied and by the following evening was out of his coma and more or less back to consciousness. Noel Duckworth was able to speak to him in the evening and Eric, whilst still worried about the state of his heart, thought that with luck he might pull through. At about 10.00 pm however an orderly reported that he had collapsed once more and within 5 minutes of Eric going to see him, he died. It is a very sad case. He was a wonderful human being, who had been up-country with us on F Force and apart from bouts of fever, which of course we all had, he had kept very well. What a damnable thing to survive three years, only to die within what will probably be only a few months of our freedom.

His funeral took place on Wednesday morning and most of us from Div. HQ attended. I suddenly realized that it was the first 'formal' funeral I had ever attended, although I had of course witnessed so many deaths, mostly in appalling circumstances. In some peculiar way, I found myself unimpressed by all the slow marching, last posts and reveilles.

Recently I have read 'The Well of Loneliness' and Gilbert Frankham's 'Peter Jackson, Cigar Merchant'. The great lesbian saga did not impress me very much – I did not find it a particularly brilliant piece of writing, although interesting in that it deals with a human propensity largely unrecognised at that time. The banning of it – why it should have been, I cannot understand – undoubtedly promoted its popularity and wider discussion of it. 'Peter Jackson' I thought excellent and one of the most effective pieces of descriptive writing about the last war that I have come across. The sort of book I wanted to read in one sitting.

Kerr is yet again in hospital, with appendicitis. He will probably be operated on by Webby in a day or so. This is undoubtedly what he has been suffering from all along, but had remained undiagnosed, until we asked John to pay him an unofficial visit. John said he either had appendicitis or amoebic dysentery after a first cursory examination. Later when Kerr had been admitted to hospital John 'sigmoided' him, found no dysentery and asked Webby to examine him, who did and immediately said "You've got appendicitis". Thank God for the few good doctors in this place. Apart from John, Eric and Webby (and of course Houston), I have very little faith in any of them and some are a public menace. For lunch today Eric made a very good stew consisting of 4 sweet potatoes, 2ozs onions at $1 per oz, two handfuls of Ceylon spinach and some taproot 'chips'. This little lot, although good, cost us about $1.50 each.

Whilst on the subject of food it is interesting that some people have taken to eating snails, which fetch 5 cents each; toads, caught in the gardens and fried rat which I am told is very good. Personally I would have to be ravenous before I could embark on this particular rodent for my diet. Perhaps we shall all descend to this before we get out of here. I wish to hell the Nips would hurry up the Red

Cross supplies, about which there is still no further news, The Nip air force has now blossomed out with three bi-planes which fly around this part of the island, looking like something out of the last war. One and a half tons of taproot now have to be lifted from the garden daily in order to make up the rations. This is by order of the IJA. When all this has gone – it will last about three months – our reserves will have gone. The day before yesterday the Nips supplied us with only 9ozs of food per man. We are very hungry. Smoking helps to allay the pangs but is too expensive to keep one going from one day to the next. Drinking large quantities of water also helps but this keeps me up all night. One cannot have it both ways. Thank God the weather has returned to normal i.e. sun, which if very hot is preferable to continual rain, when all our clothing and bedclothes, such as they are, become damp and it is too cold anyway with the small amount of clothing we possess.

Cronin's play 'Jupiter Laughs' being shown at the Coconut Grove Theatre, badly produced, I hear. Saw James Moodie the day after he had had his appendix out, very cheerful and full of chat. An orderly had just brought him a Marmite jar full of sugar telling him to eat some whenever he felt like it. Sugar is, of course, an incredible luxury even for people in hospital.

16 March 45 Went swimming this morning. Pleasant sun and the water almost cold and thus very refreshing. Philip Jones told me that Takahashi received a 25 word card from Nippon yesterday telling him that his wife and child were well and that his mother in law had died. This is the best I can do for gossip today. Many rumours flying about the camp, most of them unfounded; for instance that 1500 ORs are to be moved out of the gaol to make way for the officers, who are to go inside. As from next Thursday we are to receive 60gms of maize in lieu of 60gms of rice. The number of calories will remain unchanged. Soap now more difficult to get and very expensive. A half bar costs 50 cents. Eric Hinde went into hospital yesterday with suspected amoebic dysentery. Finished reading 'Treasure Island', an old friend.

17 March 45 Red Cross party returned today. Many versions of what the stores consist of; 80,000 x 8lb parcels of which we may with luck receive two per head. They are of course to be pooled and issued to messes.

A story from Outram Road Gaol about a US airman, shot down over Kota Baru on 7 March. Said to be a Captain and a fighter pilot, brought down while escorting a force of B29s. The fighter is said to have been based on a British aircraft carrier. God knows if it is true as at present there is no way of checking. It suggests that things are steadily moving closer and is very encouraging. The Red Cross stores are expected in the camp at the end of the month.

19 March 45 The SCF, (Senior Chaplain to the Forces, alias 'The Changi Tree'), was holding the usual evening service yesterday in the Coconut Grove for his somewhat limited flock. During his sermon, which he delivered from in front of the stage, standing tree-like in his white surplice, he spread out his arms at one moment in order to illustrate a point when a voice from the huts near the Coconut Grove shouted "Wide, scorer"!

I heard yesterday that Takahashi's platoon sergeant, Sgt. Fukuda, went into Singapore a few nights ago on a blind. He is currently in charge of Kranji Hospital, having some time previously been with Takahashi in Manchukuo, before they came down to Singapore. Towards the end of the evening he was quite drunk and he thought he would like a lorry to take him back to Kranji. So he went to the nearest police station and insisted that they should provide him with the necessary vehicle. This was not regarded as a good move by the police, since petrol is obviously strictly rationed. But when the policeman picked up the phone, Fukuda thought that it would all be fixed, particularly as a few minutes later a lorry drove up and stopped outside. It must have been a slightly sobered Fukuda, who found himself soon afterwards, not on his way to Kranji Hospital, but in the hands of the Kempeitai, being escorted to their nearest HQ. Takahashi related this story subsequently with great relish.

The effect of the cut in rations is already badly felt by the men working on the aerodrome. Many are fainting from lack of food. We were weighed yesterday and I have lost another 7lbs. Found 'My Sister Eileen' very amusing. I did not go for George Arliss's autobiography 'Up the Years from Bloomsbury'. Have now taken out of the library two plays by Tchekov and one by Alfred de Musset, an odd mixture. I found lifting and carrying sacks of vegetables on the gardens this morning just about as much as I could do. Only a month ago I found it no trouble at all and could throw them up on my back myself. Now I have to get somebody else to give me a lift up. I notice it particularly in the back of my knees and my leg muscles. We are at present managing to supplement our evening meals with a little taproot, which we can have baked in the cookhouse, but it is very expensive, being $2.30 per lb now. 1 1/2lbs does not give much bulk for four people. Yesterday we made a stew out of 2lbs sweet potatoes, 2ozs onions, two handfuls of taproot chips, two spoonfuls of sago flour to thicken it and a dash of curry powder. It was quite excellent, the onions giving it a delicious flavour and reminding us very forcibly of a soup we might have had in the outside world. There was enough for a pint each. It is at lunch that we feel the pinch most, not that the other two meals amount to very much. Looking back over my last few entries, I realize that the accent is very much on food. I can only say that it is not exactly surprising under conditions akin to starvation.

21 March 45 Sent card as follows "Fifth card. Health remains good. Very cheery hopeful. My thoughts always with you. All my love to you, Denison and others. Impatiently yours Harold". Received first whisper of another up-country party, believed 3000. My policy now definitely "Better the evil you know than the one you don't". Col. Banno said to be going in charge. Now we shall see some duck shoving. Spent yesterday evening with John and Eric. I took Peter Coope round to meet John as he also comes from Nottingham. Kerr has been successfully operated on and looks fit and cheerful. He was sitting up reading, the evening after he had had his appendix out, but we were not allowed to see him.

23 March 45 A three foot cobra was caught in the gardens this morning. It was under a tank that was being shifted. Its head was lopped off with a shovel. A glorious morning, sunny with a fresh breeze. No further news yet about the working party of 3000. It is said to be going to Singapore to work on ARP trenches and defence works, chiefly the latter I would think! Work on the aerodrome is said to be due to finish at the end of this month. The Singapore party will presumably not leave until that is finished since most of the fit bodies would have to be taken from the aerodrome parties. It is said that the party will receive 500gms of rice per day and consequently most of the men want to go; particularly those who have been working on the aerodrome every day for a year now, some of them much longer. I should hate to go myself. Having done one little jaunt up-country with Banno I do not wish to repeat the experience.

I am reading a book on the Brontes edited and compiled by E.M. Delafield. It is an account of their lives, as recorded by their contemporaries and is the second of a new series of such biographies published by Hogarth in 1935. At the same time I am also reading quite an amusing book on ships by Hendrik van Loon. Spent yesterday with Kerr, who has survived his operation very well and already, only three days later, looking better than when he was admitted to hospital a week ago. Met Peter this morning, who was about to make a seaweed stew with some weed he had collected while bathing this morning. It seems to me that there are very few things that one cannot eat amongst the flora and fauna of this world, if one is sufficiently spurred on by hunger. Whether seaweed or snails or toads or rats do any good it is impossible to say. At least they seem to do no harm.

24 March 45 Heavy rain all the afternoon, cold and most depressing. The morning not too bad. I went down bathing with Peter, instead of gardening. The sea was like a mill pond, hardly a ripple, with miniature waves only a few inches high rolling up the beach. Collecting seaweed is now a very popular pastime. It is very good fried, going crisp like shredded wheat and is delicious in a stew. It was delightful to sit on the top of the cliff and look out over the grey expanse of sea, Moisture was in the air making visibility over a short distance very good and the islands of the Rhio Archipelago and the tip of the mainland to the east of the island stood out darkly on the slate-like sea. We rarely see any shipping these days, entering or leaving Singapore, and the fishing pagars of the Malays dotted about along the coast, a mile or so from the shore, are the only things that break up the grey monotony of the water. Occasionally a Malay fishing boat passes close in shore, moving very leisurely. The general air of peacefulness and laziness is accentuated by the slow, effortless seeming movement. Peter and I, sitting on the beach after one of our swims gradually relax under the influence of the scene and our mood is transformed into one of peace. Time, for the moment, ceases to exist and we feel as though we have been sitting there always and will go on doing so into the illimitable future. Suddenly, Peter breaks the silence by remarking how wonderful it would be if a ship were to come round the headland and carry us away. But it seems impossible that anything could burst its way into that scene. We shall be here always and this is the only reality for us – nothing else exists. My thoughts try to turn to home, at such an infinite distance as though separated from me by countless light years. I dream lazily on, wondering what the family is doing and whether any of them are thinking of me. I make a conscious effort to get nearer to them and achieve some feeling of proximity, but the distance is too vast.

Suddenly my daydreams are broken by a whistle blast and it is time to make for the forming up point, where the Nip guard will count us before escorting us back to camp, We get up and the present surges back to us as we make our way laboriously through the rubber trees.

26 March 45 Two B29s over yesterday. One in the morning, the second in the evening, while we were eating. We also saw one this morning from the gardens. General Shaito expressed a strong wish the other day that at least a token issue of Red Cross stores should be made to POW for the 'Easter Festivities'. Yesterday rumour had it that the Nip WO in charge of transport received orders to make available the necessary transport for bringing Red Cross supplies up by Wednesday. Yesterday Major Jansen and a party of 10 ORs went into Singapore and are expected to be away about five days. This is assumed to be the working party charged with assisting with the distribution of the stores. Shaito is said to have asked Newey for a signed receipt for supplies but Col. Newey replied that, not having received any or even seen any, he was in no position to sign anything.

There the matter apparently rests. Yesterday Dick Underwood, who works in the office, saw several receipt forms, one of which was made out for the Representative Officer in charge of POW Malaya, presumably Col. Newey, so it looks as though he will have to sign in due course. Spent yesterday and Saturday evenings with John and Eric. On Saturday evening a Korean, whom John had cured of gonorrhoea, came in to see him and handed round 'Kooa' cigarettes. Did they taste good! They are made of Virginian tobacco and are, I believe, made in Java. This particular Korean is in peacetime a clerk in a newspaper office. He told us: that English £1 notes fetch $35 in Singapore and that the Nips receive five packets of Kooa cigarettes per month.

It will be nice if we get anything for Easter. At the moment I feel that just one Virginian cigarette would be acceptable. Saw Kerr yesterday. He is doing very well and hopes to be allowed to sit up today, when he is having the rest of his stitches out. Heavy rain again today; I wish to God it would stop. Great speculation as to which officers will go on the 3000 working party. There are strong rumours amongst the Koreans that all officers are to be moved to Johore Bahru lunatic asylum, which strikes me as being an eminently suitable place for us. Another Red Cross ship is said to be anchored seven miles off the harbour. I am at present enjoying Charles Morgan's 'The Voyage'. I am having more trouble with my digestive organs. I think it must be caused by taproot which I shall cut out for a few days and see if there is any improvement. It looks as though it is Hobson's choice – an upset stomach or loss of weight accompanied by a feeling of greater hunger.

27 March 45 One B29 over this morning. We seem to be receiving regular visits by reccy planes now. A working party of 350 Australians is to leave tomorrow, or the day after, destination unknown but rumours say Ipoh No 2 camp is now to become the HQ camp for all Singapore Island working parties. It will be completely separate and will have its own hospital. Am now reading Joseph Hergesheimer's 'The Three Black Pennies'. Still no sign of any Red Cross supplies. There is a move to put in an additional $1 or $2 to the mess to buy something extra for Easter Sunday. I personally think that, to make it worthwhile, it will have to be more than $1, as that will only buy us a third of a pound of taproot per head. Weather still continuing very thundery and we get rain practically every day. Must be the influence of the monsoon up North. Much enjoyed re-reading Charles Morgan's 'The Voyage'.

3 April 45 A night raid on Wednesday. Sirens sounded at 2.30 hours. Planes came over quite low at 5000/6000 feet. Single B29s were over on Thursday and Friday mornings. Another raid on the night of Thursday/Friday. The crump of bombs audible from Singapore. For the two nights following, the glare from an oil fire on Pulau Sambu was plainly visible. Spent last Wednesday night with Peter May and John talking about South Africa. Peter, when on this particular subject always succeeds in making the country sound very attractive. On Good Friday we received the long awaited Red Cross stores for issue on Easter Sunday. We received one parcel per 22 men, or about 5oz per man and no cigarettes!

Now, after a delay of two years, we each receive 1/22 of a parcel! Nearly. 2,000 men have now left Changi for working camps in Johore Bahru, Kranji and other places on the island. The men are to be employed in building air defences and gun emplacements. I now have to wear a belt to keep my trousers up and my weight is rapidly dropping. Eric Cruickshank says that many of the hospital patients are dangerously underweight and one is beginning to see men about the camp resembling the skeletons we had up-country.

I am told that I look like a stick insect – I certainly feel like one. For the evening meal on Friday we had a very good hot cross bun made of rice, maize, towgay, fried in palm oil.

Saturday morning was spent digging up taproot in the garden. This is not yet mature but so much is being stolen that we have decided to cut our losses and have it all up. 400 returned from Kranji hospital on Saturday and Sunday. The Bradshaw party of 1000 is said to have gone to Kranji, many scandals being unearthed. Officers caught stealing taproot from outside the gardens. Easter Sunday meals were as follows:- Breakfast the usual pap, 1 pt of 'coffee' (burnt rice) and milk, rice and fish kedgeree and whitebait on fried biscuit. Lunch, 1 pt of sludge, fish pasty and 1 biscuit with butter and apricot jam. Dinner, soup, mixed grill of beans, tap chips, Ceylon spinach, brinjals, whitebait, rice, bully pie and pea meat roll. Cake made of rice, maize, towgay, raisins and prunes with butter on top. Our first European food for over a year. Sunday morning had coffee with Peter Coope, Jacky Lewis and Charles Charlton, who were all participating in a darts match. After this John and Eric came round for coffee with us. Visited Kerr in hospital. Spent Sunday evening with Eric and later Miles Barrett (US Marines) and Bags Baggot (US Air Corps) came in unexpectedly and we spent a pleasant evening. John was out playing bridge. Have run out of newspaper for making cigarettes. I now smoke a mixture of Java weed, sliced cheroot and tapioca leaf, this is quite good in a pipe. Books read:- 'Don Burns' 'The Power of the Dog', Peter Fleming's 'One's Company' and 'News from Tartary'.

Since giving up the purchase of extra taproot, my stomach has been behaving far better, only once in 48 hours. It is a hell of a relief and makes a great difference to one's outlook. We are now all impatiently awaiting the arrival of the main Red Cross supplies. If we get two parcels per man – surely not too much to hope for – we shall be able to live more or less as we did on Sunday for 44 days. It is impossible to say how much this food will mean to us, we have been almost completely cut off from European food now for over three years

There has been a lull in air activity lately, even the daily reconnaissance planes have not been over. This must be due to the Easter weekend; give them a week or two to recover and after that they will, with luck, start thinking about the war again and the fact that we want to be let out. Kerr came out of hospital exactly two weeks after the operation. He has made a wonderful recovery under these conditions and on the present rations.

Yesterday evening had supper in the hut with Kerr, Peter and Donald and celebrated Kerr's return with a pie, which we made for ten of us. It consisted of 5lbs of taproot, one coconut, 1lb onions, some sprouted towgay and one egg, this latter cost us $2.50. We then made a tomato sauce with 40 tomatoes, grated taproot, onion water, santan from the coconut, total cost about $4 per head. It tasted good. We also had the last of our Easter Red Cross food, the chocolate being sufficient to make a very good imitation chocolate éclair. The chief thing we lack is sufficient rice to make full use of the Red Cross food. The actual weight of the tinned food is only about 5oz, so that although we greatly appreciate eating food with a taste to it, we did not really feel satisfied.

4 April 45 The Nips have again been trying to get Colonel Newey to sign a receipt for Red Cross stores. This he once again refused to do for the very good reason that only a small fraction of what is due to us has actually been received. Yesterday he was sent for by a Japanese Red Cross representative, who asked him why he had not signed. "Because I have not received all the goods" was his reply.

"Don't you trust the Japanese Red Cross?" "It is not a question of trust but of procedure". As usual the Nips are up to something. If the receipt were not to be signed, it is doubtful if we would receive anything at all. As it is, it is a month since the goods were received on the island. For some reason best known to them, the Nips seem to be very loath to let us have it all up here at once. Even the badly needed drugs and general medical supplies are still sitting in St Andrew's School in Singapore. Yesterday afternoon we were inoculated against dysentery, the inoculation according to Eric and John is completely ineffective. However, by 9.00 pm yesterday evening I felt so doped and generally lethargic that I went to bed and apart from the usual nocturnal interruptions slept solidly until 8.00 am this morning. I awoke feeling as though I had just completed another bout of fever. This disappeared after a gentle work-out on the gardens. Colonel Cox is the latest name to come up in the great camp scandal. Yesterday afternoon Takahashi visited the quarters of several officers and personally searched their kit. In the course of conversation with 'gunner' Harris, Takahashi remarked: "Well, I see a Colonel is now involved in this trading!" Harris merely smiled and agreed that this was so whereupon Takahashi said: "I wonder how long it will be before your name turns up". Col. Harris gave a sickly grin and tried to laugh it off.

Yesterday, I read 'Prosper Merimee's 'Carmen'. A party of a hundred left this morning for Singapore to prepare a camp for a working party of 1100. To date, approximately 2,000 have left. How many more are to go is not known, but it cannot be many because soon only the sick will be left behind. Shaving is soon going to become a problem as I am now finishing a small piece left from a shaving soap stick I bought nearly a year ago, which is all I have, and I only have three of my original blue Gillette blades left. How one longs for hot water for shaving and washing and for hot baths. We have now been without such luxuries for 3 1/2 years.

Amongst the items in the seven parcels received for Easter were seven tablets of soap for every 150 men. These were cut in two and were drawn for but needless to say I was unlucky. Sunday's food will live in my memory for some time to come, although the full enjoyment of eating it was so ephemeral. It was difficult to decide which was the most enjoyable snack, since it was really no more than that. The half biscuit, butter and apricot jam, or the bully beef pasty, or the chocolate pudding. The chocolate reminded me somewhat of Toblerone; it brought home to us more forcibly than any larger amount could possibly have done, how much we miss in the wretchedly inadequate rations we have existed on for so long and in particular for the last few months, during which we have been, to all intents and purposes, at starvation level. Things may of course get worse yet. Some of the Dutchmen in the camp, who have been working on an island somewhere off Singapore, received only 90gms of rice per day for three months. Perhaps the day will come when we shall look back with longing to the time when we received 230gms, our present scale. We are expected to work on this! How our enjoyment of all the smallest things will be accentuated for us by the three or four years of our imprisonment.

It is all those myriads of things accepted normally as a matter of course, which we shall derive such enjoyment from when we return home. If only we could be told when we are to be free, it would be so much easier to bear. I would like to have a fixed prison sentence and to get rid of the hopeless uncertainty as to how much longer we have to go. I often feel that this is the only life I have ever had and that nothing will ever happen to prevent its continuance into the illimitable future. No outside world exists and the people I am with here will be those I am fated to live with for the rest of my life. Our remembrance of home and family and close friends is becoming ever dimmer and ever more unreal.

5 April 45 Peter Fleming, in his 'News from Tartary', expressed his feelings better than I can: "Our hunger was not of dimensions to be reduced by snacks, and sooner or later we began involuntarily to talk about food. It was our favourite topic; all others were remote and academic by comparison. The present was empty of incident, the immediate future was maddeningly uncertain, and the rest, our respective pasts and our respective futures, seemed so infinitely far away, that as subjects for discussion, they only had the irrelevant quaintness of a dream related at the breakfast table. Food was the one thing that we could always talk about with feeling and animation".

8 April 45 Imperial Rescript Day. On Friday a Red Cross truck full of boots and clothing arrived; yesterday, there arrived three loads of Canadian food parcels and in the evening we received a similar issue to last Sunday, i.e. one parcel per 20 men. This time, however, the milk was taken to the hospital and we were to have received 5 Old Gold cigarettes per head, but these are now being held pending the departure of working parties for Singapore. These parties do not share in the allotment of cigarettes for this camp apparently. Until these parties leave, therefore, we shall see no cigarettes. In any case, I gather the total number we are likely to receive is only 18 per head. All entertainments and swimming have been stopped for the officers' area; no reason given. Loss of entertainments will not be felt because the shows have recently been of a particularly low standard. Peter May has been warned to leave as officer in charge of one of the working parties in Singapore. Whilst he is not particularly thrilled at the prospect of leaving the camp, he is looking forward to having a job to do and this he should do well, being very conscientious and, above all, interested in the none too easy task of administering prisoners of war after three years' incarceration. I shall be sorry to see him go. Am reading a very interesting book on Napoleon, post Waterloo until his death, 'St Helena', written by Octave Aubry, translated from the French.

I rather overdid things yesterday on a trailer party hauling wood up from the gardens on a Changi trailer and did my back in – not for the first time. These trailers consist of a flat platform, usually without sides, built on the chassis of a lorry, in some cases a 3 ton army lorry. Its only controls consist of a steering wheel on a long shaft, which sticks up at an angle of about 20 degrees from the horizontal and a foot brake of variable efficiency. Power is supplied by about 24 men, hauling on 6 traces, 4 men to a trace and an inevitable sprinkling of 'old soldiers' grouped around the sides and back of the truck, always a very popular place as one can either push gently or merely lean on the side, according to one's energy. I always seem to find myself on the traces. There is a very steep hill up from the gardens into Half Moon Street, which usually involves a rest half way up.

We used to be able to get up in one long pull and rest at the top, but conditions have altered and our leg muscles show up badly. This hauling of trailers reminds me of a slave scene out of the film of Ben Hur. Give the man, who sits on the trailer and steers, a whip and the picture would be complete. The rows of wet, sun baked backs, shining in the blazing sun tugging, almost horizontal, in the traces, the sickly sweet-sour smell of unwashed bodies pouring out sweat in large drops from every pore, gasping for breath, the creaking of the springs of the truck and the shouts of encouragement from the driver: "Keep her going, we are nearly there", or: "Now together, heave!" will never be forgotten; not least the nauseating contact of one body against another, as though there were a thick film of hot oil between one's own skin and that of the other men in the same trace. The hot foul air we breathe is saturated with the stench of overworked, straining bodies. At last we reach the top of the hill and someone shouts "OK, rest" and we let the traces drop, collapse on the ground, gasping, to replenish our lungs with fresher air. Sometimes one suffers from blackout, a common experience nowadays, but this soon passes off.

Last night I think I must have fallen asleep as soon as my head touched the pillow. Thanks to the Red Cross issue, meals so far today have been good. Breakfast: porridge followed by fried whitebait and salmon and sardine on a fried rice biscuit. Lunch: sludge, a pork roll and half biscuit, with butter and strawberry jam. What a heavenly flavour!

10 April 45 A general air of deep depression has seeped over the camp. We appear to be forgotten by the outside world. The possibility of freedom remains as remote as ever. Even the Air Force is no longer paying us any attention; no planes have been over to our knowledge since the end of last month. It is all very depressing. Doesn't anybody want Malaya back? Surely to God somebody wants tin and rubber, even though they do come from such a God-forsaken part of the world.

Yesterday evening Donald and Roy kindly invited me to share in a pie, which they had made. Roy produced a tin of bully, which he had conserved for three and a half years (what self-control) and this formed the basis of an excellent pie consisting of 4lbs of taproot, a handful of onions, some ladies-fingers, tomatoes and Ceylon spinach. We all felt satisfied after eating this, the first time for months. With the evening meal, we had the rest of the last issue of Red Cross goodies; a cheese savoury and a chocolate sweet, there being so little of each that the new flavours were barely apparent. We are to receive a third issue tomorrow. Unfortunately the small quantity of food and the fact that we are only to receive two issues per week, can neither provide us with much physical benefit, nor make us feel less hungry. We have still not received any cigarettes. However 3 1/2 years under the Japanese have taught us never to expect anything good. We just have to be content with whatever bone is thrown to us. I have no doubt that we shall receive a small percentage only of the goods actually destined for us and the rest will go astray. Already a large quantity of cigarettes has been stolen. I cannot write any more at present, I am too bloody-minded and in the depths of hopelessness. Frayed tempers, sullen, tired faces, eternal conversations on food, the same old camp gossip. The standard greetings of "What do you know?", 'What's new?', or "Have you heard anything?" drive one crazy.

16 April 45 Last Wednesday quite a good issue of Red Cross food. The day's menu: Breakfast, normal except for some 'coffee', burnt rice, of course. Lunch, soup, fried whitebait with tapioca chips, potted meat and rice, hash & vegetables. Dinner: soup with oil (the mark of a good soup here), whitebait, angel on horseback, cheese tart, sweet potato and meat pie, greens, cake with sugar and butter sauce, biscuit, butter and jam, real coffee. Our best meal yet although not the largest. Very hot digging in the gardens. On Thursday 12 April, 400 other ranks under the 'Pig Baron' (Lord de Ramsay) moved into number 2 area to form a base camp for Singapore working parties, The IJA has stopped the issue of Red Cross rations due to non-signature for medical stores, which have not yet been received. This is typical of the Nips.

Hutch in thoroughly bad temper and behaving like a small, spoilt child all Thursday afternoon. He is quite insufferable when he has these tantrums, which are not frequent, thank God. Wednesday evening Kerr, Peter Coope and I went chez John and Eric and spent a very amusing evening. Books – Webster's 'Duchess of Malfi', L H Mayer's 'The Near and the Far'. I am going through another period of senior officer phobia, which I hope will pass off soon.

Thursday morning; busy digging and composting in gardens. Friday – only one B29 over. Planting sweet-potato cuttings all the morning. I don't know why we bother with these;. they never come to anything and the tops are usually very tough to eat, however long they are boiled.

Thursday evening Kerr and Donald came down for the evening; I had the quarter to myself, Harwood's poker school playing elsewhere for once. Donald is much happier these days. Peter May with 250 ORs left on Friday morning for Bukit Timah where 100 of his party are already.

Base camp in number 2 area now out of bounds. This is now to have the base hospital staffed by 8 MOs under Major Bloom – a gynaecologist and including Major Goodall, 3 1/2 years in charge of the officers' ward. He is in the IMS and not very inspiring. Major Fagin, a very good Australian surgeon. Latest smoking material – cheroot stalks at 15 cents per ounce. I tried soaking them and then putting them through a mincer. It seems to be the only way of dealing with them. The result is very indifferent and smells of stale, mildewy tea-leaves. It is not so bad in a pipe.

Our lunch stew on Friday was made with portulaca, or some such name, a plant normally associated with hedges. Quite disgusting. A heavy day on the gardens, watering and feeling very tired at the end of the week. Sunday's issue of Red Cross parcels appears to be definitely postponed.

57 officers and 2500 other ranks have now gone to Singapore camps leaving a total of 8100, all ranks, in Changi including the 100 of the Hamilton party returned from Singapore as a consequence of a shortage of guards. They have been under Nip civilians guarded by IJA troops resting from Burma. Apparently they were treated well. Major George de Niro back from Normanton Camp and into hospital with beriberi and dysentery. He was drained of fluid and lost 3 stone in 14 days.

15 April 45 B29 over in the morning. Some gun-fire from the direction of the naval base. It is reported that there were another five over but we did not see them. Coffee in the morning with Kerr, Bags Bourne and Strath from the Argyles. A Manchester other-rank brought in yesterday from Normanton camp suspected of cholera. Fortunately a false alarm.

Gaol cookhouse scandal – 15 tins of bully beef have disappeared. A soldier in the gaol received two weeks stoppage of pay for taking urine and putting it on his own garden plot. At this rate we shall soon be having disciplinary action taken against us for not passing sufficient. This evening all messes have unexpectedly been ordered to collect issues of Red Cross stores immediately. The Nips are being true to form. We received eight parcels between 150 men. We shan't get fat on this.

16 April 45 Spent yesterday evening with John and Eric. They were both called away to deal with a case of MT 4+ malaria, threatening to turn cerebral. This is becoming too frequent for comfort. A Nip came to see Eric with bronchitis. Eric gave him a gargle and examined his chest, receiving a packet of cigarettes in return. He kindly gave me two, of which I am keeping one for this evening. Late last night, half-an-hour after lights out, we were roused and called out on roll-call. Some men had apparently been found missing in the gaol. We remained on parade until 12.30am when the dismissal sounded and we all returned to bed. Today's menu:

Breakfast, porridge, salmon and sardine paste on fried rice biscuit;

Lunch, sludge, sweet potato and bully pie, half a biscuit, butter and jam;

Supper, soup, fried whitebait and tapioca chips, cheese tart and whitebait pie, M & B pasty, sweet with jam, raisins, butter and sugar sauce, with a prune on top, reminiscent of bread and butter pudding. Quite the best sweet we have had yet.

Another issue of Red Cross food on Wednesday for consumption on Thursday. A certain number of Red Cross comforts have made their appearance and are apparently going to be drawn for.

19 April 45 Eating Red Cross food again today. Roughly the same issue as last week. 2oz bully, 1oz fish paste, 1oz milk, sweetened condensed (not powdered this time), 1oz jam, 1oz pudding, sweets of various types.

Still no cigarettes although it is said that there is to be an issue of five at the end of the week. Strong rumour that an Australian Red Cross ship arrived on the 10th of the month carrying bulk stores. Issue of Red Cross comforts yesterday. We had a choice of the following (one article only):-one tube Barbasol shaving-cream, 1 Tec toothbrush, 1 tin tooth-powder, razor, one razor-blade, packet of 800 sheets of lavatory paper, pencil, shoe polish, comb. Some were unlucky and drew things they did not want. I drew my first preference, which was a tube of shaving soap. What a great thrill to be able to have one of these articles at the end of 3 1/2 years! Many misfits, such as people without right arms drawing pencils, bald pates drawing combs etc. Naval people with beards drawing razors or blades, people without shoes receiving shoe polish, men without teeth receiving tooth-brushes.

Working party in number 2 area reported to be employed on digging earth-works for defensive positions in the area of Singapore. Work on the aerodrome said to be nothing compared with this. Bulldozers, levelling machines, and other heavy machinery seen leaving the aerodrome during the past few days. It looks as though work there must at last be drawing to a close. They have been at it now for nearly two years. Yesterday the heavy equipment even included two elephants, which we saw lumbering along the Changi road in the general stream of traffic.

Busy day on the gardens uprooting bean plants and digging over beds.

Have started reading a biography of Theodore Roosevelt by H F Pringle. It is one of the American Red Cross books.

The day before yesterday I borrowed the Ski Club of Great Britain's Year Book for 1936. It contains articles on the Olympic Games at Garmisch, skiing in Chile, the state of Washington, the Canadian Rockies and on the Arlberg Kandahar. Nothing could have given me greater nostalgia.

I have been able to think of nothing but skiing for two days as a result and have quite decided that one of the things I shall do at the first opportunity, when I am free, is to go skiing again. How long before conditions in Europe will allow such a holiday, I wonder? How I long for the cold, crisp sparkling exhilaration, the glorious freedom, the silent beauty of the scene, the glistening peaks, the branches of trees weighed down by the last fall of snow, the crunch of ski boots on frozen snow, the glorious smell of skis and wax. Even the smell of ski socks; quite unlike anything else.

How long ago since I last experienced all this, so remote from the ugly environment here.

Last Saturday, Norman Renton played the Emperor, followed by a Brahms Symphony on his gramophone. The records are by now very worn and in some cases are cracked right across, or even missing to the extent of whole movements, whilst the spring of the gramophone is so weak after more than three years of over-work, as to be barely able to turn the record against the needle. The sound box vibrates badly in the 'fortissimos' but we seem to notice none of this. Not even the noise made by the less appreciative people in the hut, or the constant coming and going of others, detract from our enjoyment of the music. There must be a certain pathos in the scene of 8 or 10 officers crowding round a small portable gramophone under such conditions and listening to what, to anybody from the world outside, would appear in reality to be a cacophony of sound.

20 April 45 Weighed again this morning at 10 stone; down about 7lbs since 19 March. A suicide last night in one of the boreholes inside the gaol. An Australian soldier, said to be a well-known racketeer, was found head first down the hole, the top of which had been broken in. The last time he had been seen alive was in the officers' area, making for the bore holes and dressed only in a towel, which was found later nearby. This is the most novel method of committing suicide I have yet heard of. Medical opinion thinks that approximately forty seconds would be enough for a man to lose consciousness in such an 'umgekehrt' position in such a foul atmosphere. What a ghastly, sad, unsavoury death. As the result of this, and before he had been found, we were paraded for a roll call at 10.30 pm and search parties were sent round the camp. We were finally dismissed at 12.30 pm feeling very tired and no success having been met with by the search parties. The body was not

293

found until this morning. We are not allowed out on the gardens today. This suits me as I could do with a rest.

25 April 45 Last Friday an issue of 5 Old Gold Cigarettes per man. I kept mine, except for one which I smoked on Friday evening, so that I would have something to smoke on Sunday, when we had another issue of Red Cross food. It was wonderful to be able to taste a real cigarette again and there was a general air of contentment and quiet satisfaction in the camp on Sunday evening as I took a stroll round the huts. The delicious aroma of American tobacco, being wafted past one's nostrils in the cool evening air. We are of course now back on chopped-up cheroot and brinjal leaf until the next issue, due next Friday. I hope to increase my issue this time by exchanging cheroots, some people preferring the latter. On Thursday we had the best sweet for supper yet. It consisted of a mixture of puddings of different sorts, raisins and creamed butter.

A 1000 metre trench, 2 metres wide at the top, 3 metres deep and 1 metre wide at the bottom is being dug from the guard room at the east end of the camp to the south-west corner of the gaol. Nobody knows what its purpose is. It is believed to be the product of Takahashi's brain. 1000 men have been taken off the IJA gardens to work on it. Last Saturday another two truckloads of Canadian food parcels were received. Some of us listened to Brahms' third symphony again last night. We have had a further issue of Red Cross comforts last night. The following were received for 160 men:- 27 sewing kits, 1 pair hair clippers, 1 pair nail scissors, 3 glass razor blade sharpeners, and 22 pieces of Wrigley's Spearmint chewing gum. We now have enough rice in the gaol to last until December. The supply of maize is due to finish shortly and also that of raji beans, for which we are to receive tapioca chips in lieu. A 10% rice cut, due to short weight in the sacks, was restored last Monday.

I decided to spend all day on the gardens on Monday as I was suffering from intense camp claustrophobia. My companions have been getting badly on my nerves. I do not think it would be possible to live with any other three people, with whom I had less in common. But it is amazing what one puts up with day after day, week after week, when there is no alternative. One is compelled to exercise all the tolerance and self-control one can muster. However, we would be nothing more than robots, if we were able to keep this up continually and not, now and again, have a bad day when natural inclinations surge up and all self-control goes by the board. On such days I feel that I am near breaking point. I go out on the gardens as soon as I have finished breakfast and by lunchtime feel better. As often as not I return, however, to find everybody else's faces in the quarter as long as ever and I realize that they are still having a bad day and lunch will probably be eaten in dead silence. Fortunately, lunch only takes about 5 minutes to eat if no one speaks, after which each of us picks up his book and tries to read, without much success on my part and the afternoons pass in the same intense silence; nobody ever attempting to make conversation. There is really nothing to talk about anyway, apart from the interminable and inevitable camp gossip and speculation, which it is futile to embark upon.

It is extraordinary how some days can quite spontaneously and inexplicably begin well or badly. One can go to bed at night feeling on top of the world, at peace with everybody, and wake up the following morning, after an apparently perfect night's rest, with a feeling of intense hopelessness.

Another issue of Red Cross food today, this time English parcels, chiefly tinned bacon and tomatoes with a little sugar, and a few odd puddings, about half a dozen 1 lb tins of the latter amongst 150 people. What an utter farce these Red Cross supplies are. Just enough to realise what one has been missing for 3 1/2 years, but not enough to have the slightest effect on one's constant and gnawing hunger.

All Monday afternoon and yesterday morning spent in putting urine on the gardens. This is taken down in the usual tank mounted on a trailer chassis and is, to say the least, an unsavoury job. Yesterday evening with Ken; a long talk about the upbringing of children. Monday evening with John and Eric also Cyril Wild who came round later. Somebody came in half way through the evening with a packet of 100 cheroots. This was a God-send as we had been without anything to smoke for some days. We managed to get two per man.

29 April 45 13 bags of mail have arrived including British, American and Australian. Some of it is said to have been here before; chiefly letters for the thousands of up-country dead. Some post cards from England, said to go up to October of last year. Magnificent dinner last Wednesday. A bacon and tomato pasty and an excellent pudding, which really tasted of plum pudding. An issue of 1 3/4lbs wet and damaged rice today. This caused great excitement yesterday evening when we heard about it, particularly when the medical authorities passed most of it as being fit to eat. It would have to be very bad before being refused in this camp. This morning we were able to start the day off with a pint of porridge instead of the usual 3/4 pint.

Stuart Kloter's 'Watch for the Dawn', about the 'Gotverdommers', vortrekking in South Africa at the time of Georges III and IV, very interesting. Scott's 'Quentin Durward', last read when I was at prep school. Another issue of Old Gold cigarettes on Friday, a grand total of five per man. I was able to get an extra ten by swapping 10 cheroots for them. Actually, in cash, cigarettes fetch one dollar each or even more.

Another issue of Red Cross food today, 20 men per parcel. It is said that we shall receive the present twice weekly issue for another six to eight weeks. Life is particularly stagnant at present, the days passing with monotonous regularity. 240 Red Cross books were received yesterday for the officers' library and will be available for taking out as soon as they are catalogued.

3 May 45 Yesterday I received a postcard dated 5 Oct 44 from Denison with a Sawbridgeworth, Herts, postmark. How I envy him being in England still, although knowing how anxious I was to get abroad and take a more active part in the war in 1941, I can well understand his disappointment at being kept in England. I wonder if he is still there now. He says he has just received a letter from my New Zealand girl friend, Dorrie Duigan, whose home is at Forest Row. She is the niece of a well-known General. The only news I have had of her for two years.

Camp gossip is considerable just now. 1000 arrivals are expected in the camp within a few days, but it is not known where they are coming from or what their nationality is. I saw Bill English last night who said that 600 men from the aerodrome parties may be going to work at Sembawang aerodrome near Nee Soon. The gaol cook-houses are to be prepared for fuel oil burning instead of wood. This is presumably because one day we will be unable to get out to collect timber. The gaol alarm bell has been shifted from its position inside the gaol to somewhere in Half Moon Street. Another issue of Red Cross food yesterday, also more Red Cross comforts from which I received a third of a bar of Fells Naphtha washing soap. I also received an American shirt. This was issued to Aggie and me so we tossed for it and I am delighted to say that he lost. I am particularly pleased about this as of the two shirts I had, one was far too big and the other was in rags. The last time it went in for repair the tail had been cut off to do the necessary patching.

Yesterday evening I listened to Dvorak's 'New World' and Tchaikovsky's 'Serenade for Strings', the latter pleasant but shallow with some good melodies and a lovely waltz. The slow movement of the 'New World' suited my mood. I was sitting on the steps of the hut gazing out over the top of the gaol, the outlines of which stood out darkly against a velvety sky, studded with brilliant stars. The effect of the music on this scene was quite transcendental and I began to feel that I was no longer in Changi. Experiences like this are very rare here and are all the more accentuated when they do come. Some cables have been received recently dated April. Some of which acknowledge receipt of those we sent off last Christmas. Severe headache and intense feeling of sickness and nausea yesterday afternoon possibly due to a very hot sun yesterday morning on the garden. Luckily I was considerably better by the time supper appeared and was able to cope with the Red Cross food. Woke up this morning feeling much better, as though I had just recovered from a bout of fever. Giving myself a day off the gardens. Books: 'Royal Dukes' by Roger Fulford, about the father and uncles of Queen Victoria. Just received a postcard from Mother dated 2 Oct 44.

9 May 45 Issue of five cigarettes last Friday and I bought some for 60 cents each and exchanged them for ten cheroots. Talking to Philip Jones, who said he had seen two ships leaving the harbour and a hospital ship entering. The first shipping he had seen for some time. He spends much of his time down by the sea, as he is still working for Takahashi in the IJA officers' mess down near the beach where General Shaito, Col. Banno and Lieut. Takahashi have their bungalows. Last Friday a postcard from Father dated 16 Oct and today I have just received an August card from Denison.

On Monday Donald, Kerr, Rawl Knox and I queued up for an hour for the Red Cross books which have just been put into the library. We all decided beforehand which ones we should go for and we were quite successful. I got Stephen Crane's 'The Red Badge of Courage', a book I have so often seen referred to by critics writing on American literature that I felt it was high time I read it. It is very good, eminently detached from time and place and an extraordinarily good psychological study of a youth fighting for the North in the Civil War. Considering Crane was only 22 years old when he wrote it, and had never seen, let alone experienced war, it is an amazing piece of writing. Also read John Steinbeck's 'Tortilla Flat' and am now in the middle of Sherwood Anderson's 'Winesburg, Ohio'. My name is down for a collection of five great modern Irish plays.

Last Sunday brought the end of the extra issue of rice and we came down with a bump on Monday. It is said that various people have received indications in their cards and letters that when we get out of here, if ever, we are to go to Ceylon for the initial sorting out. I dare say it would be one better than India, but I trust that we will not be kept there too long. An interesting statistic; 51,500 gallons of urine were put on the gardens last month! Today's Red Cross issue includes: mouldy tea, Lyons and Maypole, tomatoes, margarine, steak, puddings, Golden Syrup and marmalade. Last week has been insufferably hot and we have not been working particularly hard on the gardens.

13 May 45 Several truck-loads of vegetables arrived the day before yesterday including 25,000lbs tap root, 1 load sweet potatoes, 1 of pineapples.

Yesterday the men received 330lbs tap-root, 78lbs pineapple and 76lbs sweet potatoes. Great excitement caused by all this extra food. Not to say speculation as to why the Nips are suddenly being so generous.

Eric Hinde's birthday celebrated on Friday. We had a hell of a dinner with stuffed tap-root, pies and two rissoles each. Hutch produced coffee with condensed milk in the evening and this together with Old Gold cigarettes (five issued the same evening) made the day for me. In this existence one cup of coffee and a good cigarette gives one a great measure of contentment.

Peter's birthday, also on Friday, celebrated yesterday with a pie at dinner after which Kerr and I went up to see Eric and John and had to eat our way through a plateful of tap chips. Went to bed last night feeling full to bursting. But the trouble is that this feeling of satisfaction does not last and this morning I woke up feeling empty as usual. Shocking cramp in my left leg two nights ago, the third time in a fortnight. I leapt out of bed and put all my weight down hard on the toes of my left foot. This is the approved method of relieving it and I must say that it is very effective.

Eric Cruickshank says that it is a manifestation of vitamin deficiency, our old enemy beriberi no doubt. An excellent dinner last Wednesday including a bacon and tomato puree pie and an apple pudding sweet – real apples. Something I had not tasted, so far as I remember, since leaving England four years ago. Yet another indication of all the pleasures to come.

Books read include four Greek plays, Carl Sandberg's 'Storm over the Land', taken mainly from Abraham Lincoln's war years. The more I read about the American Civil War the more it strikes me how incredibly bloody it was and how bad the intelligence must have been. I am starting on Poe's 'Best Tales', also in the modern library edition. We have done very well so far with Red Cross books, having already managed to get hold of most of the books we wanted. Days are now passing quickly but not quickly enough. How I would love to get away from the people I am compelled to live with. At no point do their interests in most cases overlap mine. I could not have less in common with them. How glorious it will be to choose the people one would like to have around one and to live only with those one is especially fond of. It seems to me, in a funny way, that there is a danger of becoming over-tolerant, of no longer remaining faithful to one's views and feelings, in the sustained effort of trying to live amicably with people with whom one can share very little. It is not easy, in fact well-nigh impossible, to remain consistently honest with oneself in one's dealings with other people. Hurt feelings and over-honest opinions, where they will do harm, have to be avoided at all costs.

20 May 45 A dull week except that I have done considerable reading. Four of Ibsen's plays, Five Great Modern Irish Plays, Defoe's 'Moll Flanders', which I am reading now. Weighed yesterday 145lbs – up 5lbs on last month which pleases me a lot. My 'doovering' is evidently not in vain. It takes quite a lot to keep one's weight constant, let alone increase it. Actually the rations have been rather better this past month, particularly vegetables. Eric Hinde is in hospital again with an upset stomach. Webby also in hospital for similar reason and he is very run down and generally exhausted.

Friday, Peter, Kerr and Donald came down and we had a chip party. 4lbs tap-root chips between us. I went to bed feeling tolerably satisfied but the feeling never lasts long. A soldier in the gaol is said to have had a meal in Singapore with P Party consisting of a pork chop, vegetables, two eggs, etc. It cost him $109. Last night Peter and I went up to suburbia to listen to the Kreisler and LPO recording of the Mendelssohn violin concerto. Also listened to 'L'Aprés-midi d'un Faune' and one or two extracts from the Messiah. Records are now unfortunately badly worn and Norman Renton's gramophone has such a weak spring that someone has to maintain pressure on the handle all the time it is playing.

Red Cross food last Wednesday and again today. It should, I believe, last another month at the rate of two days a week. Takahashi is reported to have said that Changi aerodrome is no good, it would be better to plant vegetables on it. General Shaito had a plate of snails the other evening, after which he was violently sick.

23 May 45 Reading Balzac's 'Droll Stories'. 'Round up Time', a collection of south-western writing published in 1943, both of these American Red Cross books. Early morning watering on gardens, so I am taking the morning off. Weighed myself the other day, glad to say I have gone up to 10st. Red Cross day but unfortunately of the seven cases of food for our men, one complete case is blown. The weather is very hot and insufferably so in our coolie quarters at night.

25 May 45 Work on the aerodrome finishes today. Tomorrow 500 men move into Number 2 camp. Bill English is going across as interpreter.

Thank God it rained last night and is still raining this morning. Pleasantly cool after days of intolerable heat. Yesterday I fried 3lbs of tapioca chips and in the evening had a chip party with John and Eric who were in very good spirits. Eric Hinde in hospital now and has BT. I must say that I can do with a rest from him. I have been feeling very well for the last few days, both mentally and physically. Our five tomato plants are doing very well in the front garden, giving us enough for one or two tomatoes each most mornings. We also have 6 bayam plants and 6 Chekur Manis cuttings. Our flowers consist of red and orange marigolds and white balsam and daisies. Also three brinjal plants, from which we have had one brinjal, which was quite delicious fried. Our outside gardens are getting very tired. We are planting more and more sweet potatoes, as these seem to do best now. Spinach never comes to anything and bayam suffers badly from caterpillars.

27 May 45 Red Cross again. How we look forward to these days, Wednesdays and Sundays. Have read 'Two Survived', the story of the two survivors of the ship Anglo Saxon, who spent 70 days in an open boat, before being picked up and 'There Go the Ships', the story of an Allied convoy sailing to Murmansk from Iceland, told by an American seaman and journalist Robert Case. The latter I thought rather over the top. Am currently reading Melville's 'Moby Dick', which I don't think I have read since leaving school. Yesterday evening listened again to the Mendelssohn Violin concerto, of which I am particularly fond. Also a Stokowski recording of one of Bach's well known fugues for the organ. "Il est formidable, mais ce n'est pas Bach".

1000 Dutch and some British expected from Sumatra. Some Dutch already arrived. They look underfed and worn out. I guess we all do now. They were on aerodrome construction 80 miles from Palembang. I wonder why they are being brought over here. Yesterday afternoon we heard aircraft flying very high and we all turned out to see if they were allied or not. Bright blue sky, very brilliant sun but we eventually picked out a silver dot, which appeared to be stationary and turned out to be Venus! Apparently it is visible during the day at this period. Two planes were later spotted flying so high as to be two minute silver dots in the sky, probably Nip by the way they circled round and round the end of the Island.

Reading has now become a real drug to me. Fortunately, I still need something more sustaining than badly written fiction, which so many people seem satisfied to hurry through day after day. I think I have at least developed a better appreciation of good literature here, and I shall return home better read than when I left. One of the few benefits of being locked up. Naturally, one has been unable to systemise one's reading, which has been unavoidably catholic and often, over a period of months, an unbelievable sort of Russian salad.

4 June 45 Arrival of party from Palembang on Saturday. Cdr. Reid RN, who had been attached to us during the battle, spent two days with us. He had heard from his wife that Tufton was in India. Reading 'Story of San Michele' again, Hardy's 'Tess of the D'Urbervilles', much enjoyed in spite of Hardy's style which I do not much like. Air raid sirens sounded last Wednesday and Thursday. We only saw one plane, the first visit since 15 April. Various hut moves due to arrival of officers from Palembang. They are in very bad physical condition and reminiscent of F Force. Wore boots on gardens on Saturday for the first time in months. I found them very heavy and I much prefer bare feet now. Yesterday Red Cross day again. One parcel per 18 in lieu of 21 due to blown tins. This morning had coffee (now $25 per 1lb). Saturday pm listened to Beethoven's 4th symphony and the Emperor concerto. Coffee on Sunday evening for all of the old Divisional G Staff still remaining in Changi. Last issues of Red Cross parcels today and Saturday. 450 sick expected in from Keppel harbour.

We learned last night that many Red Cross books have been stolen from the men's library in the gaol. They are being cut up to make cigarette papers for sale at 1 cent each. One Australian has been caught at this and has received 90 days detention for stealing and 50 days for damaging Red Cross books. Some of us tried fried curried snails yesterday, the snails having been collected in the long grass around the camp. They were very good and slightly reminiscent of mushrooms.

15 June 45 Warning received yesterday that 4000 men would be leaving this camp. Party of 800 approx. to leave 'almost immediately' followed by small party of 200 specialists. Had a long talk this morning with Dick Austin. We drank tea and smoked Japanese cigarettes. Dick had been studying law in Sydney before the war. He was born in Australia and had been to England twice. His parents live in New Zealand, and he is one of the interpreters in the gaol. Also talked to Mackenzie, who is in hospital with severe blood poisoning and has had to have his thumb nails removed. He was with the Commercial Union Insurance Co. in Malaya and is the most recently married man in the camp, having got married on the day of the capitulation of Singapore. His object, so it is said, being amongst other things, to ensure that she would get a marriage allowance during the time he is a POW and she is interned as a civilian at Sime Road. Although it will not matter much, the authorities certainly will not catch up with this until the end of the war, as we are well aware that no information was dispatched from Singapore about casualties etc immediately prior to its fall.

17 June 45 Last issue of Red Cross food! 500 sick in from Keppel Harbour. Brownout sounded day before yesterday. P Party say a recce plane was over Singapore. Nothing seen here. Reading R C Hutchinson's 'Testament'. Tinea almost cured and am hoping to return to gardening soon. 3 bags of mail and 500 cables reported to have been received in the camp. Dates not known. Some of the cables were distributed last night.

Hutch produced his emergency ration yesterday and with this I made a chocolate and santan sauce to go over a coconut sweet, which went down very well. Life continues in an endless monotony of days and weeks. I find now I cannot read for more than a short time at a sitting, as my mind begins to wander. No cheroots have been received in the camp for about a fortnight now. IJA plans said to be to reduce this camp to the hospital, 1200 ORs and the bulk of the officers, making a total of about 4000 in all, who would be concentrated inside the gaol. However, it now seems doubtful if we can produce enough ORs, who are fit enough to be sent away to other camps. The 3 'Hs' (Hutch, Harwood and Hinde) are getting on my nerves again. This must be the result of my not having been out on the gardens for ten days, since normally, I just tolerate them assuming, of course, that I make enough effort. Weather insufferably hot day and night. God! How I long to live in a temperate climate once more.

20 June 45 Another Red Cross issue yesterday. Canadian parcels. Back on the gardens again this week. The officers' gardens are to become part of the main greens gardens, whilst the remainder of the outside gardens are to be cropped and then planted with tapioca. This will mean more work, as we shall have to get manure and compost. Tinea pretty well cleared up but I cannot remain all and every day in the camp any longer.

24 June 45 Last Wednesday we listened to Brahms 2nd Symphony in the afternoon; in the evening the Tchaikovsky 'Serenade for Strings' and Dvorak's 'New World' were played at the Coconut Grove on the gramophone. Never enjoyed the New World so much as I did that evening in spite of the interruptions caused by the 'screamers', taking off from the aerodrome. Glorious evening with a gibbous moon shedding a silver shimmer on the palm fronds. Some more mail in. Two cards from Father dated 15 Feb 45 and 16 Aug 44. Went bathing yesterday morning; water almost cold. Delightful morning, but very homesick making.

Books: R C Hutchinson's 'Testament', much enjoyed and 'The Fire and the Wood', very indifferent.

Nips said to be busy building bunkers and holes all over the island. Some Koreans have rejoined their units in Singapore. Crippled Splendour (Hutch) has been in a hell of a state during the past 24 hours.

30 June 45 Very depressed over the past week. Working hard on the gardens as we now come under the area to be turned over to concentrated greens production. This means digging over beds, opening them up, digging over the second layer, putting in grass compost, putting on urine (a delightful job!), re-covering with earth and raking. Finally comes the planting. All this entails a hell of a lot of work.

Last Monday and Tuesday, Ken and I went swimming in the morning, which for some peculiar reason makes us feel homesick. Perhaps it is because being in the water, one feels more directly connected with home. Feelings possibly aggravated by receiving a 25 word message and photograph from Mother last Sunday. This was dated 2 Dec 44. On Tuesday a card from Father dated 20 Nov 44, informing me that he was arranging to invest my accumulating bank balance. Good news; this marks my first ever investment. Wonderful to receive a photograph after all this time although I should have liked one of the whole family.

Cheroots now prohibitively expensive – $1.40 each and tobacco unobtainable, Have been forced to give up smoking completely for two days, which has been hell. Life is bad enough when one does not get enough to eat, but even that is tolerable when one can smoke away the more immediate hunger pangs. With nothing to smoke it is rather grim.

The 'Three Hs' continue to get on my nerves and I would be very glad of a change – particularly to be able to live with people of my own age and interests once more. As it is, I spend a great deal of my time up in the hut with Peter, Ken and Donald, and in the evenings Philip Jones usually comes down from Admin. Group. Some 1300 men are due to leave during the next few days. This reduces the total in camp to 6400 all ranks, including the hospital.

Talk of officers having to do some camp fatigues such as wood trailers etc. I do not mind what I do but now feel justified in claiming my 'heavy duty ration', if I have to continue working as a two legged cart horse. Hitherto no differentiation has been made in the ration scales earned by officers, those of us entitled to heavy duty scale pooling ours with the rest. However, I think now the time is not far distant when we, as heavy duty workers, will have to consume what we earn.

Takahashi said to be off in next few days to an engineer unit at Bukit Timah. The screamers left the aerodrome at the beginning of the week and none have returned. Last Tuesday evening with Eric and Webby, who had been unable to eat his evening meal. Eric and I helped him to finish his by eating 1 1/2 doovers each!

Have been re-reading 'Jane Eyre', also reading J M Thompson's 'Lectures in Foreign History', T S Elliot's 'Selected Essays', and 'The Ship' by C S Forster, a novel based on the action of a light cruiser in the Mediterranean. Meals have recently been silent, heads buried deep in books. Heavy, laboured conversation, which creaked with forced politeness until I could take no more and shouted to them to shut up. How much longer can this bloody existence go on?

Nothing in the canteen now, apart from soap at $2.80 and talcum powder.

Last Wednesday afternoon listened to the Eroica. The more I listen to this, the longer the 2nd movement appears to become. The last movement stands out above the others, although the scherzo is rather fine.

1 July 45 Thank God we have embarked on the 2nd half of the year. Yesterday another great day as I received another three cards dated 17 Dec 44, 1 Jan 45 and 16 Jan 45. Have now received 7 cards and a photograph of Mother in the present batch of mail. Am busy trying to find a piece of glass for her photograph – not an easy thing to come by in this camp. 'Crippled Splendour' is at present suffering from a slight chill. He is a hopeless patient. What he would be like if he had malaria or was really ill I can't imagine. He goes around now looking like a whipped dog with his cap, now almost in shreds, on the back of his head and a cigarette dangling almost vertically downwards from his mouth, as though it were glued there. A party of 1000 (mixed Dutch and British) left this morning for No 2 area on South side of the gaol. Cpl. Chandler, our old mess cook, left on this party. The Australian, who escaped some days ago, has not yet been found. Kempeitai have been in the camp – all entertainments and bathing stopped once more. Weather delightfully cool during the past week. Some cables have been received in the past few days, dated as late at June 45. I understand replies may be sent. I suppose it is too much to hope that I shall be one of the fortunates to receive one. I attended an auction of drakes belonging to the hospital 'Duckery' this morning. Birds only 2lbs 15ozs maximum (alive) fetched up to $115. Birds of 1lb 8ozs went for $65. Very illuminating to see who did the purchasing – all the people one would expect to have money!

7 July 45 One week of July already passed. Lieut. Takahashi has left and a Lieut. Miura has taken over the job of Camp Commandant. He is a small man with a Charlie Chaplin moustache. 'Taka' refers to him to Philip Jones as a 'gentleman'. 'On verra'. Before leaving, 'Taka' ordered Andy Dillon to assume the position of representative officer in place of Newey. This, needless to say, is a very popular move. Last Tuesday I went out on a wood trailer party in the afternoon – some three miles down the Changi road. It was pleasant to see something different after all these months – twelve to be precise – in this camp. We saw some

Nip fighting troops looking very sunburnt by the side of the road. Malays seem to be more cheerfully disposed towards us and even ready to smile. Quite a change after their earlier surly expressions. I felt very low yesterday after inoculation the day before yesterday for TAB and spent most of yesterday in bed, reading Philip Guedalla's 'The Duke', which I find fascinating. I have also been reading 'The Philosophy of William James'. A grey, overcast day – no gardening – have been reading 'The Duke' all day.

10 July 45 Yesterday inspection of officers' area by Lt. Miura and the IJA QM. There was a retinue of 7 or 8. He took offence at private cooking, but this has not been stopped yet. Rumours of move into gaol in near future. 'Crippled Splendour' (Hutch) at present in such an insufferable mental condition that I almost welcome the possibility of such a change.

Books: Emmerson's 'Essays' and 'Conflict' by George F Milton on the American Civil War.

Recent news from Sime Road Camp: husbands and wives now allowed to meet once a week. Camp has been increased by 1500 Jewish internees, but I do not know where they have come from. St Andrew's school still contains Red Cross stores, some packed ready for Borneo, Java and Sumatra, but not yet sent. Coffee with Philip after putting urine on gardens earlier. Yesterday spent pm collecting sludge from farm; very hot and stinking. Tap root theft on officers' outside gardens thought to be by an officer. Monday evening lecture by Maj. Carl Gunther on Pidgin English in New Guinea.

Poor Hutch seems to be turning into a mental case. He does nothing but complain all day long about the food, smells etc. He lies on his bed all day long, complains of not sleeping at night and has been told by John that he must rest. Personally, I think he needs a job of work to do to exercise his white, unhealthy looking body.

He has become a 'malade imaginaire'. I have now adopted the policy of ignoring him as far as possible and this seems quite effective. He is one of many who, if left here long enough, will die mentally and eventually physically, through sheer lack of exercise. Mother's photograph now sits beside my bed on the table behind a glass frame. All I need now is a photograph of Father and Denison.

13 July 45 Friday. No worse than any other day in spite of the date. Busy on garden yesterday collecting human excreta in the morning, later horse manure, followed by an afternoon of putting sludge on beds. Piss slinging this morning. C.S. still bloody. Life unbelievably dull and as Hitler would say "My patience is exhausted".

14 July 45 Planted about 250 bayam seedlings this morning. Reading 'The Making of Modern Britain', by Brabner and Nevins, a popular history of England by two Americans, published in 1943.

15 July 45 Yesterday evening listened to some operatic records, mostly Italian, two songs (one by Leoncavallo) sung by Caruso, a pre-electrical recording, and Lalo's 'Symphonie Espagnole' played by Menuhin and the Orchestre Symphonique de Paris. Why this is called a symphony I do not know; it is, I would have thought, a violin concerto. C.S. due to move up to the 'White House' with Andy Dillon.

25 July 45 Hutch moved to the White House on the 16th and Stanley Kent (Major in 118 Field Regt.) came in on Tuesday. Kent is quiet, negative, suburban middle class outlook on life, but quite easy to live with. Pleasant feeling of freedom from suppression without Hutch, who had become very difficult to live with. After six months, I can now give vent to my changing moods. This makes life considerably easier. Have been out on three wood trailers now – work heavy but a change to see something new. Wednesday last listened to Leonora Overtures 1 and 3 and the 3rd Piano Concerto, Mark Hambourg. Records in good condition.

Afterwards spent evening chatting with Dick Austin. He is from 2/19 Bn, whose CO, Lt. Col. Anderson won the VC at the Moore battle. His battalion was practically wiped out. Books: 'History of World Literature,' (US publication), 'An Introduction to Conrad' by Frank Cush was excellent; all the autobiographical passages and sections of Conrad's books, collected so as to construct Conrad's autobiography. Huxley's 'Beyond the Mexique Bay'; disappointing. Now in the middle of V Hugo's 'Les Miserables', which is great stuff. There is a possibility of officers taking over the work of the forestry party. Volunteers have been called for. Donald, Ken and I and one or two others in 18 Division have volunteered.

Last Saturday evening listened to Lalo's Symphonie Espagnole again, scherzo rather fun, lovely slow movement, 3rd movement mostly missing unfortunately. Sunday evening spent with John and Eric, my usual Sunday date. John in bed with a bad foot. Today a great day! Fighters over for the first time. Said to be Lockheed 'Lightnings' by the American air force people. Four of them escorting a large four engined bomber, probably a Liberator, about 3 pm. Clear blue sky. Fighters estimated at only 8 - 9000 ft. 3 AA bursts. Brownout sounded after planes had disappeared to the West. This is an excellent sign. Made a good sweet yesterday. A steamed pudding. Grated taproot, coconut, 1 lb gula, some tamarind and a gula/santan sauce. The nearest thing to a treacle pudding I have had for years! It went down particularly well, as I had been out trailing in the afternoon. Rumours of the canteen closing down soon. Still busy on gardens. Magnificent night last night; full moon, cool breeze. Far too good to be incarcerated here. God! How impatient we all are to get out. If only we knew how long it was going to be. It's almost unendurable.

I wonder what it feels like to be full again and not feel perpetually hungry. Every meal one eats, one could eat two or three times over. We are all wondering whether we shall be able to digest European food and how long it will take us to re-adapt ourselves to a meat diet. Even with the extra 'doovering' we are never anything like satisfied. At best only blown out for an hour or two and then this hopeless, nagging feeling of hunger descends over one once more.

27 July 45 Plane over yesterday for 3/4 hour, but not seen, only heard.

A Korean, by name Ono, committed suicide with rifle behind IJA guardroom. Shot himself through the head. Ken, Donald, Tommy Bond and me selected for forestry work. Total 50 officers, out each day from a pool of 80, two days out, one day in. Heavy duty rations, thank goodness. Wednesday evening listened to the Beethoven 9th still in comparatively good condition. What a glorious thing it is. The poignancy of the slow movement.

5 August 45 Day off from forestry work after being out 2 days. Several visits by Lightnings recently. 3 over low on Wednesday. Yesterday seven flew over this end of the island after coming in from the direction of the naval base, flying one behind the other, weaving in and out like a flying serpent and 'tail-arse Charleying'. Said to have shot down a Nip 'Navy 0'. Nips busy patrolling now, but no sign of any of our planes. Last two days on forestry have been very wet and yesterday was spent corduroying the road for the trailers. We had to winch out a 6 wheeled Nip truck, which was bogged down. Reading 'Flowering of New England' by van Wyck Brooks. Less time for reading now I am out two days in three. Last Thursday evening with John and Eric; the former still in bed. Last Wednesday heard the Rubinstein recording of Chopin's 2nd Concerto, followed by the Rachmaninov 2nd. Yesterday listened to the lst. Chopin piano concerto which I prefer to the 2nd. It will be more difficult to get hold of records in future, as they are now all concentrated in the gaol.

Visit by Nip C in C Malaya some days ago. Did not appear to take much interest in the camp. Why should he? I don't really blame him, why should he care what happens to a few thousand POWs. He must have plenty to worry about apart from us. There is an atmosphere of intense impatience in camp. All feel that things cannot go on much longer as they are and yet there is no sign of anything significant happening to bring about our freedom apart from air activity, but perhaps this should be enough for us. The time passes quickly, working two days at a time but reading suffers. Wondering how my weight will be affected as all we get extra by way of food is one small rice rissole!

15 August 45 The delight and shock of sudden incredible, wonderful news. 3 1/2 years to the day and the war appears to be as good as over.

Busy on forestry for the past fortnight; two days out, one in. Paraded this morning but working party cancelled. Suppressed excitement over the momentous news outside the gaol that the war is over. None of us have slept since the first hint of Japan's unconditional surrender. It seems impossible and utterly incredible that everything can really be over. My brain is in a whirl and I cannot concentrate on anything, let alone reading.

It is difficult to believe that in a week or two we might be free. Our Korean guards mostly appear to be quite cheerful, otherwise there is no visible evidence that the situation must be changing rapidly. The Nips have said nothing officially and we have to play the idiot boys for the time being, since our fear that they might find our radios still runs deep. Grim overcast day. How different to the brilliant blue skies and sun which accompanied our capitulation more than 3 1/2 years ago! The whole camp has gone doovering mad and money is steadily depreciating. The sappers are building huts near the Ford works at Bukit Timah under Takahashi, who pumped Philip about conditions in their camp. He said he supposed we had already received our further issue of Red Cross food. Philip rather naturally looked very surprised and said he had heard nothing of a further issue. Cases of diphtheric ulcers and throat cases have increased during the past few days. We have just heard a rumour that the Nips intend to fight it out. Personally I doubt it. Particularly if orders for the surrender come from the Emperor himself. Great speculation now as to whether we shall go all the way home by sea or whether we shall fly part of the way. Rice ration increased by 50gms and oil ration doubled.

18 August 45 In bed this morning with a bad cold. A good sign perhaps, as I left England with a cold, so perhaps we shall be leaving here soon.

Day in yesterday, out on Thursday. Local Nip reaction now noticeable. Saw one crowd of about 200 Nip soldiers in their full uniform of tunic and breeches being addressed by an officer. All looked rather subdued. Also passed a truck-load of one star privates (in full uniform, rarely seen under normal circumstances) with all their equipment, bedding and personal belongings. About 50 Nip guards arrived two days ago and have established a guardroom about 1 mile down the Changi Road. Many sick are expected in from Singapore camps. Kerr's operation scar refuses to heal up and he is worried about the possibility of having to return home on a hospital ship and not being able to enjoy the trip home with us. The initial enjoyment of being free is going to be far richer and more intense if we are able to remain in our own circle of friends and can thus enjoy everything together.

Philip went into Singapore yesterday, still working for Takahashi at Bukit Timah. They were told to put a wire fence round the environs of Taka's house and to include one or two huts on the opposite side of the road. While they were working a truck load of IJA arrived and about 50 troops in full uniform and all their equipment and personal gear got out. They were fallen in in the road and after a cursory inspection put their rifles and ammunition down in the roadway. The bolt mechanism of the rifles had recently been smeared with wet mud. They were then addressed for about ten minutes by a captain and after him by a 2nd Lieut. Each man was given a form to fill in and after much sucking of teeth, the men extracted stub ends of pencils from different parts of their equipment and started to fill in the information required, to the accompaniment of much head scratching and reference to the man next door for advice.

Philip and his little party of 12 sappers watched all this from the garden of Taka's house. By now a crowd of Malays and Chinese had congregated and watched the proceedings with increasing interest and in the case of the Chinese, I've no doubt, with mounting pleasure. Here, to their puzzled minds was an extraordinary sight. A party of POWs putting up wire round the billet area of some Nip troops, who appeared to be handing in their rifles, as though they had no further use for them! Philip had a long conversation with Taka, each assuming that the other was fully aware of the transcendental events taking place. Philip asked if his party would be coming down again the next day, to which Taka replied "No, prisoners would not be working in Singapore in future and would be returning to Changi in the next few days". After exchanging mutual thanks, polite and suitable remarks, the two of them parted. A grim future for Takahashi, one of the very few Nips, who have shown understanding and have taken an interest in our welfare. He has always, I believe, done his best, within the confines of the IJA, to help us under extremely difficult circumstances.

At 12.45 pm three planes, believed to be RAF Beaufighters have just flown over from the direction of the Naval Base and were fired on. Is this war over or not? 2000–3000 men have come in from Singapore camps. Books: Somerset Maugham's 'The Summing Up', his autobiography and Jenegan's 'The American Colonies.'

19 August 45 Things seem to be moving at last. It now appears to be recognised by the Nips that Japan has surrendered. Working parties from Singapore are flooding in, among them L.V. Taylor's party. Three truckloads of Red Cross food arrived this morning. The Nips are allowing us to put the rice ration up to 500gms, but this is to be limited to 325gms on the recommendation of the medical authorities, who are afraid that to put it up further would lead to too unbalanced a diet and incipient beriberi would return. A service is to be held on the padang tomorrow and the possibility of putting on a show is being discussed. There is a distinct end of term feeling in the air.

20 August 45 By 11.00 pm last night 9 truckloads of Red Cross stores had arrived. Last night we received our issue of 20 cigarettes per man. Choice of Chesterfields or Camel. The present consignment of Red Cross food is part of that which arrived in January 44. It is absolutely criminal that all this food should have been sat on for over 18 months. There is still said to be a large quantity of stores left from the Awa Maru consignment.

We are to be allowed to send a five word message home. Lieut.

317

Miura informed Andy yesterday that the war was nearly over, but that he, Miura, would continue to command the camp until orders to the contrary. All Outram Road prisoners are to come up here; some have already arrived. They were paraded yesterday at Outram Road (The Kempeitai gaol). They then had their respective sentences read out to them, after which they were calmly informed that their sentences were finished. Amongst the officers and men to come up were some American B29 aircrews. 13 of these are unaccounted for. This lends credence to the story that 10 of them were executed some few weeks back as a reprisal for indiscriminate bombing of Japan. It is reported that 1400 people of different nationalities have died in Outram Road Gaol in the past 6 months. Starvation and torture, probably. My cold is running its course and at present I cannot enjoy a good cigarette. I shall have to postpone the opening of my packet. Reorganisation of the camp, prior to the ultimate 'dispersal' of POWs starts today. Lunch time score of Red Cross trucks was 15. Supplies are still flooding in. Started on Red Cross food today, coffee and sweetened milk for breakfast. Hutch gave me an egg two days ago, my first for over 18 months. It is incredible to think that the past years of malnutrition and semi-starvation can really be over.

21 August 45 Everything seems to be happening at once. Red Cross stores continue to flood in and we received one parcel per man up to last night. Today fresh pork arrived, but only 8lbs for our mess of 150, but these are quite unbelievable days. We have managed to get hold of quite a bit of coffee and it is wonderful to be able to sit down to an 11 o'clock cup of real coffee with sweetened milk and to smoke a Chesterfield cigarette. I think I enjoy this as much as anything else.

Rumour today of Mountbatten meeting the Nip Commander of the

Southern Regions in Rangoon on Thursday. With luck our people may be in by the end of the week. This waiting is a nerve racking business. There has been trouble between the INA (Indian National Army) and loyal Indians in Singapore and machine gun fire and rifle shots are reported to have been exchanged. It is said that 60 casualties were caused. Some American B29 pilots in from Outram Road Gaol speak very highly of Mountbatten as a commander. Here of course, he has been criticized for doing nothing. Unfortunately a POW easily gets an exaggerated idea of his own importance and considers that all operations should be aimed at getting him out. This is somewhat natural. Our five word messages are being handed in today. These are being sent under IJA auspices. Gaol cookhouse now cooking for 8000. Considerable difficulty in opening Red Cross tins as a lot of labour and space are required. All Outram Road prisoners are now up here. Saw Henry Phillips, the adjutant of the Beds & Herts yesterday. He had completed a month of a 2 year sentence for disseminating news in Thailand and had been in Bangkok Gaol prior to Outram Road. Many of the incoming troops from Singapore working camps had heard nothing of the surrender until arriving here. In one camp, L V Taylor's at Johore, two men pinched a wireless set which they saw in a private house, took it back to the vicinity of the camp and tuned in. The first thing they heard was the King's speech! What a moment that must have been. Two marines, survivors from the sinking of the Prince of Wales have just come into the camp. They have passed themselves off as Eurasians for the past 3 1/2 years and have been living in Singapore.

I expect other similar stories will come to light when all is over. For the last two days I have made some very good shortbread, which we have had for tea. Recipe was quite simple, tap flour, sugar and palm oil in proportion 2-1-1. I then put on a gula sauce which formed a sort of icing on top. Result very satisfactory.

22 August 45 Clothing in addition to food now coming into the camp; even coffee beans, sugar, wheat flour (2oz per man per day for 8 days) and pork have come in. Troops continued to pour into the gaol up to 1.30 am this morning, the last people to arrive being Dutch civilians who have been working on an island off Singapore. Wonderful to feel not only full but satisfied once more. I am getting much more interested in taste now and bulk takes second place. Peter, Kerr and I went to see John and Eric last night. We had coffee and ate shortbread with Charles Charlton, Peter Coope and some others this morning. It is great to be able to coffee-house and smoke good cigarettes again. The atmosphere of the camp is that of the end of a winter term at school accentuated a thousand times. Many of the Outram Road prisoners had been undergoing life sentences for attempted escapes made from camps in Thailand, in particular the survivors of the attempt from our camp at Sonkurai, which ended so disastrously.

Some of them are suffering considerable nervous reaction after suddenly being freed and discovering that the war is over. From what we hear, there seem to be good hopes of Count Terauchi, the Nip C in C, signing the surrender of the Southern Regions tomorrow or Friday in Rangoon. In that event our forces should be in here by the end of the week. It is reported locally that all roads in Singapore Island have to be clear of all traffic by Thursday midnight. A dozen 'Navy Os' flying around the island this morning. Having their final joy ride? There seem to be indications that some of us may go home by air. What utterly fantastic days these are. I just cannot take in all that is going on and I certainly can't concentrate for long on any reading. I was weighed four days ago and have at last reached over 9 stone. I feel very fit. Had a magnificent chocolate sweet for dinner last night. It tasted unbelievably rich. Morale in the gaol is very high and the troops have maintained excellent discipline, taking the news of the Japanese surrender relatively calmly. This was just as well, as we received news of the surrender some days before the Nips let out any hint of it. The Koreans have been going around the camp obtaining references! They are in high spirits.

24 August 45 General Shaito called for Andy Dillon, Holmes and Neal this morning. He told them that General Terauchi's envoys were expected to go to Rangoon on Sunday 26th and that everything would be completed by 1 September. He asked Andy if there was anything he wanted. The result of this was as follows:

1. The IJA would supply towgay and rice polishings and the rice ration should be increased.

2. General Shaito offered Alexandra Hospital for hospital patients. Andy delayed decision on this as he was fully aware what movement of patients under the IJA involved.

3. Bathing Parties would be arranged starting tomorrow.

4. Visiting camps in Singapore would be allowed and would start this afternoon.

5. General Shaito stated that Allied doctors and medical supplies were expected to arrive by air from 1700 hrs this afternoon.

6. Andy said that he required a wireless set for news. General Shaito replied that this would only give us a one-sided picture. Andy riposted with the remark that at present we only received the Japanese side. (Not strictly true).

7. Bugle calls would be changed back as soon as possible.

Ken and I coffeed with John and Eric last night. John gave me a sleeping draught, which like a b.f, I took. Have been half asleep all day. Peter May in the camp today from Adam Road but did not see him. He is remaining at Adam Road pro tem. Have just had daily bulletin read out.

Glad to hear that our relations are allowed to send airmail letters to us. Perhaps news from home will be awaiting us on release or may even be flown in to us. Another issue of 10 cigarettes today. I was amused to hear today that ARP shelters at Reigate had been used to store whisky, but worried at stories that there will be a worldwide whisky shortage until 1953. Difficulty of getting showers now; due to large numbers in camp.

Water not available in evening and we have to rely on wells, which are inadequate. Lt. Col. Nee Soon, Indian Hospital Camp, produced one day's ration for 1 man and a duck to demonstrate to Japanese that the camp ration for one man was insufficient to feed a duck. Charles Charlton met some of his Indian soldiers, who offered him a live chicken. He replied that he could not take a live chicken through the wire into the camp. The Indian replied: "The Sahib is quite right. We will kill it at once."

The news that the return of AIF 8th Division is to be celebrated by a public holiday has caused considerable amazement. The Divisional Commander, General Gordon Bennett, must have a thick hide to believe that, as a deserter, he ought to take part in any celebrations, let alone the formal surrender of Singapore. Not a popular figure here. There is widespread annoyance at hearing that General Percival has been freed before us.

There have been three deaths in the past two days. One, reportedly, through over-eating; the man apparently ate, amongst other things, three pounds of sugar. Eric says that many of the Dutch half-castes are over-stuffing themselves. Generally speaking, the Dutch have too often not shown up very well during the past 3 1/2 years. This is borne out by our people from camps in Java, Sumatra and up country. All are unanimous in stating that the Dutch in general are selfish, greedy and often dirty, although the latter refers, in my own experience, to the Eurasian Dutch. Certainly, in this camp they have been all out for themselves and have shown little or no willingness to co-operate in the interests of the camp as a whole.

25 August 45 Woke up this morning to British reveille again, followed by, 'Come to the cookhouse'. Issue of 20 Kooa cigarettes last night. Said to be total of 150 Kooas, Old Gold and Nip issue cigarettes per man.

Nips standing by as from 0500 hrs this morning for air drops of Red Cross supplies and drugs. Letters 'POW' in yellow on black cloth have been put on Padang and Nip sentries have been posted. Entertainments are allowed once more. Light classical music at Coconut Grove this evening. Swimming probably tomorrow. Issue of beef and fish last night. Beef 1 1/2ozs per man. Fresh fish 5ozs per man. Heard yesterday that the plane taking General Wainwright to freedom is missing. What a tragedy if he has been killed.

27 August 45 My 27th birthday fast approaching and it does not look as though anybody will arrive before the end of the week. Conference this morning between General Shaito and Swiss International Red Cross representatives. One result of this is that we are to be given a wireless set tomorrow and a news sheet will be published daily. Rather amusing under the circumstances since we have had radio sets operating practically throughout our captivity! The rice ration has been put up to 400gms as from today, and we are now on 20gms of rice polishings per day. Tomorrow the issue of Red Cross parcels will be increased to 1 per 15; we are at present on 1 per 20.

We went bathing yesterday and today, although the weather has not been good. Rain and little sun. The sea looks much more friendly now, whereas it used to strike me as being an infinite barrier separating me from home. It now forms a link with the outside world and it is pleasant to sit up on the top of the cliff and let my mind wander idly over the days soon to come, when we shall be sailing steadily homewards. Yesterday evening with John and Eric. John's foot is no better and is completely raw on top. Yesterday fresh butter and cheese from the Singapore cold storage were received. The butter ration is approx 1lb per head and fresh milk has been received for the hospital. The Koreans are reported to have gone out on their first fatigue today, collecting wood!

Yesterday we received an issue of IJA vests, shorts, socks (no heels), G strings and boots (small sizes only). It is atrocious stuff. I find five people in a coolie quarter, as we now are, very crowded and with the exception of Eric, the three Majors, all equally useless and idle, get on my nerves. However it will not be for much longer. Everybody, I think, is finding the present period of waiting very trying. Still no mention of when any relieving forces may be expected to land and speculation about our trip home continues. It would help greatly to have something definite to go on. Heard today that the Rangoon conference is to continue until Wednesday and that matters to be discussed include mine sweeping operations, dropping medical officers and supplies for POWs and arrangements for Allied naval shipping to enter 'Japanese' waters etc. But no mention of the, for us, all important date for the relief of Singapore. It looks now as though we shall have to wait until the beginning of next month.

29 August 45 A Liberator appeared at 2.00 pm over the camp flying low, at about 500 ft. After circling twice it came straight over the gaol area and dropped hundreds of leaflets. We could easily see the two airmen in the plane's doorway throwing them out. The leaflets are in Japanese and addressed to our guards. There are two. The first reads:

Instructions to all Japanese forces throughout Malaya:

After the unconditional surrender of the Japanese forces, Tenno Heika, who stands under the orders of the United Nations Supreme Commander, has issued an Imperial Rescript on 13 August telling the Japanese forces in all Malaya to cease fighting. It goes without saying that this Imperial Rescript does not only apply to the Regular Forces but also to all personnel continuing resistance by means of guerrilla warfare or other extraordinary methods. We quote below a passage from Tenno Heika's Imperial Rescript:

"We, embodying the Government of the Empire have had the Governments of the United States, Great Britain, China and the USSR informed that we accept their joint association. We urgently warn against all acts which, due to excessive feelings would cause Allied planes dropping pamphlets announcing the end of the war, disturbances or worsen the situation to the detriment of their fellow countrymen, thereby setting virtue at nought and causing the loss of the trust of the world".

Tenno Heika's Imperial Rescript has already been issued and it will therefore be transmitted to you before long by your commanding officers and so you will have to obey the orders of the Supreme Commander of the United Nations. You should by no means commit acts of violence against Malays or Chinese. Furthermore you are strictly prohibited from leaving the appointed areas arbitrarily. If you should resist the United Nations Armies in the slightest, this will be severely punished as an infringement of the surrender signed by Tenno Heika. In other words you should be well aware of the fact that your actions will not only decide your own fate, but will also influence the fate of your fatherland Japan.

The second pamphlet is addressed specifically to our Japanese guards:

Instructions to Japanese Guards:

The land, sea and air forces of Japan, have completely surrendered to the United Nations, Tenno Heika has personally signed their capitulation and the Pacific War is over. In the next few days United Nations aeroplanes will be dropping pamphlets written in English, Dutch and the Indian languages, to United Nations soldiers and civilians in the hands of the Japanese forces, containing instructions for them.

The United Nations soldiers and civilians should maintain their calm and remain in their present positions. When these pamphlets have come into the hands of the Japanese Guards they must hand them over immediately to the United Nations prisoners of war and civilians and treat them with care. After handing over these pamphlets the guards are to return to their own barracks. Japanese officers and men are to give United Nations prisoners of war and civilians such good food as they require and treat them without stint.

This is their responsibility. Within a few days one or more United Nations officers with wireless sets will come into internment camps of the United Nations soldiers. Their main task will be to maintain contact with United Nations personnel and to transmit their needs to the Supreme Commander of the United Nations Armies.

Therefore the Japanese guards should not interfere with the activities of these United Nations officers, but should help and protect them.

This was dropped in the POW camps on Tuesday 28 August 45. The pamphlets were thrown out by one of the crew standing in the doorway of the fuselage, who afterwards waved to us, as the plane circled around Changi.

The camp was an amazing sight. People crowded on roofs, balconies and all the open spaces. It was an intensely exciting moment and very many of us were in tears. I got a very odd feeling in the pit of my stomach and it was a highly emotional occasion. Later we went down to the sea for a swim, the sea being full of jellyfish. It was very funny to see most people coming out of the water as fast as they could, clutching their nether regions, either through having been stung or the mere fear of being stung. I hit several but was not stung. At about 5.00 pm a second Liberator appeared suddenly over the camp and dropped more leaflets in the hospital area, this time in English and addressed to us. Again, intense excitement. Donald and I stood on the chimney on the roof of the coolie quarters. The plane circled several times, banking steeply, at about 500ft. We were greatly amused by this pamphlet at the reference to cooking any gifts of food from natives.

The next day hundreds of copies of the following pamphlet were dropped:

TO ALL ALLIED PRISONERS OF WAR. THE JAPANESE FORCES HAVE SURRENDERED UNCONDITIONALLY AND THE WAR IS OVER.

We will get supplies to you as soon as is humanly possible and will make arrangements to get you out but, owing to the distances involved it may be some time before we can achieve this. You will help us and yourselves if you act as follows:

1. Stay in your camp until you get further orders from us.

2. Start preparing nominal rolls of personnel, giving full particulars.

3. List your most urgent necessities.

4. If you have been starved or underfed for long periods,

DO NOT eat large quantities of solid food, fruit or vegetables first. It is dangerous for you to do so.

Catalina flying boats expected today. Trying to read 'Guy Mannering' but books are difficult to concentrate on. Visit yesterday by Swiss International Red Cross representatives. Radio set for the camp received last night from IJA. An officer died yesterday from TB. God, how incredibly sad. Party standing by last night to go into Singapore to collect supplies. Presumably Catalinas will land at Kalang. Hundreds of us have got oedema of the legs and face. Can this be the effect of increased rice ration? My legs and face are very swollen and if I press my legs, great thumb marks are left on my shins and I can feel nothing! Quite like old times.

30 August 45 My birthday! I had hoped three weeks ago that by now we would have been free and I might have had something to drink. However, I had two fried eggs for breakfast – a birthday present from Hutch. John gave me a packet of Kooa cigarettes and Eric presented me with a vest! So I did very well.

In addition to birthday excitements, it had been a great day. Yesterday evening we heard on the news that officers and supplies were to be dropped on Changi aerodrome today. True to their word, at 8.00 am I woke to the sound of engines roaring overhead, jumped out of bed and rushed up to get a good view of the aerodrome. I was just in time to see about 12 parachutes open, men dropping in batches of three. Two staff officers, two medical officers and two orderlies landed and were in the camp by 10.00 am. Medical officers wearing cerise RAMC berets, jackets and trousers tucked into boots. They are personnel belonging to an Indian army Parafield Ambulance Unit, designed especially for relieving POWs in the course of active operations against the enemy. They came from Ceylon in a Liberator, having apparently left last night. They stated on arrival that more supplies were expected later today and, as I write this, two Liberators are circling the aerodrome dropping containers by parachute. Unfortunately we cannot see these actually dropping as the planes go down too low and are lost to view behind the palm trees. We can, however, tell when the parachutes open as this is greeted each time by a lusty cheer from the men in the gaol, who are crowding the windows.

The whole camp is seething with excitement and Donald, true to his journalistic instinct, is spending most of the day in the gaol office and by this evening should have picked up some interesting dope.

Hutch came down after lunch and gave me a State Express 333, given him by one of the incoming people. It certainly tasted good. He did not seem to have picked up very much in the way of news from them. They can tell us nothing of when we are likely to get out of here and reach home, which is the only thing we really want to know. In many ways these are nerve-wracking days. There have now been a number of cases of officers going down with nervous breakdowns. One or two of these have simply gone mad, one attempted to commit suicide by cutting one of his wrists, but did not do himself very much damage. A very good dinner last night with baked jam roll and cream custard, biscuits and cheese savoury! The food is really excellent now.

The wireless set received from the IJA is now working and it is intended to broadcast news by means of loudspeakers in the hospital area and the trailer park. In the gaol the news is to be read out in the form of a summary through loud speakers. The officers who have just parachuted in are astounded that we have had news all the time and at the ingenuity shown in the design of our cigarette lighters. They have seen nothing yet! If they are impressed by this, they will be astounded at what has been produced in our workshops in the way of medical equipment.

Coffee with John and Eric this morning. Aussies becoming more and more regimental as the days go by. Their bullshit is unbelievable, not least the issue of 'orders of the day' etc. Kerr, Peter and I went to a musical show yesterday evening, but it was bum and, as the lights went out and the whole thing developed into a sing-song, we left in a hurry. Very pleasant afternoon yesterday bathing, sun and a fresh breeze, but unfortunately lots of jellyfish. It seems to be jellyfish breeding season!

31 August 45 Donald did not pick up very much in the way of news after all. In fact he seemed very tired and distraught by the end of the day. Most of us, I think, are finding things altogether too much for us and impossible to grasp. Another allied plane over the camp this morning.

Our own MPs have taken over from the Nips this morning. This, of course, means that where the IJA had only 6 guards we now have about 60 MPs. Have seen a 'Daily Express' and a 'John Bull' dated June 45. The two combatant officers had lunch yesterday with Hutch and Andy at the 'White House'. A special lunch had been put on including stew, rice, greens and two Red Cross doovers. The stew they did not touch; the rice they only picked at with their forks, the greens they took one look at and left untouched; it was Kang-Kong and rubbery at that. They removed the tops of the doovers, picked at the meat fillings, leaving the casings uneaten and then produced their own lunch and knocked back half a tin of pork roll each, a tin of some other sort of meat and finished off with large quantities of biscuits, butter, jam and cheese. They then asked whether the lunch was our usual diet and were rather surprised to be told that it was far better than usual, as it not only included Red Cross food, but was a special lunch anyway!

One of the MOs landed on the roof of one of the buildings in the old 18 Div. Changi area and broke one of his legs. Apparently a Colonel Stewart was landed three days ago with a transmitter, but neither he nor his transmitter have been heard of since.

Meanwhile a party of American airmen including Bags Baggott and Longmore (RAF) visited Changi, Kalang and one or two other airfields and passed them fit for flying in B24s. However, without Colonel Stewart's transmitter, it appears to be impossible to pass on this information to SEAC, so God knows what the next move is! According to yesterday evening's news, envoys had left Singapore for the Allied fleets at Sabang and Penang to guide them through the minefields to Singapore, so they should be here soon. These days of waiting are intensely irritating, particularly as we hear of POWs already being flown to Calcutta from Thailand and others being freed in Manchuria. Trust General Percival and all those dead-wood, red-tabbed senior officers to get out before us.

The four officers, who landed yesterday, seem to know very little and can tell us nothing of how, when and by what route we shall be sent home. As these are the only things we are really interested in, they are not of any great value to us. Typical for any junior officer in the army – he is told nothing, and therefore knows damn all about anything, beyond what he has to know about his own limited responsibility. As a staff officer on a divisional headquarters one is fortunate in that one generally has a much wider knowledge of what is going on around one.

Yesterday evening, Ken, Peter and I coffeed with John and Eric. Whiskers, Cyril Wild and Hutch were also there. We were informed yesterday that we shall be able to send one free cable, two post cards and four letter-cards, the first three to be of standard text. This will save me much brain effort. Three Liberators dropped 60–70 containers on the aerodrome this afternoon but no transmitter has yet been received. The Nips will no doubt help out by providing one, if they can. Clearly the British military has not changed much, which we find rather reassuring, since it will not be quite so difficult as we have been thinking to catch up with the post-war world. Spent most of afternoon in Hutch's room reading an airmail edition of the 'Daily Telegraph' dated August 45. It made me unbelievably homesick to see it. Also read about a dozen copies of the paper published by SEAC in India, the latest dated 21 August. This afternoon the two crew members, one a New Zealand Lieut. and the other an English WO, force landed their Mosquito, 'owing to engine trouble' at Kalang. They are in our lines now. They expect to return to their base at the Cocos Islands today. They have been employed on photographic recces of Singapore for the past two months. It is said that, in fact, they did not have engine trouble and landed on purpose in order to be able to claim that they were the first allied troops to set foot in Singapore.

1 September 45 Last night we listened to the news broadcast from New Delhi at 8.30. We received it very clearly but unfortunately a particularly dull bulletin. Two signals orderlies dropped yesterday evening from a Liberator. Said to have left part of their transmitter in the plane. This sounds typical of our blundering ways. First a Lieut. Col. and transmitter are dropped somewhere in Malaya and lost. Then two men arrive and leave some essential piece of equipment behind. Obviously the army has not changed at all.

From Walt Whitman's 'Poems of Joys':

"O to realize space!

The plenteousness of all – that there are no bounds;

To emerge, and be of the sky – of the sun and moon, and the flying clouds, as one with them."

Two Mosquitos over this afternoon very low, flying straight over the camp. More wireless sets have been received from the Nips.

2 September 45 Red Cross rations increased to one parcel per 10 and rice to be decreased. Three truckloads of tinned pineapple were collected from Singapore today – 1 tin per man! More expected. Lt. Col. Stewart and seven others including one Chinese officer, Pte. Fairbrother (AIF), who escaped from here 2–3 months ago, and one or two other guerrillas arrived this morning at 5 am. Stewart has brought his transmitter with him. Great preparation of nominal rolls going on at present. RAPWI HQ set up in Half Moon Street. Party yesterday evening with Dick Austin, Philip Jones and Mel Portal, Charles Portal's brother, at which we ate frankfurters in tomato sauce and drank samsu, flavoured with fruit juices (pineapple and pear) and cooled with ice. Needless to say it was excellent and although I only had 3/4 pint, I took quite a good view even of this life by the time I went to bed. Woke up this morning with a distinctly noticeable hangover. A number of B24s over again this morning, dropping supplies on the aerodrome. Also one Mosquito came zooming over the camp and entertained us to quite a bit of low flying at high speed. Everybody crowding rooftops and all open spaces as usual. Have just been listening to New Delhi 4.00 pm news broadcast, but apart from the terms of the Japanese surrender and news that minesweepers have once more embarked on their sweeping of the Malacca Straits, there was little of interest. There are now quite a few illustrated papers, such as 'Picture Post' and 'Punch', available in the library, but I have not yet succeeded in getting hold of any to look at. Some people, who have read 'Punch', say they just cannot understand a word of it as most of the jokes refer to things which mean nothing to us.

The Mosquito, which force landed two days ago at Kalang took off again after the CO of the squadron had landed too. He had flown out from the Cocos Islands the day after the plane had put down, to bring the crew some lunch and to see if they were OK. They came over before leaving to 'shoot up' the gaol in answer to a request to do this. Donald tried to get out a story on this plane but RAPWI would not let anything go. When the hell is the Allied fleet arriving? We hear every day now of POWs in other parts of the Far East being released, but there is still no sign of things happening here. It has become an increasingly trying time.

Yesterday evening we heard that SEAC had ordered the Nips to have Government House ready for occupation by Wed 5 Sep, so perhaps something will happen early this next week. My beriberi is much better and the swelling in my legs and ankles has almost disappeared. Decreasing the rice and increasing the Red Cross food should soon cure this completely.

Still no news of any further incoming mail. How I would like to receive up to date airmail news from home. Am enjoying Walt Whitman's 'Leaves of Grass' at present. One of the Liberators, based on Cocos Island, is reported to have stalled on take-off, with supplies for Singapore POWs, crashed and burst into flames, all the crew killed; poor bastards. Two women were seen in the camp this afternoon, internees from Sime Rd.

The two officers who dropped by parachute the other day over Changi have visited the civilian internees in Sime Road camp and were mobbed by the women, which is hardly surprising. One of the two, Wishart by name, makes us all feel incredibly old. He is only 22 and the other officer with him 21. The ADMS of their division is 32. We are worn out 'has-beens'.

4 September 45 Three PROs, the advance party of the press, were dropped yesterday from a B24. An Australian, an Indian and a British Major. Their first jump. They brought the news that the 5th Indian Division is due to land in Singapore tomorrow and that a press ship with over 100 war correspondents is expected in at the same time. The Cathay building is to be prepared for their arrival. On yesterday evening's news we heard that HMS Sussex is due in this morning to meet Nip envoys off Singapore. Things are moving at last. I was very sick the night before last and consequently spent yesterday on my bed feeling bloody. Woke this morning feeling very much better, but rather empty since I ate practically nothing all day yesterday. 'Country Walks' have been arranged for the troops and bathing hours extended to 4 hours per day. Various Red Cross comforts have been received. So far I've received 1 razor blade and a pencil. This is the sum total of what I have seen of the stuff dropped from the B24s, hardly over generous. We listened to the news from the BBC last night for the first time for the best part of 4 years. Yesterday evening received 3 Craven A cigarettes. I swapped mine with Peter for Players. Smoked one after breakfast this morning. By far the best, smoothest smoke of all. The camp is becoming increasingly bullshit mad and the Australians are holding a victory parade! Yesterday the Union Jack, Stars and Stripes and the Dutch tricolour were unfurled on the gaol tower. The Stars and Stripes are rather small and the Dutch tricolour is far too big. Personally, I think they should also fly the Chungking flag, many of which are apparently flying in Singapore. After all the Chinese suffered infinitely more casualties than all the allies put together.

None of the incoming people (RAPWI representatives and others) can touch our food and they cannot understand the terrific bulk we are able to put away. I don't suppose they can, as they have not had to live mainly on very poor quality rice for 3 1/2 years to keep themselves alive.

Everyone is hoping that, when the 5th Indian Div. arrives, they will make large numbers of transports available on which POWs will be taken away without further delay. A great change in the atmosphere of the camp during the past fortnight, particularly noticeable in the evening.

Loudspeakers blaring forth all over the camp; in the gaol, in the hospital area, no 2 area, Coconut Grove and the trailer park. News bulletins, news commentaries, gramophone records and variety programmes from the BBC forces programme, New Delhi, SEAC and San Francisco. Lights blazing everywhere and lights out has been put back to 23.30 hours.

5 September 45 Arrival of cruiser Cleopatra, flying the flag of Admiral Power, off Singapore two days ago. Cruiser Sussex (Admiral Holland) arrived yesterday and 8 destroyers have entered the Naval Base. Yesterday evening PROs and Rawl Knox and Donald left for Cathay building, where the press bureau is being set up. Great break for them both to get away from here so early.

PRO Col. visit to General Itagaki, who was told that he wanted two floors of the Cathay building prepared for press representatives. Gen. Itagaki said he was sorry but the Cathay building was in the Japanese area. To which PRO. replied "No, your tense is wrong. It was a Japanese area". By late yesterday afternoon beds, desks and telephones had all been installed. We had such a belly full of news and commentaries last night over the radio that by 9.30 I decided that I had had enough. I wandered all over the camp and could not find a corner anywhere where I could be away from all the noise. It was blaring everywhere, echoing and re-echoing off all the walls and buildings of the gaol.

Peter is now in charge of the Changi end of the press organisation. My stomach is much better and I hope to go swimming today. Permission has been given by RAPWI for us to go to Fairy Point to watch the fleet enter the Naval Base, whenever that is due to take place. Yesterday I managed at last to get a look at quite a few 'Picture Posts' and 'Weekly Illustrated'.

6 September 45 Yesterday, after more than 3 1/2 years, Allied forces returned to Singapore - the 5th Indian Division. Some of our people in Singapore saw the fleet arriving. Cleopatra visible about a mile out, some destroyers and then a vast line of transports and naval vessels, stretching away in one long line to the horizon, where the smoke of other shipping was visible. Some POWs visiting Singapore met some of the Indian troops, who had already started occupying the city area, to the accompaniment of much hand shaking. A Eurasian civilian was heard to shout "It's about time you returned". IJA officers had their swords and pistols removed. The whole thing apparently proceeded very smoothly. As each crossroad, bridge or important building was reached, troops with LMGs mounted guard. Some of the occupation forces are expected up here today and are to fix the ration, medical and clothing situation. Yesterday evening news came in thick and fast. The senior PRO told us over the local radio hook up that we had shown great patience during the past days and he asked us to be patient for 2 or 3 days more! On D + 4 British and Indian POWs are expected to start leaving. That presumably means Sunday. Six hospital ships are expected and a number of empty transports have just arrived with the convoy. It looks as though it will only be a matter of days now before we are off.

Airmail letter cards are being issued to us today and it is said that these will be flown out tomorrow. An American aircraft is landing at Kalang today to evacuate 40 US nationals. The Aussies are very depressed; 1). Their paratroops did NOT land. 2). None of their representatives have yet arrived. 3). They heard yesterday evening that transports to evacuate AIF POW would not be here for another few days yet.

This morning went to see Hutch in Camp HQ. He gave me 5 State Express 555. Went up to the top of the tower and saw part of the fleet entering the naval base. Two destroyers followed by 2 MTBs were already sailing up the straits. Coming slowly round from Keppel harbour direction were two destroyers, a cruiser, two large transports, two fleet tankers, one aircraft carrier and some other vessels coming up behind. A wonderful sight.

I also saw the first European woman I had seen for over 3 1/2 years. A woman war correspondent. No doubt she saw a lot of odd sights during her walk round the camp. One of the correspondents, who visited X ward in the hospital yesterday, said he had seen many cases of malnutrition amongst POWs in German camps, but nothing approaching what he found here. They took photographs of many of the cases. Other photographs have been taken of groups of POW and such things as hut interiors etc. Newsreel cameramen have also been round. I find I am becoming rather annoyed by all these press people looking at us as though the place were a zoo. I resent being observed as though I were some oddity. I may well be slightly odd, but it need not be rubbed in, in this fashion! The camp is now full of these press people and no matter where you go, you are bound to run into some of them – British, American and

Australian. Thank God there are no Dutch yet. Another woman has just walked past the front of the quarter, large bottomed, shirted and trousered, with a wide brimmed hat and a nose like a plough.

We are due to go on to Delhi time tomorrow. What this means I don't quite know. I suppose we get up later and have supper in the dark. The Japanese system of making the fullest possible use of daylight seems to be more sensible.

7 September 45 We have just said good-bye to John, who is off by air this afternoon via Penang and Rangoon. The remainder of the Americans left this morning for Kalang. The first 40 left yesterday. Their Douglas DC4 flew off over the camp the afternoon. No hope of us being flown out. The occupation forces busily taking over the island and a battalion of the Burma Rifles is taking over Changi Gaol area. Some nurses, part of a field surgical unit have moved into Half Moon Street. Donald up yesterday with two war correspondents from Sketch and Mirror. They came to look at our coolie quarter. Sent off my airmail letter card this morning.

QM has just been round to take clothing measurements, so perhaps we shall get some clothes soon. No sign of any further incoming mail yet, but more important for us to send news out from here. The 5th Indian Division sign is a black rectangle with red circle in middle. The Japanese flag in mourning? Must be intentional. Report this morning that the 14th Army is to occupy Malaya. POWs ex Tangong Paga Camp were taken on board Sussex yesterday and afterwards given film show. I have just seen another two women go past. This is becoming an amazing place – even women.

8 September 45 Still no news of when we are leaving. Camp showing signs of impatience at the delay, particularly in light of all the press bullshit being put out. John left yesterday by DC4, Peter

saw him off at Kalang. Brandy with Hutch last night. POW description of 'South East Asia Command' (SEAC) and 'Repatriation of Allied Prisoners of War and Internees' is now 'Supreme Example of Absolute Chaos' and 'Retention of All Prisoners of War Indefinitely', respectively. A broadcast by Mrs Cranston, New Zealand war correspondent, last night over camp hook-up in the course of which she reassured us that we do not stink. Poor Donald Cathie has just read in 'The Times' of ten days ago the announcement of the death of his wife, having just written an airmail letter card to her. He is, of course, absolutely stunned and we feel there is no way in which we can help him, much as we would like to. What a perfectly bloody war and what a perfectly bloody way in which to hear such news.

Admirals Power and Holland visited the camp yesterday. Naval personnel have already received European food, bread, etc. Many people have been contacted by friends of theirs in the incoming forces and are being taken off to Singapore. One has gone to stay on the Pasha, one of the supply ships. He is a friend of the captain. I still cannot manage to get out of this bloody place. Ken and I are very fed up. We still live just as we have done for the past year and we read in the papers that we have been 'relieved'. As far as we are concerned we might just as well be under the Nips still. Their guards are still around the camp, armed with rifles.

Harwood's visit to Sussex and Vigilant. He tells us that Admiral Power was not expected and is here unofficially. He is nevertheless issuing orders himself. There is consequent chaos caused by both Power and Holland issuing different orders. Things don't seem to have changed much. Meals today have been shocking. Ghurkha officers left this morning to join their troops. 3000 Indian troops expecting to leave tomorrow.

Hospital ships to be loaded in next day or two. We are now without water for 48 hours. God, I'm fed up. If only one could get out of this bloody camp. Everybody is very nervy this evening. Heaven knows how much longer the men will be able to contain their impatience. General Christersen broadcast over the camp hook-up this afternoon telling us to be patient. No comment.

9 September 45 Col. Harris and some others left by air early this morning. A party of 99 sick are leaving by air today and another party of 500 due off by sea transport on Tuesday. European rations received last night and about time too. Managed to get my hands on two airmail letter cards and sent one off to Denison and one to Allan and Catherine. We expect to be issued with clothing in the next day or so. Issue to include:- Two bush shirts, 1 pr slacks, socks, underclothing, shoes, two pairs pyjamas, two sheets, pillow case and blanket, head gear and 1939 - 45 ribbon! The latter is hardly what we need - we are only too well aware that we have been at it for six bloody long years. There is no need to remind us. Peter in Singapore yesterday. He returned in a Chrysler with 5 FANYs, so he obviously had a very pleasant day, having also had tea at RAPWI HQ in the Goodwood Park Hotel with various women. Canteens possibly opening here in the next day or two. A visit by the marine band from the cruiser Sussex yesterday evening. They played in the hospital area.

11 September 45 Peter and I spent from Sunday afternoon until yesterday evening with the Navy. We went down by jeep with the Captain, Commander Bingham RNR, then by launch out to his ship, HMS Barracuda, one of two depot ships for two flotillas of motor torpedo boats. The ship was originally Danish, 4000 tons, built in Hong Kong and taken over by the Admiralty. Arrived in wardroom to find a birthday party in progress and we had pink gins in our hands within 30 seconds of setting foot inside. Hospitality overwhelming - I shall never forget it.

Wonderful to feel free again and to be treated like a human being. We slept in beds specially provided on the deck, just under the bridge outside the commander's day room. Lovely cool breeze, lights of the harbour and shipping twinkling all round us. The light from a new moon shimmering over the water reminded me of Halifax harbour in 1941. A breath-taking sight. Transports, frigates, MTBs, cruisers, battleships. No mosquitos or flies, everything spotless. I thought I must be dreaming and am only now gradually coming down to earth. My drink capacity surprisingly normal in spite of 3 1/2 years gap. Pink gins, beers, whisky and cherry brandies, cigarettes by the score. Australian butter and bread, toast, marmalade, ham, steaks - all the good things of life for the first time for over 3 1/2 years. We hope to go down again today.

Yesterday evening with Eric. Drank brandy; the hair of the dog that bit me. Went to bed feeling on top of the world. Returned to camp to find rations greatly improved. No more rice and plenty of biscuits, margarine, cheese, jam, milk, tinned meats, sugar, chocolates, cigarettes, even port and sweets, the latter a present from the FANYs. We heard this morning that all 18 Division personnel will probably embark on Saturday on either a Dutch ship or on the Orduna, whatever that is. Lady Louis Mountbatten visited the camp yesterday and created an extremely good impression. She spent one and a half hours in the hospital wards and broadcast over the camp hook-up. She certainly has enormous charisma. Lord Louis is expected in today. On return from Collier Quay yesterday I watched Nips clearing up the Padang ready for Lord Louis' arrival.

13 September 45 Still no further news of when we are leaving.

Yesterday, I was on board the Barracuda again, having spent the night before last on board. We visited the minesweeper flotilla leader and we were taken on board by the flotilla commander, Cdr. Bailey RN. Had drinks with him in his cabin and then on to Barracuda for dinner. We listened to the surrender celebrations over the radio and watched RAF fly past, which all thought very disappointing. Singapore harbour is now completely filled with shipping. Two days ago the battleships Nelson and Richelieu (French), four more aircraft carriers, two more cruisers, one the Cumberland, destroyers and a large number of minesweepers, corvettes and sloops. Making a quick count of all types of shipping visible, I counted over sixty. On shore, the naval ratings appear to outnumber the army. I returned from the Barracuda with three sack loads of bread, baked specially for us to bring up to camp. Naval hospitality something I shall never forget. Film show last night in Coconut Grove. First since leaving England four years ago. Four newsreels showing such things as V2 bombs, fighting in the Pacific, the Berlin Conference, victory parades in Berlin. Some magnificent photography.

I am feeling incredibly tired after two visits to Singapore. We all get tired very easily. I think it must stem from the mental strain of being in a room full of people from the outside world. Here, with people one has been living with for so long, little effort is required. God knows what my reactions will be to being in a room full of women. We are expecting to draw kit today. AIF received mail yesterday, but none for us. Transports still lying in harbour with no sign of activity and no further sign of any of us leaving yet. Nobody seems to know anything, the great RAPWI organisation, who are after all supposed to be responsible, least of anybody.

14 September 45 It now seems we may be off on Wednesday. Two boats are leaving tomorrow, one on Monday and the main party of 18 Division on Wednesday. Had a hell of a day yesterday trying to

draw kit. None of it fits at all, everything being either far too small – hat, bush shirts and footwear, or far too big – trousers, pyjama trousers etc. The army has not changed a bit so far as I can see. I was given trousers and pyjamas, which would fit a man 4ft tall with a 6ft waist admirably. The pyjama trousers are certainly wider than they are long. We watched another film yesterday called 'Thousands Cheer'. Most of the actors being new faces to me.

General Slim visited the camp yesterday and today Lord Louis is expected. Both he and Lady Louis have gone over big here. Admiral Power evidently unpopular as he has a reputation for working to get to the top and not minding how many toes he treads on to reach it. Another ten bags of mail received at RAPWI.

I saw Donald for a few minutes yesterday. He hopes to join us on board when we embark.

Liberation

The one and only time throughout our captivity that our secret radio failed to work was when the two atom bombs were dropped on Hiroshima on the 6th August 1945 and three days later on Nagasaki , leading to Japan's surrender. This meant that we did not learn of this momentous news until a few days later. The first evidence of what had happened was the arrival of an RAF Liberator flying very low over Changi Gaol to drop thousands of leaflets addressed to the Japanese stating that they would be held responsible for the safety of all prisoners in South East Asia until the allies had reoccupied Singapore. The following day a second Liberator dropped more leaflets, this time in English, addressed to the prisoners, saying that they would be released as soon as the Allies landed and that transports would be arriving to take them home. The leaflet included one piece of medical advice to the effect that rice water was good for dysentery - what the hell they thought we had been doing for nearly four years was beyond belief!

One morning two RAF pilots made an unauthorised landing on Changi airfield in their Mosquito to be the first to greet us personally. Thereafter events speeded up with the air-drop of a Major, the official representative of the C in C, Louis Mountbatten, and his team. Their first job was to set up direct radio communication with GHQ in Burma. All the essential equipment was successfully dropped except for one vital piece, which the Japanese kindly supplied immediately. The Major was followed by a medical team, including two army doctors, one of whom broke his leg on landing and had to be taken straight to hospital.

With the main task force taking over Singapore, the next to pay us a visit were two Australian nurses. They suddenly appeared round the corner to find a group of us taking showers outside our huts. A somewhat surreal conversation ensued between the two nurses in their smart white uniforms and our unfit little group, all stark naked. It was wonderful to see women again and our reaction was one of surprise rather than embarrassment.

A New Zealand woman war correspondent, a Mrs Cranston, visited Changi some days later and was shocked to find that we were still on Japanese rice rations. She returned immediately to Singapore, somehow managed to commandeer trucks and had them loaded with proper food rations for delivery to Changi before our own army, in the form of the Royal Army Service Corps (RASC), finally got around to it. Still on the subject of food, when I and two thousand others were returning home on the Polish ship *Sobieski*, it ran out of potatoes and served rice, over which there was almost a mutiny.

It was thanks to Mrs Cranston that I had my first hot bath for four years. She had taken over the top floor apartment in what was then the tallest building in the centre of Singapore. In the course of conversation with two of us in Changi, she asked if there was anything we would particularly like - a hot bath was the reply. She drove us there and then to her flat, which a few days later was commandeered for Louis Mountbatten, the C in C, on his visit to receive the formal surrender of the Japanese.

We found the many cock-ups most reassuring because we had thought that the world would have changed beyond recognition during our captivity whereas in reality things were just as inefficient as they had always been. Our voyage home ended in Liverpool opposite the Liver Building, where we were greeted by the mayor of Bootle, a small group of army officers and a brass band. We thought we were worth at least the Mayor of Liverpool until reality hit me that we only represented a minute part of the millions of people throughout Europe who, by the end of the war, were quite simply in the wrong place and had to be returned to where they belonged.

It was not long before we woke to the fact that, throughout our captivity, a grateful government had been deducting income tax from our army pay.

Appendix

∽

JIM BRADLEY AND RONALD SEARLE

JIM BRADLEY

In the foreword to this book, I referred to a book written about Cyril Wild by Jim Bradley -"The Tall Man who Never Slept". Jim Bradley also wrote "Towards the Setting Sun", which was published in 1982, describing his experiences as a POW. He was a captain in one of our divisional engineer regiments and I knew him quite well. He was one of a party of ten men who escaped on the night of 5 July 1943 from Sonkurai Camp. The majority of this group were officers in the 18th Division and we all lived together in one half of a hut, the other half of which was occupied by Japanese engineers. Jim was lucky to survive.

By the end of the first two weeks of their attempt five were dead. He and I were in the same camps and our experiences, particularly at Sonkurai, were identical up to the time of his escape, a few months after we had arrived there. Jim died in 2003, at the age of 91. I am including the quote below from The Times obituary, because it is such a vivid record both of the conditions we faced and of an incredibly brave, but hopeless, attempt to get news to the outside world of the conditions facing us on the railway. Whilst I feel that there was an element of irresponsibility in the venture, since they were all half-starved and suffering from numerous diseases, it was their condition that drove them to try, and it was nevertheless a gallant, if vain, attempt.

"Jim Bradley was the last survivor of a party of nine British service men and an Indian civilian, who made an audacious attempt to escape from the Thailand Burma Railway in 1943. In May that year Bradley was one of 1600 British prisoners of war at Sonkurai, a camp just south of the Three Pagodas Pass on the Thailand-Burma Border, 1200 of whom were to die within the year. These prisoners, already in poor health after confinement at Changi in Singapore, had been forced to undergo a 200-mile march and then build the new camp in a jungle clearing, hampered by the breaking of the monsoon. Food and medical supplies were minimal, which depleted their reserves of energy and resistance to diseases such as malaria, dysentery and cholera. The task given to the prisoners at Sonkurai was the construction, under the command of a Japanese engineer, Lieutenant Hiroshe Abe, of a three-span wooden trestle bridge. The bridge rose 30ft above a fast flowing river and the huge logs had to be carried by the prisoners through knee-deep mud.

Work began at seven in the morning and continued under arc lights until far into the night, with no time to rest or wash. When progress fell behind schedule, the prisoners were beaten by Abe's engineers with whips made from strands of fencing wire. Morale collapsed. Cholera broke out soon after the prisoners arrived at Sonkurai, and Bradley had the misfortune to be identified by the Japanese as a carrier. The carriers were ordered to live in isolation and Bradley was put in charge of the crematorium. Wood had to be collected to build the funeral pyres for the cholera corpses and then kept alight in the pouring rain. Death was so swift that men who helped in the morning could themselves be on the pyre by the evening.

The prisoners had been warned that any attempt to leave the camp was futile because of the density of the jungle, the monetary rewards offered by the Japanese in Thailand and Burma for the handing over of escapees, the language problem and the lack of maps, food and medicines. The Japanese also threatened draconian punishments on camps from which anyone escaped. Nevertheless, Bradley and his friends reckoned that the likelihood of survival at Sonkurai was minimal and every effort should be made to alert the Allied powers to the plight of the prisoners in the railway camps. The escape party was put together by Lieutenant Colonel Wilkinson (Wilkie) of the Royal Engineers, Bradley's former regimental commander and a very lovable man.

On 5 July 1943, the ten men set out on a track through the jungle that Bradley had prepared near the crematorium, an area avoided by the Japanese. They had for guidance only a rough map of the Burma coast drawn on a silk handkerchief, which suggested that the distance they had to cover to Ye, their initial objective, was about 50 miles. This they hoped to accomplish on foot and by raft in about three weeks.

They had accumulated a quantity of rice, soya beans and fish and a few medicines such as prophylactic quinine; the rest of their equipment amounted to an axe, three parangs, lighters and compasses together with blankets, groundsheets and a few treasured personal possessions. Strict secrecy was observed, Wilkinson merely leaving a note listing their names beside the bed-space of the British camp commander. Covering their tracks by wading up a swollen river, the men set course due west, forced a path through dense undergrowth and initially made fair progress. The incessant rain hindered attempts to light fires, which were needed not only for cooking but also warding off tigers at night. Soon the country became hilly, the primitive map having given no indication of the range of mountains that ran in an unbroken line south of

Moulmein. The jungle was so dense with interlocking fallen bamboos that even half a mile a day became a challenge. By 25 July food supplies were reduced to a little rice and a tin of pilchards. During the next fortnight five of the party died, including Colonel Wilkinson. Of all the deaths, that of 'Wilkie' affected Bradley most deeply. On 18 August, having eaten nothing for three weeks and fully aware of the risks involved, the five survivors allowed themselves to be taken into a village by two Burmese. Their subsequent discovery that the headman of the village had claimed a large reward from the Japanese for revealing their whereabouts came as no surprise.

The Japanese at first refused to believe that anyone could have crossed the mountainous jungle, presuming that the men had landed by parachute. This factor almost certainly saved them from immediate execution by bayonet or firing squad, the usual fate of recaptured officers. After formal identification and prolonged interrogation by the Japanese military police, the five were informed that they had been sentenced to death. Allied officers brought by the Japanese from surrounding camps to witness the executions made every attempt to negotiate a reprieve.

Captain Cyril Wild, who was fluent in Japanese, managed to persuade Lieutenant Colonel Hirateru Banno to make an emotional cancellation of the death sentence by impressing upon him the disgrace he would bring upon the Emperor and the Imperial Japanese Army if he permitted the deaths of such brave men. Wild's appeal was successful; years later Bradley was to pay tribute to him in a biography, The Tall Man Who Never Slept (1991).

At the end of 1943 Bradley was removed to Singapore for further interrogation by Japanese military police at Outram Road gaol. Two months of this treatment left him unable to stand and he was sent to Changi where he remained until 1945, except for an interlude in June 1944 when he faced a Japanese court martial and was sentenced to eight years' penal servitude for his part in the escape.

After the war, Bradley's attitude towards the Japanese was always generous. In 1995 he shook hands with Abe after travelling to Tokyo to appear in a television programme to mark the fiftieth anniversary of VJ Day. Abe recalled with great emotion Bradley burning the bodies of his comrades on the funeral pyres at Sonkurai and he offered an apology, which Bradley accepted. 'I still have nightmares,' Bradley wrote in 1998 before the visit of the Emperor of Japan to London, 'but these are not caused by the present or immediate past generation of Japanese. We have reached a time to forgive, if not to forget'."

The story of his escape reminds me vividly of the never-to-be-forgotten occasions, of which I wrote in my diary, when my turn came round to burn the bodies of those who had died. Most had died of cholera within twenty-four to thirty-six hours of falling ill and were unrecognisable. Others succumbed to malaria, dysentery, beriberi, jungle ulcers and pellagra, or a combination of these or other diseases, but overwork and starvation were common to all. In 1995 I was interviewed at Conduit House by a film crew from ITV, who were making a programme about Jim Bradley's emotional meeting with Lieutenant Abe. I told them that I did not think that I had much to contribute, although I remembered Abe only too well, as he supervised work on our section of the railway. He frequently rode up and down on a Mongolian pony, carrying a large bamboo stick in his right hand, with which he clouted anyone who crossed him, including myself, whom he knocked out on two occasions.

Only quite recently, I was reminded of the poem written by Cyril Wild after our return to Changi from Thailand at the end of 1943, and quoted by Jim Bradley in his book "Towards The Setting Sun":

Sonkurai Labour Camp

(Thailand Railway 1943)
Qui ante diem perierunt
At Sonkurai, where hope lay drowned
Beneath the bridge, the earth is browned
With mould, sad monsoon-vapours veil
The jungle, and the creepers trail
Like snakes inert, their coils unwound.

And there our rear-guard keep their ground
(Eight comrades laid beneath each mound)
A thousand, dead 'without avail'
At Sonkurai.

Freed from the captive's weary round,
Homeless, a lasting home they found.
Let not our faith their courage fail,
Till with the dawn the stars turn pale
And (silent long) our bugles sound
At Sonkurai!

Singapore, June 1944

RONALD SEARLE

I owe a great debt of gratitude to Ronald Searle who, when I wrote to him some ten years ago, asking if I might illustrate my diary with some of his drawings, replied saying "Use, choose what you like. The copyrights are mine". Today most people in Britain who know anything at all about his work, remember him as the creator of the schoolgirls of St Trinian's.

To quote from The Times obituary, published after Ronald's death in December 2011:

"Searle was more than just that; an aficionado of the grotesque, the false, the inhuman and the destructive, his drawings were often obliquely political, pointing to the greed, folly and exploitation that lie behind so many of the world's promises. His picture of the world was a dark one of broken heads, and hypodermic needles, lasciviousness without desire, madness, ugliness and victimisation. We are at the mercy, his drawings tell us, of totalitarian brutes, military hardware and the obsequiousness men who serve authority.

More and more towards the end of his life it became clear that he was forever haunted by the cruelty he saw and endured as a prisoner of war helping to build the Burma Thailand railway.

His artistic career was interrupted when he was called up, and in 1941 sent by sea to the Far East with the 287th Field Company. In the Army he continued to sketch every day. "Our Commanders simply said to us, "No problem, you know, they are slit eyed, they can't shoot straight, they are just a lot of yellow dwarves".

There was to be a rude awakening when they reached Malaya with the Japanese advance in progress, and they found themselves facing their skilled Infantry in the jungle. He was forced to work 12 - 18 hours a day breaking rocks for the Burma Thailand Railway in stifling heat.

"The terrifying thing was that you were with your friends, people you grew up with, or people you joined the Army with, and you would wake up in the morning and find that on each side of you one of your friends was dead".

His anarchic imagination was influenced not only by William Hogarth, but by the other great cartoonists and illustrators of the 18th and 19th centuries, particularly Gillray, Rowlandson and Cruikshank, and he in turn was to be a great influence on younger draftsmen, caricaturists, reporters and satirists.

In 1959, at the invitation of the United Nations, Searle and his wife Kaye Webb toured some of the refugee camps of Europe, and produced a hauntingly poignant account of what they saw.

In the 1990s Searle produced occasional political drawings for the main editorial page of Le Monde. He commented that he found it difficult to know whether "In these days of computer educated visual barbarians, satirical graphics can have the slightest impact on public opinion. On the whole I am pessimistic, and fear that I am exercising a moribund art".

He welcomed the chance, nevertheless, to comment on current events, and particularly "On those situations involving mankind's propensity for self-destruction". These grim drawings – in one a skinhead carrying a box of eyeballs confronts a man with a box of teeth – were the inspiration for The Face of War, a book of poems by Simon Rae.

Searle remained as he had been during the Second World War, one of the world's great witnesses to cruelty and exploitation.

A fellow prisoner said of Searle, "If you can imagine something that weighs six stone or so, is on the point of death and has no qualities of the human condition that aren't revolting, calmly lying there with a pencil and a scrap of paper, drawing, you have some idea of the difference of temperament that this man had from the ordinary human being".

Most of the many thousands of prisoners held by the Japanese were beaten up at some time or other, but Ronald himself was beaten up on several occasions, once with an iron bar which practically killed him.

I shall always treasure the lunch my wife, Sally, and I had with him and his lovely wife Monica, in the little restaurant "La Table" in Provence where they frequently entertained their friends. We started with a bottle of Champagne, which Ronald referred to as his "engine oil", followed by delicious white and then red Sancerre. We then returned to their house and continued talking long into the afternoon over coffee and more engine oil.

He was more honoured for his work in countries other than his own. He was given The American National Cartoonists Society's Advertising and Illustration Award in 1959 and 1965. He was appointed CBE in 2004, when he should have received a knighthood. He became a Chevalier of the Legion d'Honneur in 2007 and the German Order of Merit in 2009. Ronald never felt that he was properly appreciated in this country and left his personal collection to the Wilhelm Busch Museum in Hanover.

It is sad that in his own country he continued to carry the label of St Trinian's until he died. He was so much more than this, and I have little doubt that he will in time be regarded not only as an outstanding cartoonist and illustrator, but one of the greatest satirists of all time.

GLOSSARY

ADMS Assistant Director of Medical Services.

'Aggie' Agnew, Major, HQ, 18 Div. A Scot with large moustache, always carried a shepherd's crook. A lawyer, responsible for legal matters. Appeared never to have left his Scottish estate.

AIF Australian Imperial Force.

Andy Dillon, Lieutenant Colonel, RIASC. GSO 1, 18 Division. Outstanding regular officer, who had seen action on North West Frontier in India. Unflappable and very popular. Responsible for all supply and administration.

Archie Bevan Captain, Welsh Guards. ADC to Major General Beckwith-Smith.

ARP Air Raid Precaution

Banno, Colonel. Senior Japanese officer in charge of all POW in Singapore and Malaysia. Weak, little authority but by no means entirely bad.

'Becky', Major General Beckwith-Smith, Welsh Guards, GOC 18 Div. An outstanding soldier and human being, died of diphtheria whilst POW. Had brought Guards Division out of France in 1940. Urged Gen Percival to allow full divisional counter attack by 18 Div, in vain. This might well have saved Singapore.

Berkeley Quill, Captain, One of three MCOs at 18 Div HQ. Married to a very beautiful wife, who had been a model. On our release he learned that she had left him for someone else; a fairly frequent occurrence during the war.

Bill English, Captain i/c Military Police 18 Div. Member of a family undertaking business pre-war. Much to his amusement he was 'accused' of making a fortune by re-using the same coffin for all funerals. Ordered to clear the ship Empire Star of Australian deserters, which proved impossible, in spite of firing on them.

Bryan Barrow, Captain i/c Div Defence Company. His family lived in Reigate and were friends of my parents. Mortally wounded before Singapore fell. First news of his death reached his parents via my first post card received in 1943.

BT Benign Tertiary malaria.

Cyril Wild, Major. Bilingual in Japanese. With F Force at Sonkurai and chief prosecution witness in Japanese war crimes trials. Tragically killed in air crash in Hong Kong, September 1946.

DAPM Deputy Assistant Provost Marshall

Diana Bean my girlfriend whilst 18 Div HQ was at Bewdley. We met at a cocktail party given by Becky and his wife. She was working as a Land Girl and her family owned an engineering and car manufacturing company near Birmingham. I often spent the evening with her and her family at their home.

Doover a roll made basically, from rice, but with different flavourings and ingredients depending upon what was available.

Doovering Australian slang – used to mean cooking in my diary.

Eric Cruickshank, Captain RAMC. Served in Singapore General Hospital. Member of leading medical family in Aberdeen, where his father had been professor of medicine. A brilliant diagnostician, who saved many lives. Great friend of John Phillips and me. Took up professorship in West Indies after the war.

GOC General Officer Commanding

GSO General Staff Officer. There were three grades: 1, Lieutenant Colonel; 2, Major; 3, Captain.

Gula malacca dark brown unrefined sugar sold in blocks, used by POWs as sweetener and as one of the ingredients for making artificial tobacco.

Harold Atcherley, Captain. Born 1918 in Epsom, Surrey. Spent my first seven years in the Argentine. Returned to England to go to boarding school in 1926. 1935–1937 studied at Heidelberg and Geneva Universities. Joined Shell as Eastern Staff trainee in 1937. Planned appointment to China aborted by onset of war. Joined 2nd Battalion, the Queen's Westminster Rifles in 1939 as a rifleman. Equipped as wartime soldier at Liverpool Street Station gymnasium with battle dress, 1917 rifle, civilian gas mask (packed in a cardboard box attached to a piece of string) and London bus driver's blue overcoat, due to supply shortages. Commissioned Intelligence Corps in 1940. Appointed Intelligence Officer HQ 18 (Motorised Infantry) Division. Ordered away from Singapore on 15 February 1942 but failed to make it and became POW.

Harwood Harrison, Major, Royal Suffolk Regt. Brigade Major.
Became Tory MP for Woodbridge constituency after the war.
Pompous, humourless, bridge playing fanatic.

'Hutch' Lieut. Col. Hutchison, GSO1 18 Div. Highly
professional soldier. Unfairly criticised in my diary; was in fact
respected and liked by all junior officers. Never recovered fully
after release and died a few years after the war.

James Bull, Major RAMC. Singapore General Hospital. Leading
Harley Street radiologist. A close friend.

John Phillips, Major RAMC, DADMS 18 Div. A GP pre-war
and later emigrated to Canada. An outstanding doctor, who
saved many lives. A close friend of mine and with me throughout
our captivity.

Fitz Barrington, The Hon., Captain Intelligence Corps. There
were 3 I. C. grade 3 staff officers at Div HQ. He did the office
job, I the leg work and Stanley Lemin, Field Security. Highly
civilised, charming, unselfish. Became 7th Baronet and publisher
after the war.

IJA Imperial Japanese Army.

Jean Palethorpe friend of Diana, Tufton's very pretty girl friend
when 18 Div stationed at Ribbesford. We regularly went out
together whilst at Bewdley.

Kempeitai Japanese KGB

Kerr Paxton, Captain Divisional Education Officer, 18 Div.
With British Council in Rome pre-war and returned there in
1946. Suffered badly as POW and never fully recovered. Became
an alcoholic and later committed suicide. A lovely human being,
gentle, well read, always stimulating and original.

Kinsley Weller My cousin. Served war in East African Rifles Lived most of his married life in Chester. I never had much contact with him.

Nip a word for Japanese people.

OC Officer Commanding

Peter Fane, Captain, Royal Artillery. He and I were both members of party ordered away from Singapore in Feb 1942. Tried in vain to obtain tug from Malaya Command to take some 100 others away from the island.

'Puss in Boots' Tompkinson, Lieut. One of three MCOs at HQ 18 Div. Son of Kidderminster carpet manufacturer. Wartime officer, who tried to imitate the regulars by affecting riding breeches and boots, hence his nickname.

Richard Sharpe, Captain, Northumberland Fusiliers. Staff Officer 18 Div HQ. A civil servant, who later became Deputy Secretary at No 10 responsible for processing honours recommendations. Known as 'Dead Ned' for reasons now forgotten.

MCO Motor Contact Officer. Three at Div HQ, liaison between Div HQ and Brigades. Vital in Malaysian campaign because our radios did not work.

MT Malignant Tertiary malaria.

Peter Jamieson, Lieutenant, MCO at HQ 18 Division. Had served in France in 1939–40. A very close friend, who very nearly died as POW at Sonkurai. Journalist before war and after war joined Shell.

RAMC Royal Army Medical Corps

RAPWI Repatriation of Allied Prisoners of War and Internees. Known by prisoners as 'Retain All Prisoners of War Indefinitely'.

RIASC Royal Indian Army Service Corps.

Ronald Searle A sapper with Royal Engineers, 18 Div. A brilliant artist and cartoonist; with 'H' Force on railway. Went to live in South of France in 1961 with his French wife. Generously allowed me to use his drawings, made whilst he was a POW, to illustrate my diary.

SEAC South East Asia Command.

Shaito General, C in C all Southern POW Camps. Executed at Changi Gaol in 1946 for war crimes.

South Looe The name of my Uncle Lance's house in Ewell, Surrey, happily spelt with an 'e'.

Stanley Davis, Captain Ex Guards Warrant Officer, in command of Div HQ defence company.

Stanley Lemin, Captain 'I', 18 Div. Responsible for field security, i.e. denying information to enemy, as opposed to my job, obtaining information about the enemy. One of the lucky ones, with Tufton, in drawing lots for escape from Singapore. With Tufton in escape to Ceylon and served in India.

Tenko Japanese for Roll Call.

Tenno Heika The Japanese Emperor.

Tufton Beamish, Captain GSO Ops 18 Div HQ. Regular soldier, in France 1939/40, ordered out of Singapore and reached Ceylon by dhow. Served India, Burma and North Africa. Twice wounded. Later MP and Baron Chelwood. A close friend.

'Webby' Webster, Major RAMC, Singapore General Hospital. Surgeon

'Whiskers' Sutherland, Major, Argyle & Sutherland Highlanders. GSO 2 18 Div. Hutch's second in command and a regular soldier. Had a huge handle bar moustache, hence his nickname.